A
BOOK
ABOUT
LOVE

———————————

JONAH LEHRER

SIMON & SCHUSTER

New York London Toronto Sydney New Delhi

Simon & Schuster
1230 Avenue of the Americas
New York, NY 10020

First Simon & Schuster hardcover edition July 2016

SIMON & SCHUSTER and colophon are
registered trademarks of Simon & Schuster, Inc.

For information about special discounts for bulk purchases, please contact
Simon & Schuster Special Sales at 1-866-506-1949
or business@simonandschuster.com.

The Simon & Schuster Speakers Bureau can bring authors
to your live event. For more information or to book an event,
contact the Simon & Schuster Speakers Bureau at
1-866-248-3049 or visit our website at
www.simonspeakers.com.

Manufactured in the United States of America

1 3 5 7 9 10 8 6 4 2

Library of Congress Cataloging-in-Publication Data is available.

ISBN 978-1-4767-6139-8
ISBN 978-1-4767-6141-1 (ebook)

CONTENTS

. . . and to prove/Our almost-instinct almost true:
What will survive of us is love.

—Philip Larkin, "An Arundel Tomb"

"God breaks the heart again and again and again
until it stays open."

—Hazrat Inayat Khan

AUTHOR'S NOTE

IN EARLY AUGUST 2012, a book I wrote called *Imagine* was taken out of print and pulled from stores. This happened because I made several serious mistakes in the text. The worst of these mistakes involved fabricated quotes from Bob Dylan. In addition, there were passages where I relied on secondary sources that were not cited.

In the months that followed, other mistakes and failures came to light. In one instance, I plagiarized from another writer on my blog. My second book, *How We Decide*, was later taken out of print due to factual errors and improper citation.

I broke the most basic rules of my profession. I am ashamed of what I've done. I will regret it for the rest of my life.

To prevent these mistakes from happening again, I have followed a few simple procedures in this book. All quotes and relevant text have been sent to subjects for their approval. This also applies to the research I describe: whenever possible, my writing has been sent to the scientists to ensure accuracy. In addition, the book has been independently fact-checked.

A
BOOK
ABOUT
LOVE

———————

INTRODUCTION

Habituation

As we know, love needs re-inventing.

—ARTHUR RIMBAUD[1]

1

Two psychological laws shape much of human experience. They exist in opposition to each other.

2

The first law is habituation. It's a law of brute simplicity. When we are repeatedly exposed to a stimulus—no matter what the stimulus—we gradually come to ignore it. We become desensitized to the sensation, bored by its constancy. Consider your underwear. Do you feel it? Are you conscious of it? Of course not. The garments are rubbing against some of the most sensitive nerves of the body, but you've learned to tune those signals out. The cotton has become an invisible fabric, as imperceptible as the air.

The most important implications of habituation have to do with pleasure. Although animals are programmed to seek out rewards, the law of habituation means that these rewards come with diminishing returns. That's why the first bite of chocolate cake is better than the second, and the second is better than the third. It's why that new gadget is exciting the first few times you touch the screen, but then it becomes just another device, gathering dust in the corner. The delight always vanishes, replaced by the usual boredom and indifference.

Habituation is a phenomenon of sweeping power.[2] It is one of the only mental properties shared by every species with a nervous system, from fruit flies to humans. The biology of habituation has been carefully studied in sea slugs and drug addicts; economists have used the phenomenon to explain the surprising disconnect between money and happiness;[3] the concept has even been applied to the short life cycle of fashionable clothes, which lose their allure long before they wear out.[4] Habituation is not *a* fact of life—in many respects, it is *the* fact of life. We spend our days chasing after the most fleeting things, those desires that never last.

3

But habituation does not ruin everything. There is a second law of human experience and this law is about what persists. Amid all the vanishing, some delights endure. We find joys that never disappear. We meet people who never get boring. And you know what we say about these things? We say *we love them.*

Here is the thesis of this book: love is the only meaning that lasts. It the opposite of underwear. It is the antithesis of chocolate cake. It is not pleasure or passion or joy. Or rather, it is all those things, but it is only those things when they go on. While we typically define love in terms of its intensity—it is the highest of highs—the power of the feeling can only be understood over time, for it is what time cannot destroy.

Love is just another name for what never gets old.

4

This is a strange way of thinking about love. In Shakespeare's *Romeo and Juliet*, love is described as the most wonderful form of madness, a rapture that makes the randy teenagers say the most romantic things. The emotion is a reminder of what our nerves can do, of all the potential energy that flows along their wires. This is life as it's meant to be lived: ecstatic, exultant, every detail etched permanently into the circuits of memory. To fall in love is to learn, at long last, what it is like to want another body more than we've ever wanted anything else before.

Shakespeare didn't invent this story—he just told it better than anyone else. The basic plot is the engine of nearly every great romance, from Orpheus and Eurydice to Tristan and Isolde. It's what Paris feels when he first sees Helen and what Taylor Swift is always singing about in her pop songs.

This narrative is not just an entertaining cliché. Rather, the Romeo and Juliet version of love has come to define nearly all investigations of the subject. Evolutionary biologists, for instance, have explained away the emotion as merely a temporary surge of sex hormones, which traps males in a monogamous pair bond.[5] Neuroscience, meanwhile, has concluded that love's delight is nothing but a flood of dopamine, a spasm of neurotransmitter lingering too long in the synapse.[6] (There is no mystery, only chemistry.) Most recently, brain scans of loving couples have shown where these chemicals come from: a short list of brain areas, all of which have been previously associated with the processing of hedonic rewards, such as addictive drugs and sugary foods.[7] According to the scientists, love is just an excess of lust, a pleasure so intense it hijacks the mind.

But this description of love—the Romeo and Juliet version—is woefully incomplete. It describes love as a binary state, an all-or-nothing phenomenon. This can make love seem easy, as if we just fall into the feeling and then the feeling takes care of itself. But love is a process, not a switch. And here the standard science of love—an attempt to reduce the emotion to a set of wires and ingredients—reaches its limits, since it cannot explain the mystery of love's endurance. After all, the same neurotransmitters that are the supposed source of the feeling are also known to habituate with a vengeance. The chemicals cannot explain why love abides. They cannot show us how it lasts.

That is why it's not enough to describe the hormones of Romeo, or the fMRI results of Juliet. These scientific results are interesting, but that is mostly because of what they *cannot* reveal, of all the reality they leave out. ("Love's function," E. E. Cummings once wrote, "is to fabricate unknownness.")[8] I write here about many scientific studies, but these are not studies of temporary chemistry. Instead, this book will focus on research that attempts, even in glancing ways, to deal with the long-term and the everyday. It features mostly longitudinal projects, those messy attempts to track our lives and our loves over time. When Romeo meets Juliet, he speaks in poetry, his pickup lines unfolding in iambic pentameter. It's a glorious scene. It's also a fantasy. Real life is lived in prose.

This book is about real life, an attempt to detail all the hard work that love requires. It's not a memoir or a how-to manual. But it is an investigation with selfish motives, an attempt to learn about this feeling that has sustained me. When I write that love survives, even in hard times, I am not summarizing an abstract truth. I am telling you what happened to me.

My favorite part of every scientific paper comes at the end, when the researchers qualify all of their claims. It's a ritual of modesty, a way of reminding the reader that these ideas are bracketed by uncertainty, that we know so little and understand even less. So here are my caveats, most of which are blindingly obvious. Love is a vast subject; this is a small book. What I have written here would be better if I were older, if I were wiser, if I had loved more and lost more. Much of the research I write about is relatively new, which is another way of saying it might turn out to be wrong. This book dwells on aspects of love that speak to my own life. As such, it is an inherently subjective work, framed by my own memories and experiences.

Yet, the basic mystery I'm interested in—how does love hold us together, when everything else falls apart?—remains the essential mystery of our lives. It's a question we take for granted, a daily wonder that's often ignored. It doesn't help that we've come to define love in terms of Romeo's fickle desire. Instead of praising the ordinary pleasures of intimacy, we celebrate the fleeting high. Rather than focus on what endures, we obsess over what happens first. (To restate the problem in psychological terms: we focus on the passion and neglect the attachment.) And so we miss the real miracle of love, which is that it goes on and on.

The meaning of life is that it ends, wrote Kafka.

The meaning of love is that it does not.

1

ATTACHMENT

If I can stop one heart from breaking,
I shall not live in vain.

—EMILY DICKINSON[1]

J OHN BROADUS WATSON didn't believe in love. He was
one of the most influential psychologists of the twentieth
century,[2] yet Watson insisted that the feeling was just a
fantasy, a fairy tale, a four-letter word used to sell lipstick and
sonnets and movie tickets. If love were real, he said, then it
must be measurable, a cause with tangible effects. But Watson
concluded that love was not like that—it could not be held in
the hand or weighed on a scale—and so he declared it an empty
cliché, as useless as poetry.

His doubt led to a discovery. When Watson said that love
was not real, other scientists tried to prove that it was, and that
no subject mattered more.

The Scientist

Watson was born, in 1878, into a destitute family. His mother, Emma, was a devout Baptist. His vagabond father loved whiskey and disappeared for weeks at a time to drink in the backwoods of South Carolina.[3] They scratched out a living as tenant cotton farmers; Watson remembered laboring as a young child, "handling tools, half-soling shoes and milking cows."[4] He was bullied as a boy and then became a bully.[5] Fighting, specifically with African-Americans, was one of his "favorite going-home activities." He never went to high school because the local county didn't have a public one.

But Watson wasn't held back by his childhood. A self-styled truth-teller, he described his life as a testament to the possibilities of the modern age, a time in which people started to shed their old superstitions. After enduring five "bitter" years at the local college,[6] Watson sent a letter to the president of the University of Chicago, promising to be an "earnest student."[7] The letter worked. In 1900, Watson headed north with $50 to his name, determined to prove his worth and change the world.[8]

Although Watson had intended to study philosophy at Chicago, the subject "wouldn't take hold." (He seems to have failed his class on Kant.)[9] However, Watson soon became enchanted with experimental psychology, a young field that matched his ambitions. Human nature had always been a mystery, a subject full of myth and lore, but experimental psychology promised to finally reveal the truth. It could show us who we really are.[10]

Like many of these new psychologists, Watson began by stripping us down, searching for the simplest laws of the mind. In his 1913 manifesto, "Psychology as the Behaviorist Views It," he declared that researchers had wasted too much time chasing after ideas that couldn't be quantified, such as love and consciousness.[11] They'd squandered centuries speculating about emotions and dreams and other airy nothings. Watson argued, quite rightly, that any real science had to be rooted in measurement. That meant focusing on *behavior*, studying the link between stimulus and response and ignoring everything in between. "The behaviorist . . . recognizes no dividing line between man and brute," Watson wrote.[12] Every living thing is just a reinforcement machine, responding to the primal incentives of food and sex.[13]

This strict view of psychology turned Watson into an academic star, a symbol of progress and potential. (Among young psychologists, Watson was hailed as a "second Moses," leading his field out of the wilderness.)[14] Before long, he was chair of the Johns Hopkins psychology department and, at the age of thirty-six, the youngest president of the American Psychological Association. But Watson was only getting started—his real goal was to apply his new science to the practical questions of everyday life. His most famous experiment featured "Little Albert," a nine-month-old infant.[15] First, Albert was exposed to the sight of a white rat. As expected, the baby boy reacted to the rodent with curiosity, reaching out to touch the animal. However, after the rat was paired with a loud noise—Watson clanged on a steel bar, held behind the infant's head—Albert grew to fear every kind of furred thing, including rabbits, dogs, a sealskin coat, and even a Santa Claus mask. The lesson of the experiment was that fear, like every other emotion, was a learned reflex. Children didn't love their mothers. They simply paired her face with the pleasure of milk, just as Albert learned to pair the fur with a feeling of fear.[16] The theory was compelling, and the Little Albert paper would become one of the most frequently cited studies in American psychology textbooks.[17]

Watson's collaborator on these experiments was a young graduate student named Rosalie Rayner. During their research, John and Rosalie began having a passionate affair. Unfortunately for Watson, his wife discovered a stash of their letters, which would be released during their divorce trial. The affair became a public scandal, featured on the front pages of Baltimore newspapers. Watson and Rayner's correspondence was full of behaviorist language, an awkward attempt to describe their emotions in "objective" terms: "Every cell I have is yours individually and collectively," he wrote. "My total reactions are positive and towards you. So likewise each and every heart reaction."[18] Forced to choose between his science and his love, Watson resigned from Hopkins. It was an ironic choice for a scientist who had spent years insisting that love was not real and certainly couldn't influence our behavior.

But Watson was not one to stay down. He soon reinvented himself as a popularizer of behaviorism, a salesman for science.* He remained convinced that a psychology focused on observable facts—and not the invisible urges of emotion—could transform society, creating a world of maximum happiness. His first popular book was a primer on child care, since he believed that parenting was still mired in the mistakes of "emotional-

---

*Watson's first job after quitting academia was in advertising, as he sought to apply the techniques of behaviorism to the marketing of consumer products. It was a lucrative shift; Watson was good at selling things. In a campaign for Maxwell House, he coined the term *coffee break*; he created an early infomercial for Pebeco toothpaste; he even convinced the queen of Spain to endorse Pond's facial cream. "It can be just as thrilling to watch the growth of a sales curve of a new product as to watch the learning curve of animals or men," Watson later wrote.

ism." (Watson dedicated the book to "The first Mother who brings up a happy child.") First published in 1928, *Psychological Care of Infant and Child* became a bestseller and remained the definitive guide to parenting until Dr. Benjamin Spock's *Common Sense Book of Baby and Child Care* was published in 1946. (In a laudatory early review, Bertrand Russell proudly endorsed Watson's child-care techniques, while even Watson's critics admitted that "Watsonism has become gospel and catechism in the nurseries and drawing rooms of America.")[19] The appeal of the book was obvious: Watson pitched it as an empirical guide to parenting, a how-to manual inspired by the careful study of "more than five hundred infants" at Johns Hopkins Hospital.

So what could parents learn from this science? Watson's fundamental message was that love wasn't just overrated—it was *unsafe*. In one chapter, "The Dangers of Too Much Mother Love," Watson insisted that all the kissing and coddling of parents reinforced the very behavior it was supposed to prevent. For instance, when a child cries, the typical mother reacts with soothing affection, which only encourages the child to cry more. (The tenderness rewards the bad behavior.) The result, Watson wrote, is "invalidism," which will "wreck your adult son or daughter's vocational future and their chances for marital happiness."

Instead of loving our children, Watson advised that we treat them like coworkers. "Shake hands with them in the morning," he wrote. "In a week's time, you will find how easy it is to be perfectly objective with your child and at the same time kindly. You will be utterly ashamed of the mawkish, sentimental way you have been handling it."[20] Watson's ultimate goal was to do away with parents altogether: he imagined an America in which infants were raised in scientific nurseries, with trained caretakers doling out rewards and punishments in response to the babies' behavior. While some mothers might protest such a system—isn't love a natural instinct?—Watson dismissed their concerns. "Only one thing will bring out a love response in the child—stroking and touching its skin, lips, sex organs and the like," Watson wrote. "This is the clay out of which all love—maternal, paternal, wifely or husbandly—is made. Hard to believe? But true."[21]

Watson's science of parenting no longer seems scientific. Yet, his theories of love continue to influence our lives. They endure as a collection of parental techniques—Watson has been credited with inventing the time-out as a form of punishment[22]—and as a larger belief that children need boundaries, and not boundless affection. What's more, the experimental tools that Watson helped invent—his obsession with rat mazes, reinforcement, and quick changes in behavior—are still the central tools of modern psychology. If a phenomenon can't be quantified or dissected or reduced to a list of molecular ingredients, then we assume it doesn't exist. The study of the mind remains a study of what can be measured in the lab.

But the real legacy of Watson's popular science is a belief about human beings. The behaviorist argued that what the poets called love was merely a sentimental lie, used to disguise a more primal set of pleasures. It was time to admit that we are just Darwinian machines, driven by a short list of biological rules and base instincts.[23] Life is not romantic. Life is sex and death and survival.

Watson's cynicism has the tang of truth. It seems like one of those disenchanting facts that science is always discovering: the earth is a lonely speck, floating at the edge of the Milky Way; man is a brute, made of monkey parts; the universe is just dust and old starlight. Maybe love is like that, too—another marvel ruined by too much reality.

But was Watson right? Is love really make-believe? What's at stake in this debate is nothing less than the nature of human nature. If we are just a bundle of learned habits and selfish genes, a wet computer made of dopamine and instinct, then lovers are fools. Our most intimate relationships are made of flimsy stuff. What's worse, believing in love is a dangerous illusion, a romantic mistake that leads us to spoil our kids, ruin our marriages, and become the sort of neurotic people who need pills and therapy to cope with existence. We waste our lives chasing a fiction. No wonder we aren't happy.

Of course, if love is real—if the feeling is more than a cultural trope or a chemical trick—then it remains our great consolation, a source of meaning in a meaningless world. The poets are right. Love is a feeling we can't live without.

The Young Thief

John Bowlby was born on February 26, 1907, the fourth child and second son of Sir Anthony Bowlby, a baronet and surgeon to King George V. John Bowlby's childhood was typical of the British upper class. John and his siblings were raised almost entirely by a procession of wet nurses, nannies, and governesses on the top floor of a London town house.[24] Every afternoon, the children spent a single hour with their mother; John recalled having to get dressed up in silk shirts and velvet shorts for the occasion.[25] Amid all this luxury, what Bowlby remembered most was the loneliness, describing his childhood as leaving him "sufficiently hurt but not sufficiently damaged."[26] During infancy, Bowlby was cared for by a sweet young nursemaid named Minnie. When Bowlby was four, Minnie left the household. He never got over the loss. "For a child to be looked after entirely by a loving nanny and then for her to leave when he is two or three, or even four or five, can be almost as tragic as the loss of a mother," Bowlby would later write.[27]

At the age of eight, Bowlby and his older brother were sent to boarding school. It was a miserable experience; Bowlby was desperately homesick.[28] Nevertheless, he survived his education and, while an undergraduate at Cambridge University, chose to study medicine like his father.[29] But Bowlby wasn't interested in surgery or the royal court. Instead, he decided to pursue the new field of psychoanalysis, as he'd become convinced that Freudian theory could transform the lives of troubled children. After completing his psychiatric training, Bowlby began working at the Child Guidance Clinic, a mental hospital for youth in North London.[30] He cared for children with all sorts of conditions, from hysteria to violence. Bowlby, however, grew most interested in those sent to the clinic for "thievery."[31] (These children had repeatedly been caught stealing or destroying property.) In addition to giving these young thieves a battery of cognitive tests, Bowlby and the social workers asked them questions about their parents and siblings.[32] Their stories were heartbreaking: Fred's mother "shouts and terrifies the children," while Winnie's father "often beat her." Cyril's mother "openly stated that she wished he had died instead of the baby," while Kathleen's mother "had curious sexual ideas about the children and had been seen thrashing the dogs in a sadistic way."[33]

These sad stories were not unique to the thieving children. Rather, they were a common theme in the lives of many of the disturbed children at the clinic. But Bowlby would soon identify a variable of childhood that, he believed, was more unique to those who stole. His hypothesis began with a six-year-old named Derek who had been sent to the clinic for stealing and skipping school.[34] At first glance, Derek's childhood appeared perfectly ordinary; his middle-class parents were affectionate and his older brother displayed none of his symptoms. However, Derek's medical file contained one notable event: when he was eighteen months old, Derek was hospitalized for nine months with diphtheria. He was completely isolated from his family, cut off from everyone he loved. According to Derek's mother, this separation changed her son. When he returned home, he called her "nurse" and refused to eat. "It seemed like [I was] looking after someone else's baby," she said.[35]

Derek's story led Bowlby to review the histories of his other thieving patients. What he discovered next would define the rest of his career. According to the case files, approximately 85 percent of "affectionless" children prone to stealing had also suffered, like Derek, from a prolonged separation in early childhood. This became their defining trauma. These kids stole candy and toys and clothes, Bowlby argued, to fill an emotional void. "Behind the mask of indifference," he wrote, "is bottomless misery."[36]

Bowlby was haunted by this apparent connection between separation from loved ones and emotional damage. His study of these young thieves would lead him, in 1939, to oppose Operation Pied Piper, the ambitious attempt to evacuate children from British cities in anticipation of a German bombing campaign. (Over four days in September 1939 nearly 3 million people—most of them children—were put on buses and trains and shipped off to live with strangers in the countryside.)[37] In a letter published in the *British Medical Journal*, Bowlby and his coauthors warned that the noble military exercise came with an unintended cost, as the separation of kids under the age of five from their parents would result in a "very serious and widespread psychological disorder" and a subsequent increase in "juvenile delinquency."*[38]

As the war dragged on, Bowlby followed the reports from wartime orphanages. He spoke often with Anna Freud, Sigmund's youngest daughter and the head of the Hampstead War Nursery, who described the suffering of the kids in her care. (Anna Freud was also against Operation Pied Piper, writing that "Love for parents is so great that it is a far greater shock for a child to be suddenly separated from its mother than to have a house collapse on top of him."[39]) In many instances, the toddlers at the Hampstead War Nursery were simply not able to cope with the sudden absence of their family. Patrick, for instance, was a three-year-old whose mother had to work in a distant munitions factory. The boy was distraught, but he refused to cry because his parents said they wouldn't visit if he cried. So Patrick constructed an elaborate routine, telling himself over and over that "his mother would come for him, she would put on his overcoat and would take him home with her again." As the days turned into months, Patrick's monologue became increasingly detailed and desperate: "She will put on

---

*Bowlby was also moved by stories from foundling hospitals, institutions established in the nineteenth century to care for orphaned children. Although these hospitals supplied infants with adequate nutrition, they struggled to keep them alive. A 1915 review of ten infant foundling hospitals in the eastern United States, for instance, concluded that up to 75 percent of the children died before their second birthday. The best hospital in the study had a 31.7 percent mortality rate. Robert Karen, *Becoming Attached* (Oxford: Oxford University Press, 1994), 19.

my overcoat and leggings, she will zip up the zipper, she will put on my pixie hat." When the nursemaids asked Patrick to stop talking, he began mouthing the words silently to himself in the corner.[40]

These tragic anecdotes made Bowlby determined to conduct his own study on the impact of an extended separation between children and parents. His subjects were patients in the pediatric wards of hospitals. British doctors enforced a strict visitation policy, as frequent family contact was believed to cause infection and emotional neediness. Many London hospitals limited parental visits to a single hour on Sundays, with no visits allowed to children under the age of three.[41]

Bowlby soon realized that these separations were traumatic, and that the trauma followed a predictable arc, much like the progression of a physical disease. (Bowlby would later compare the damage of separation to a vitamin deficiency, in which the lack of an "essential nutrient" causes permanent harm.)[42] When first left alone at the hospital, the children collapsed in tears and wails; they didn't trust these strangers in white coats. Their violent protest, however, would soon turn into an eerie detachment, especially if the separation lasted for more than a week. Instead of crying, the children appeared withdrawn, resigned, aloof. It was as if they had forgotten about their parents entirely.[43] The hospital staff referred to this phase as "the settling down."[44] Bowlby called it despair.[45] In an influential 1951 report for the World Health Organization, Bowlby reviewed his hospital data and concluded, contra Watson and the behaviorists, that "the infant and young child should experience a warm, intimate, and continuous relationship with his mother (or permanent mother substitute) in which both find satisfaction and enjoyment."[46]

Although Bowlby was convinced by his data—the loneliness of these children left scars—his research was criticized. Many of the critics attacked the nature of his evidence, which they regarded as anecdotal and confused. They complained about Bowlby's small sample sizes and failure to control for other variables, such as physical illness or nutritional deficits. How could he be so sure that the lack of "mother-love" was causing these behavioral problems? Perhaps these thieves needed more discipline, not affection? The skepticism of love ran deep.

So Bowlby went searching for more evidence. He found it in the work of Harry Harlow, a psychologist at the University of Wisconsin. In the early 1950s, Harlow decided to start a breeding colony of monkeys, as he needed subjects for his research on primate learning. He raised the baby monkeys according to the latest science, feeding them a formula of milk and sugar out of doll bottles. In addition, he gave them a slew of vitamins, antibiotics, and iron supplements.[47] To minimize the spread of disease, Harlow kept the animals in individual cages, away from parents and siblings. (He had accidentally created the kind of "baby farm" dreamed of by Watson.) The resulting litter of primates looked bigger and healthier than their peers in the wild.

But the appearance of these young monkeys hid a devastating loneliness. Because their short lives had been defined by total isolation, they proved incapable of even the most basic social interactions. In the company of other primates, they appeared nervous and withdrawn, staring at the floor. "We had created a brooding, not a breeding colony," Harlow said.[48] For the Wisconsin scientists, these troubled primates demonstrated that the developing mind needed more than proper nutrition. But what did it need?

The first clue came from the cloth diapers that had been used to line the cages. Harlow noticed that his monkeys had become obsessed with these rags, clinging to the fabric like a young child clings to a favorite blanket. (The animals would throw "violent temper tantrums" when the cloth pads were removed.) This poignant behavior inspired Harlow to come up with a new experiment. He decided to raise the next generation of baby monkeys with two different pretend mothers. One was a "wire mother," formed out of metal mesh. (An internal lightbulb provided glimmers of heat.) The second mother was a wooden sculpture, covered in soft rubber sponge and wrapped in terry cloth. In some of these cages, the wire mesh sculpture was fitted with a nipple and feeding tube, while the remaining monkeys were able to feed while cuddling with the soft terrycloth mother. If the skeptics of love were right, and milk was the cause of the mother-child bond, then the infant monkeys should prefer whichever maternal substitute gave them food.

That wasn't what happened. It didn't matter which "mother" held the milk—the babies preferred the one made of rubber sponge and fabric.[49] By the age of five months, the monkeys were spending nearly eighteen hours a day nuzzling with their cuddly parent; they would only climb onto the wire mother to eat.[50] For Harlow, the lesson was clear: the developing mind desperately craved the pleasures of closeness. "Psychologists, at least psychologists who write textbooks, not only show no interest in the origin of love and affection, but they seem to be unaware of its existence," Harlow said, in a speech about his monkey experiments to the American Psychological Association.[51] But this was a tragic mistake. "If monkeys have taught us anything," he later wrote, "it's that you've got to learn how to love before you learn how to live."[52]

Bowlby grasped the implications of Harlow's experiments. The monkeys with their wire mesh mothers were like those toddlers alone in a hospital room: What they craved was closeness. Affection. A feeling that could not be measured in ounces or calories, but instead fulfilled a deeper need. So Bowlby concluded that love was not some frivolous luxury—it was part of a larger process that allowed children to cope with a difficult world. He called this process attachment.

The Strange Situation

Mary Ainsworth, a lively midwesterner with a fondness for basketball, board games, and dinner parties, arrived in London in the summer of 1950.[53] She was following her husband, Leonard, who had been accepted into a graduate program. Although Mary had worked as a researcher at the University of Toronto—her most recent project focused on Rorschach inkblots—she struggled to find a suitable job in England. After a few months of unemployment, Ainsworth got an interview at a psychiatric hospital, where a doctor was looking for an assistant to help analyze his interviews with children.[54] His name was John Bowlby.

Ainsworth got the job. She would spend the next three and a half years working closely with Bowlby, studying the long-term effects of separations at an early age from loved ones.[55] They had no shortage of subjects: postwar Britain was overrun with orphans and refugees, the legacy of a violent decade. The interview data was usually heartbreaking—the children's lives were already marked by absence—but it convinced Ainsworth that Bowlby was right. Attachment is a basic need, writ into our nature.

In 1954, Ainsworth left London behind, following her husband to his new job, this time in Uganda. Although she had no official academic position and little funding, Ainsworth began an ambitious study of infant behavior.[56] She recruited twenty-six families with young babies and visited them for two hours every two weeks in their own homes, many of which were made of mud and wattle.[57] (To gain access, Ainsworth offered the mothers free rides to a nearby medical clinic and dried skim milk at the wholesale price.)[58] Because of her work with Bowlby, Ainsworth was primarily interested in observing the development of the mother-child relationship, but she approached the subject from a different angle. If Bowlby had measured the devastating effects of love's absence, Ainsworth wanted to watch its ordinary beginning.

Ainsworth's research method proved essential. An outsider to everything—Ainsworth was a midwesterner in Africa, a childless woman observing children—she watched these mothers without any preconceptions.[59] In Ainsworth's book about her field research, *Infancy in Uganda: Infant Care and the Growth of Love*, she makes her case not with theory or speculation, but with detailed vignettes of home life. She describes, for instance, an infant named Sulaimani, and the struggles of his mother to care for him:

Sulaimani's mother was a slip of a girl, still in her teens. This was her first baby, and both she and he were unhappy. She had to do most of the garden work, but had no satisfactory arrangement for Sulaimani's care while she was gone. He cried so much that his mother was at her wit's end, and could not behave consistently. Sometimes she was tender and indulgent, and sometimes she was rough and angry in the way she picked him up, slung him over her back, and rocked him. Sometimes, she just let him cry and cry.[60]

Even as Ainsworth describes clear failures of parenting, she withholds judgment. She is careful to remind herself that these mothers are living arduous lives. If they are inattentive, it's often because they need to work the fields; if they are anxious, it's usually because they don't have enough food to eat. The tragedy is that their child-care issues became a downward spiral. The women with the hardest lives often had the least time to attend to their children, which led to more crying and even more stress.

The Uganda observations were an important extension of Bowlby's research, but Ainsworth knew that mere observation was insufficient. If she was going to really understand the mother-child bond, then she needed to find a way to calculate its strength. After two years in Africa, Ainsworth followed her husband for the final time, settling in Baltimore. (She would divorce Leonard in 1960.) Ainsworth accepted a position as a lecturer at Johns Hopkins University, working in the same department that Watson had once chaired.

In 1965, Ainsworth and her assistant, Barbara Wittig, pioneered an experiment known as the Strange Situation task.[61] The task was a twenty-minute melodrama of science, a scripted play unfolding in eight distinct scenes. In the first scene, a mother and her one-year-old baby are introduced to a new room, filled with toys. Most children soon begin to explore the space, bouncing on the red ball and playing with the Raggedy Andy doll. A few minutes later, a strange woman enters the room and begins talking with the mother. In scene three, the first separation occurs: the mother abruptly exits the room, leaving the child alone with the stranger. A few long minutes unfold; the child is observed through a two-way mirror. Scene five is the first reunion, as the mother returns to the room and the stranger departs. Once the baby is "settled in play"—this usually takes a little while—the mother leaves again. In scene six, the baby is left alone for three long minutes (unless he or she was so distraught the experiment had to be terminated early) before the stranger returns and tries to play with the infant. Then, in the final scene, the mother enters and comforts her child.

Not surprisingly, the Strange Situation experiment was controversial when it was first introduced. Many of Ainsworth's colleagues thought it needlessly callous, revealing nothing new about the parent-child bond. But Ainsworth was unfazed. She believed that her scripted experiment revealed a basic truth of life. Only in the midst of high drama—when a baby was repeatedly lost and found, abandoned and reunited—was Ainsworth able to learn about our attachment habits.

At first, the results seemed to confirm Bowlby's basic theory: separation from the mother is stressful.* That's why a clear majority of one-year-olds wept when left alone and expressed

---

*One of the persistent criticisms of attachment theory is that, at least in the early decades, researchers focused solely on the role of the mother, making it seem as if she were the only parent who mattered. This is a mistake that Bowlby, toward the end of his career, took pains to correct. "Looking after babies and young children is no job for a single person," Bowlby declared in a 1980 lecture. "If the job is to be well done and the child's principal caregiver is not to be too exhausted, the caregiver herself (or himself) needs a great deal of assistance. . . . In most societies throughout the world these facts have been, and still are, taken for granted and the society organized accordingly. Paradoxically it has taken the world's richest societies to ignore these basic facts."

affection after their mother returned. But Ainsworth wasn't interested in generalities—she wanted to understand *every* child, even those who violated her theoretical assumptions. This led her to study those outlier infants, the kids who didn't cry when abandoned or couldn't stop crying when the experiment was over.[62]

The problem with outliers is that they're unusual. As a result, Ainsworth was forced to repeat the experiment again and again; the sound of wailing became the sound track of her lab. It took a few years, but some patterns eventually emerged from the muddle of tears and hugs. While approximately 66 percent of kids engaged in affectionate touches when their mother came back—this was a sign of secure attachment—the remaining 34 percent consistently exhibited a form of behavior Ainsworth labeled "insecure" attachment.[63] In most instances, this insecurity manifested itself as indifference, as the children didn't seem to mind the departure of the mothers; the separation wasn't that upsetting. (Later studies revealed that these stoic infants were in fact quite stressed, as their heart rate and cortisol levels spiked whenever they were left alone.)[64] When the mother returned, these children would turn away, seemingly uninterested in reunion. Ainsworth referred to these babies as having "avoidant" attachments. However, a third of the insecure infants, or 12 percent of the total sample, reacted in the opposite manner. Some of these babies never settled into the new room and refused to play with the unknown toys. Others became distraught after the first separation, clinging to the mother or pushing her away when she returned. (If the mother picked them up, these infants did not "sink in" to her embrace.)[65] Ainsworth labeled this category of response "resistant" attachment, since the children seemed to resist the comfort of their caregivers. Instead of being affectionate, the interactions of mother and child had an "unmistakably angry quality."[66]

Such variation isn't surprising. Human nature is a bell curve, every behavior exhibiting a spectrum of differences. But Ainsworth discovered that these differences weren't random, but instead were closely correlated with parenting style as observed during a series of lengthy home visits conducted every three weeks.[67] ("We got to know our families very well," Ainsworth wrote, noting that this familiarity made it easier for the mothers to forget they were being studied.[68]) Those infants with secure attachments were far more likely to have mothers who scored high on a sliding scale of "parental sensitivity."[69] These moms engaged in constant baby-talk and expressed more interest in the infant mind. When asked about their child, their answers were far more detailed, entertaining, and emotive. The highly sensitive mother is "able to see things from B's [the baby's] point of view," Ainsworth wrote. "Her perceptions of his signals and communications are not distorted by her own needs and defenses."[70]

This doesn't mean that these sensitive mothers were pushovers, always obeying the whims of their kids. Ainsworth was careful to point out that true sensitivity also included plenty of boundaries; the most effective parents knew when to push back. "When she feels that it is best not to comply with his demands—for example, when he is too excited, over-imperious, or wants something he should not have—she is tactful in acknowledging his communication and in offering an acceptable alternative," Ainsworth wrote."[71] While Watson and his followers dismissed the "mawkish" love of parents as a dangerous influence, weakening the will of their kids, Ainsworth pointed out that even effective discipline requires warmth. It wasn't a coincidence that the babies with the most loving mothers spent the least time crying.

Ainsworth's research is often taken as a guide to parenting, but its real legacy concerns the nature of measurement. John Watson and his followers disregarded love because it couldn't be quantified. The feeling was just another vague mystery, unfit for a rigorous science. But Ainsworth's Strange Situation experiment—her short drama of separation and reunion—found a way to test the strength of the loving bond. Although modern psychology had always been obsessed with variables of the individual—intelligence tests, personality quizzes, and so on—Ainsworth's research documented the stunning influence of relationships. What mattered most, at least for these babies, happened *between* people.

In her later years, Ainsworth and her colleagues would show that attachment security closely predicted a wide range of seemingly unrelated childhood behaviors. One of her most important findings was the connection between sensitive parents and the willingness of young children to explore novel situations, whether it was a new room or a new toy. Bowlby explained this finding with an elaborate military metaphor, comparing the attachment figure to a "secure base," which allows an expeditionary force to "press forward and take risks."[72] The same logic applies to parents. Unless children have a secure base at home—a loved one to retreat to in times of stress—they won't be able to enjoy the world on their own."[73]

This finding would later become known as the dependency paradox.[74] It's a paradox because it suggests that true independence requires that we become dependent on someone else. Children don't explore because they are lacking something essential. They explore because they already have everything they need.* As John wrote in the Gospels (4:18), "Perfect love casts out fear."

Like Bowlby before her, Ainsworth faced harsh criticism from her peers. They pilloried the premise of her work—wasn't it obvious that kids would cry when left alone in a strange place?—and mocked her use of "nonscientific" language, such as "tender" and "sensitive." (Many of these attacks now seem tainted with misogyny, as if Ainsworth were incapable of looking at love objectively simply because she was a woman with maternal instincts.) The criticism was so fierce that Ainsworth's studies were routinely rejected during peer review, forcing her to write books about her research instead of publishing articles.[75]

The scorn fueled Ainsworth's self-doubts. On good days, she imagined herself, like Bowlby, as one of those stubborn scientists working to shift the paradigm. On bad days, she worried that her critics were right, that love wasn't a subject fit for science. However, the force of her ideas—her conviction that our attachments mattered, and that how they mattered could be measured—was irrefutable. But it would take another study of infants left alone in a strange room, and another few decades, for that to become clear.

---

*In his early writings on separation, Bowlby imagined the child mind as a homeostatic system, wired to seek out a balance between two opposed goals: safety and learning. His thinking on the subject was strongly influenced by World War II military technology, which used rudimentary computers to control the behavior of machines. By monitoring changes in the external environment, these "cybernetic" devices were able to adjust their own responses. This new approach helped lead to the invention of "smart bombs"—they altered their own trajectory based on radio signals—and gun mounts that automatically focused on the target. Phillip Shaver and Mario Mikulincer, *Attachment in Adulthood: Structure, Dynamics and Change* (New York: Guilford Press, 2007), 219.

Licking and Grooming

In 1975, Byron Egeland, a psychologist at the University of Minnesota, began studying a group of subjects that had been largely neglected by modern science: pregnant women living in poverty. He signed up 267 expectant mothers at Hennepin County General Hospital in Minneapolis. Their demographic data reads like a laundry list of risk factors for a difficult future. In addition to poverty, many of these mothers were teenagers, lacked education (41 percent had dropped out of high school), had dietary deficiencies (37 percent weren't getting adequate nutrition), and suffered from a shortage of social support.[76] Veronica, for instance, ran away from an abusive home at the age of twelve. A few years later, she became pregnant, probably with her drug dealer's child. When he was sent to prison, Veronica and her son, Thomas, ended up living in a shelter.[77] She suffered from depression and addiction.

Egeland's study began with limited aims: he wanted to identify the variables that predicted the "mistreatment" of children, so that social workers could offer counseling before any abuse occurred. However, the scientists were soon impressed, like Ainsworth in Uganda, by the sheer variation of parenting behavior. Some of these new mothers were attentive and supportive, even amid adversity. Others struggled to hold it together during a tantrum; Veronica, for instance, was often "harshly rejecting" toward her son.[78]

To better understand the impact of all this variation, Egeland teamed up with Alan Sroufe, a Minnesota psychologist and early supporter of attachment theory. After testing every infant with Ainsworth's Strange Situation task at the age of twelve months—the initial results confirmed the correlation between sensitive parenting and attachment security—Egeland and Sroufe decided to turn their short-term risk-assessment study into a longitudinal project that would eventually become epic in scale, spanning generations and decades. "We didn't really know what we were getting into," Sroufe remembers. "But once you start seeing these patterns emerge, and you see the continuities in behavior, you don't want to stop."[79]

The first ambitious follow-up occurred when the children were four and five years old. To capture the complexities of early childhood, Egeland and Sroufe decided to start their own nursery school, which was offered free to forty of the children in the study. In the classrooms, a team of twenty trained observers kept detailed notes on every child's behavior. In addition, the scientists recorded hundreds of hours of videotape, which were later coded and analyzed.[80]

The results were convincing. In the nursery school, children with secure attachment histories were rated as more independent, sociable, and popular than their less secure peers. They were far less likely to bully or get bullied. They exhibited more self-control, scored higher on measurements of intelligence, self-esteem, and resilience,[81] and displayed more empathy for other children.[82] (All ratings were done blindly, as the observers had no knowledge of how the subjects had been categorized as infants.) In the laboratory Barrier Box task, for instance, a child was introduced to a collection of toys, such as LEGOs, superhero figurines, and dolls. After a few minutes of free play, a scientist came along and told the children that the toys they'd been enjoying belonged in the other room. If the children wanted to keep playing, they had to get a new set of toys out of a clear plastic box that was virtually impossible to open. It was a deliberately frustrating task. However, the way these children coped with their frustration was revealing. While most preschoolers struggled with the task, either quickly giving up or resorting to brute force and displays of anger, some kids excelled at the Barrier Box. They never managed to open it, but they remained focused and persistent, patiently trying out a variety of strategies. After ten minutes, the scientists ended the experiment, opened the box, and let every child play with the toys.

What explained these differences in performance? The best answer was early attachment. Approximately 40 percent of securely attached children were given the highest ratings on the Barrier Box task, while not a single preschooler with an insecure attachment history was so rated. What's more, insecurely attached kids accounted for 75 percent of the subjects given the lowest ratings. Although the children had been given a challenge that had nothing to do with their closest family relationships, the legacy of those first attachments shadowed their behavior. The variable couldn't be escaped.[83]

Five years later. The children were invited to spend four weeks at a summer camp on the University of Minnesota campus. Like the preschool, this immersive setup allowed the scientists to gather an unprecedented amount of data as they watched the children play soccer and softball, swim in the pool, and work together on art projects. Once again, the results were a stark reminder that attachment has lasting consequences. Children with secure attachments to their parents generally showed much higher levels of "social competence," better able to develop and maintain relationships with other kids at the camp. As a result, they spent 40 percent more time with their friends. When the ten-year-olds were given challenging tasks by the scientists, such as having to navigate an obstacle course, those with "secure histories organized themselves in more effective ways, avoided scapegoating, and performed dramatically better."[84]

As Egeland and Sroufe followed the children into adolescence, they uncovered a most unexpected finding: the connection between infant attachment and the behavior of the children was getting *stronger*. The teenagers were even more influenced by their earliest relationships than when they were five or ten years old. "Isn't that remarkable?" Sroufe says. "These kids often have the physical characteristics of adults, and yet what we found is that so much of what they are doing was correlated with these attachment measures from when they were twelve months old." The Minnesota scientists found that adolescents with secure infant attachments also performed better in high school, with stronger attachments leading to higher standardized-test scores. (Attachment security was also inversely correlated with disciplinary problems.) The presence of a supportive and sensitive parent before the age of three and a half was better than IQ scores at predicting whether the children would graduate from high school. [85]

Why are teenagers so shaped by their attachment history? Like infants, adolescents are also struggling to form close relationships as they spend increasing amounts of time with their friends. "They're [teenagers] looking for a kind of intimacy," Sroufe says. "But if you're going to get that intimacy, then you need to trust people. You need to tell them how you feel. You need to open up. And that builds on emotional skills that are very much connected to early attachment experience."[86] Just as babies must learn how to express their vulnerability—that usually means crying for an attachment figure—so do teenagers have to find ways to reach out and make connections with their peers. Being vulnerable is not a sign of weakness. It's how we let people in.

The Minnesota subjects are now turning forty, with families and children of their own. Nevertheless, the correlations continue; love echoes across the generations.[87] The scientists have found that attachment quality in the first year of life helps predict adult health, as "resistant" infants—those babies who refused to be comforted by their mothers upon their return, even though they cried in her absence—were 2.85 times more likely to report a chronic illness at the age of thirty-two when compared to those who were securely attached.[*88] Or consider a recent paper led by the psychologist Lee Raby, which found that the quality of parenting during childhood was correlated with the romantic behavior of the Minnesota subjects more than thirty years later. In particular, those with less sensitive mothers exhibited a spike in skin reactivity when having discussions about a source of conflict with their partners and spouses. One explanation for these changes in skin reactivity is that subjects are holding back their feelings, as increased reactivity is associated with fear and emotional inhibition. (Lie detectors work on this principle.) Because these adults had parents who struggled to respond to their emotional needs, they learned

---

*The precise mechanisms behind this dramatic increase in illness remain unclear. One likely possibility is that troubled attachment styles in childhood increase the incidence of psychosomatic illness. For instance, a 2006 study led by Robert Waldinger at Harvard Medical School found that middle-aged adults who experience insecure attachments in early life are far more likely to experience "somatization," which is the tendency to experience bodily symptoms in response to psychological stressors. Robert J. Waldinger, Marc S. Schulz, Arthur J. Barsky, and David K. Ahern, "Mapping the road from childhood trauma to adult somatization: The role of attachment," *Psychosomatic Medicine* 68.1 (2006): 129–35.

to hide their worries.[89] Intimacy requires candor, a willingness to show your cracks, but that can be hard for people who had insecure childhood attachments.

As the years pass, this inability to discuss relationship issues can undo the relationship, which is why those with less secure attachments as children also experienced shorter and less satisfying adult attachments.[90] In a separate analysis, the Minnesota researchers looked at old videotapes of the subjects at the age of two, as the toddlers attempted to learn a new skill from their mothers. If this interaction was judged unsuccessful—the mother wasn't supportive enough, or the child refused help—the subjects were also more likely to get described as a "weak link" by their adult partners. Thirty years had passed, but they still struggled to get close to other people.[91]

In their descriptions of the study, the Minnesota scientists repeatedly return to the story of a boy named Tony, whose complicated life reflects the complicated themes of the research. In 1977, when the Minnesota scientists first tested him on the Strange Situation task, Tony appeared securely attached, the happy infant of loving parents. He excelled in preschool and scored well on nearly every measurement of early childhood, from the Barrier Box to literacy skills. But then, when Tony was six, his parents went through a bitter divorce. He rarely saw his father. When he was thirteen, Tony's mother died in a car accident. His father then decided to move to another state, taking Tony's two siblings with him. Tony was forced to live with his elderly aunt and uncle.[92]

Given this tragic series of events, it's not surprising that Tony spiraled downward in his teenage years. He failed several classes at school, had few stable friendships, and oversaw a burglary ring in an "administrative capacity." (Like Bowlby's young thieves, Tony tried to appease his sadness with stolen things.) After interviewing Tony at the age of fifteen, the psychologists described his fall: "The light inside of him seemed to have gone out. He was visibly depressed and isolated."

But Tony's tale doesn't end there. In his early twenties, he met a woman at the local community college. She was attracted "to his quietness and tender heart." They got married a few years later and had a daughter. When the scientists watched Tony with his toddler, they were struck by his devotion, how he hadn't forgotten the lessons of early attachment. "An extraordinarily supportive father," wrote the scientists. "He was patient, involved, warm and available, providing the structure, limits, and encouragement the child needed." Although Tony had struggled as a teenager to talk about his mother's death—he insisted that the loss "didn't mean that much"—he was now able to share his feelings and speculate on how her passing had shaped his life.[93] In *The Development of the Person*, the Minnesota scientists compare our early attachment experiences to the foundation of a house. While the foundation is not sufficient for shelter—you also need solid beams and a sturdy roof—they note that "a house cannot be stronger than its foundation." That's what we get as young children: a foundation for attachment. The beginnings of a structure on which everything else is built.[94]

Such stories are just stories; nothing is proved when the *n* is 1. We will never know if Tony's securely attached childhood enabled his adult recovery or if his experience of early love made his later resilience possible. It's important to remember that these correlations of personality are not certainties: many insecure babies become supportive spouses, just as many secure children drop out of high school and struggle later in life. As Bowlby first pointed out, the human attachment system is responsive to changing conditions. That means we can still learn how to love, even if our childhood was marked by loss and insecurity. Attachment is not a fixed state, or a permanent diagnosis. It is a continual *process*, a working model of relationships that can always be revised.

The Minnesota study looks at life with a telescope. By tracking its subjects for years, it illuminates our human arcs, the subtle patterns that underpin our lives. But some questions require microscopes. If we want to understand *how* love changes us—why it makes us tougher, more resilient, less likely to break—then we need to zoom in. Because the feeling is not an airy nothing. Love literally marks the mind.

Michael Meaney, a neuroscientist at McGill University, began studying attachment because of an accidental observation. After he returned rat pups to their Plexiglas cages, Meaney noticed that some rodent mothers were much quicker to comfort their offspring than others, licking and grooming the young animal until its pulse returned to baseline. Meaney became interested in this maternal variation, which led him and his graduate students to spend eight hours a day closely observing the interactions of rat families. Sure enough, some mothers spent far more time (about 50 percent more) licking and grooming their offspring. When the pups were a hundred days old—that's late adolescence in rat years—they were run through a battery of stress and intelligence tests.[95]

The results were stunning. One of Meaney's main behavioral measures is known as the open-field test. It's a simple enough design: A rat is placed in a round box for five minutes. Nervous animals tend to be wallflowers, clinging to the edge of the box like teenagers at a school dance. Less anxious rats tend to explore their surroundings, wandering into the center of the enclosure in search of food. According to Meaney's data, those pups born to the most comforting mothers—the high-LG [licking/grooming] animals—spent thirty-five seconds, on average, in the center of the box. The low-LG pups, on the other hand, spent less than five seconds there.[96] Similar patterns appeared across a wide range of assays and measurements. High-LG were less aggressive with their peers.[97] They released fewer stress hormones when restrained.[98] They solved mazes more quickly.[99] They were better at learning from their littermates.[100] They were more nurturing with their own pups.

In recent years, Meaney has shown how these feelings of affection alter the brain. High-LG rat pups have fewer receptors for stress hormone and more receptors for the chemicals that attenuate the stress response; they show less activity in parts of the cortex, such as the amygdala, closely associated with fear and anxiety; they exhibit more synaptic growth in the hippocampus, a part of the cortex associated with learning and memory;[101] even their DNA is read differently as all that maternal care activates a genetic switch that protects rats against chronic stress.[102] These neural and genetic differences suggest that pups raised by the most comforting mothers are better able to handle the upheavals of life, whether it's a scary new cage or a strange new scientist.

The same lesson applies to people. A natural experiment took place during World War II, when more than seventy thousand young Finnish children were evacuated to temporary foster homes in Sweden and Denmark.[103] For the kids who stayed behind in Finland, life was filled with moments of acute stress—regular air bombardments and invasions by the Russians and the Germans. But for those sent away, the stress of being separated from their parents was unceasing. They lacked what they needed most.

This early shock had lifelong consequences. A 2009 study found that Finnish adults who had been sent away from their parents between 1939 and 1944 showed an 86 percent increase in deaths due to cardiovascular illness compared to those who had stayed at home.[104] Although more than sixty years had passed since the war, these temporary orphans were also significantly more likely to have high blood pressure and type 2 diabetes. Other studies have documented elevated levels of stress hormone[105] and increased risk of severe depressive symptoms among the wartime evacuees.[106]

The feeling of love is not just a source of pleasure. It's also a kind of protection.[107]

Adaptation to Life

In the late 1930s, Arlie Bock, a professor of hygiene and the head of Health Services at Harvard University, received funding from the department-store magnate W. T. Grant for a long-term study of healthy undergraduates. Science was too focused on sickness, Bock said. It was time to "make a systematic inquiry into the kinds of people who are well and do well."[108] Grant agreed and hoped that the research would help him better identify those who would be successful store managers.

The project began with the Harvard College class of 1939 and continued to recruit normal undergraduates—men "able to paddle their own canoe," Bock wrote[109]—for the next five years. Bock ended up with a cohort of 268 Harvard students.[110] The subjects were run through a gauntlet of medical and psychiatric tests, from handwriting analysis to inkblot cards.

They were asked about their personal and medical histories—
When did you stop wetting the bed? How much sugar do you
put in your coffee? Do you masturbate?[111]—and given a litany
of intelligence tests, most borrowed from the army. The staff
doctors measured the brow ridges on their foreheads, the circumference of their chests, and the hanging length of their
scrotums.[112] They were asked to make sense of inkblots and
sprint for five minutes on a treadmill.

The results were not interesting. Although Bock and his colleagues hoped that their medical measurements would predict
life outcomes, that didn't happen. The "masculinity" of body
types bore no relationship to rank in the military during World
War II, nor did their responses to the inkblots predict anything
about their sex lives. Forehead structure wasn't linked to intelligence, and intelligence wasn't significantly linked to income.[113]

Despite these failures, the Grant Study—its official name is
the Harvard Study of Adult Development—continued to track
the men into middle age. The subjects were asked about their
drinking habits, political beliefs, and favorite sports to play.
They were interviewed about their experience in the war and
given a long list of questions about smoking and cigarettes.
(After W. T. Grant withdrew funding, the study was supported
in part by Philip Morris.)[114] Given the privileged backgrounds
of the Harvard men, it's not surprising that many of them became eminent and successful. One became a governor; four
ran for the US Senate; another became the president. (While
almost all of the Grant subjects remain anonymous, John F.
Kennedy's file has been sealed until 2040, thus forcing the scientists to confirm his involvement.)[115] As the years went by,
the Harvard study remained most notable for what it could *not*

find. The scientists had amassed so much detailed information—each man had his own folder, as thick as a dictionary[116]—
but it all proved useless, at least when it came to making sense
of adult outcomes. The expected associations never appeared;
the secrets of the good life remained a secret.

Most worrisome, perhaps, was that the fundamental assumption of the project—it was supposed to be an investigation of health, not sickness—was slowly being dismantled.
By the time the Harvard men turned fifty, nearly 30 percent
of them had suffered from mental illness, such as alcoholism
and manic depression.[117] (Three percent of them had been
hospitalized for their psychiatric problems.)[118] "They must
have been spoiled by you psychiatrists," Bock would later
complain. "They didn't have problems like that when I was
running the study!"[119]

If not for a young doctor named George Eman Vaillant, the
Grant Study may have remained an expensive failure. It would
be remembered, to the extent anyone remembered it, as a testament to the peculiar theories of midcentury psychology. But
Vaillant realized that this longitudinal project had vast potential if the right questions were asked. Unlike his predecessors,
Vaillant didn't believe that measures of chest circumference
would ever predict life outcomes, or that such a thing as "the
normal person" even existed. "I had gone to Harvard myself,"
Vaillant says, "and I knew that even Harvard men had their
issues."[120]

I met George Vaillant on a hot summer day in Orange, California, where he lives with his current wife, who is also a Harvard-
trained psychiatrist. Their gated clapboard house is on a quiet

suburban street, situated among towering trees that were planted before there were any houses, when the neighborhood was a private park surrounded by citrus groves. After the Great Depression, the park was sold off to local doctors, who built these estates.

Vaillant suggested that we sit on the front porch and enjoy the breeze and the birds. But then the breeze disappeared and the only birds around were crows, fighting over the treetops. After a few minutes, both of us were sweating through our shirts, water glasses already empty.

Vaillant is a spry eighty-year-old. His gray hair is fine and parted, tamed by decades of being combed in the exact same manner. He talks slowly, always pausing thoughtfully in mid-sentence, even when answering questions he's probably answered a hundred times before. When Vaillant slips into a soliloquy—and even straightforward questions have a way of turning into digressive lectures on Freud and fMRI research—he tends to close his eyes and run his fingers delicately over his eyelids. It almost looks as if he were praying.

The oldest son of a banker's daughter, Vaillant grew up in the Great Depression in a wealthy family. His mother, he says ruefully, "came from the John Watson school of parenting," leaving young George starved for affection. When he was ten years old, his father walked into the backyard of their mansion in Chester County, Pennsylvania, and shot himself in the head with a revolver. George was the last person to see him alive.

The suicide defined the rest of Vaillant's childhood. His mother took the kids away to Arizona; they didn't even stay for the funeral. A few years later, Vaillant was sent to boarding school in New England. He went on to Harvard College, where he studied literature. He stayed in Cambridge for medical school—"I had a vague desire to help people, which I guess is why I became a doctor," Vaillant says—and chose to specialize in psychiatry. When I ask him why, he holds out his trembling hands. "Look at the shake. I could never hold a knife."

As a young resident, Vaillant became interested in schizophrenic patients who no longer displayed symptoms of their illness. "Remember, schizophrenics were supposed to be incurable," Vaillant says. "They were never supposed to stop hearing voices." To understand their recovery, Vaillant began paying careful attention to the extended case histories of his patients, noticing all the ways in which their symptoms were shifted by circumstance, treatment, and even personal relationships. "This probably sounds like a very obvious idea, but I was impressed by the notion that if you wanted to understand mental health, then you needed to follow people for years and years. You couldn't just take a slice of a life and say you understood. Understanding takes time."

It was at this point in his career that Vaillant started working on the Grant Study. While he was enthralled with its longitudinal approach—"To be able to study lives in such depth, over so many decades . . . was like looking through the Mount Palomar telescope," he said in a 2009 interview in the *Atlantic* with Joshua Wolf Shenk—Vaillant was disappointed with his subjects, at least at first. "I didn't particularly want to work on healthy people," he says. "Normal seemed boring." However, once Vaillant read the men's case files, he realized that their upper-class lives hid a vast amount of angst and illness, just like his own. These subjects had been selected because they seemed so healthy and fortunate—they were the most privileged young men in the most privileged country on earth—but Vaillant came to see that none of them were living happily ever after. "Their files felt to me like a Tolstoy story or a Eugene O'Neill play," he says. "They were filled with drama. I couldn't stop reading them."

Vaillant's literary allusions are not an accident. The Grant Study began as an attempt to fit the messiness of life into a neat model, to find the biological variables that predicted health, wealth, and happiness. But the initial failures of the study to predict anything led Vaillant to conclude that a new approach was needed. "You can't fit a man on an IBM [punch] card," Vaillant says, referring to the first form of data storage used by the Grant scientists. Instead of trying to quantify the lives of his subjects, measuring their skulls and blood pressure and scrotums, Vaillant treated them like characters in a complicated novel. He wanted to hear their stories, which was why he started his interviews with a long list of open-ended questions. He asked about their wives and mistresses, their kids and their cocktails, what they did for fun and how they coped with despair. Vaillant was a good listener. The conversations were his best data.

These interviews transformed the Grant Study. If the early Grant follow-ups had been modeled on a routine physical exam—the body was supposed to be destiny—Vaillant turned it into a therapy session. For the most part, the men responded with candor, grateful for the opportunity to unburden themselves for science. Their answers confirmed Vaillant's suspicions, as the middle-aged subjects frequently confessed that all their money and success still left them struggling for meaning and happiness. In one of his first extended write-ups of the Grant Study, Vaillant approvingly quotes the conclusions of another longitudinal project. "No especially blessed individual turned up in this assessment," the scientists wrote. "The luckiest of the lives here studied had its full share of difficulty and private despair."[121]

This depressing truth—everyone struggles, everyone suffers—led to Vaillant's first revelation, which is that our mental health is defined by how we *cope*. The body responds to injury by relying on a raft of automatic defenses—when we bleed, the blood clots; when we are cut, the skin scars. Vaillant believed that the mind had its own mechanisms of protection, especially when it came to handling stress and trauma. In Freudian theory, these mechanisms are known as adaptations. Some adaptations are psychotic—we might become paranoid or start hallucinating—while others are immature and neurotic and manifest themselves as hypochondria and addiction. The healthiest defenses, however, are those Vaillant places in the "mature" category, such as humor, sublimation, and altruism.[122] Instead of drowning our sorrows in whiskey, we cheer ourselves up by helping others or writing a poem about the sadness. "The basic distinction is quite straightforward," Vaillant says. "The mature defenses are all about the other. They help you help other people. The immature defenses, in contrast, might make you happy in the moment, but they totally screw up your life and relationships." Vaillant then pauses, as if he's about to deliver a line he knows I'll like: "The essence of love is in realizing that someone matters more than you. In the short run, that's the hard part. In the long run, that's the fun part."

This theory of mental life raises an obvious question: If psychiatric health is simply the process of adaptation, what determines our adaptive style? Why do some people get back pain while others make art? Why do some people flee into affairs while others find solace in their marriage? Here Vaillant's research has been most revealing, providing yet another layer of evidence in support of attachment theory. While Freud argued that our defense mechanisms were shaped by the sexual tensions of childhood, Vaillant has come to believe that they're actually determined by our relationships with other people. In particular, Vaillant says, it is the experience of loving and being loved that most closely predicts how we react to the hardships of life; human attachments are the ultimate source of resilience. "The seventy-five years and twenty million dollars expended on the Grant Study points, at least to me, to a straightforward five-word conclusion," Vaillant writes. " 'Happiness equals love. Full stop.' "[*123]

The line seems too romantic to be true. Yet, Vaillant insists that the numbers can't be denied. When he began working on the Grant Study, Vaillant was barely familiar with the research of Bowlby and Ainsworth. "I thought of him [Bowlby] as someone who studied juvenile delinquents," Vaillant says, "and it wasn't until I was asked to write a short biography of Bowlby [for the *American Journal of Psychiatry*] that I discovered that he was big on the same things that I was big on. And I think what we both came to see is that you really can't do anything without love."

The power of love begins at the beginning, just as Bowlby and Ainsworth suspected. Based on the initial interviews with the Harvard men, Vaillant assessed the warmth of their early childhood. Did the subjects feel loved by their mother and father? How often did they eat family meals together? Did they stay in close contact with their brothers and sisters? The an-

---

*As Vaillant notes, Virgil came to a similar conclusion a few thousand years ago, when he declared, "Omnia vincit amor," or love conquers all. Unfortunately, Virgil "had no data" to back up his poetry. George Vaillant, *Triumphs of Experience* (Cambridge, MA: Belknap Press, 2012), 52.

swers to these questions turned out to have sweeping consequences, even decades later. When Vaillant compared the lives
of men in the Cherished category—those with the most secure
attachments in early life—to those in the Loveless category, he
found that the Loveless were three times more likely to have
been diagnosed with a mental illness, five times more likely
to be "unusually anxious," and four times less likely to rely on
mature adaptations when dealing with adversity.[124] A third of
the men without a warm maternal relationship suffered from
dementia in old age, a rate 2.5 times higher than those with
a warm relationship.[125] (Interestingly, a loving mother was
far more protective against memory loss than "vascular risk
factors," such as low cholesterol.)* The variation in childhood
warmth even predicted success in the workplace, as subjects
from the most loving homes earned 50 percent more money
over their careers than those from the bleakest homes.[126] Early
attachment is more predictive of achievement than any other
variable measured in the Grant Study, including IQ scores.[127]

But love doesn't only matter at the start of life; the need for
attachment is not just a phase of development. As the men entered their fifties, Vaillant increasingly focused his interviews
on their closest relationships. (Vaillant likes to compare longitudinal studies to good wines—they tend to get better with
age.) He asked about their marital lives and "patterns of entertaining"; about their oldest friends and their parenting habits.
This mass of biographical data allowed Vaillant to rank the
Grant subjects based on the quality of their relationships in

---

*The importance of the maternal relationship doesn't mean fathers don't
matter—it was merely a by-product of the age, as the scientists largely neglected to study the typical father-child relationship.

middle age. According to the data, nothing counts more than our attachments. Nothing even comes close. The loneliest subjects in the Grant study were ten times more likely to suffer from a chronic illness before the age of fifty-two, five times more likely to be diagnosed with a mental illness, and eight times more likely to rely on immature defense mechanisms. These men often feigned self-reliance, pretending not to need other people, but Vaillant discovered that they actually lived life in terror. They were three times as likely to become heavy users of alcohol and tranquilizers.[128]

Such numbers are mere distillates, a scientific summary of anonymous men. But there is still value in knowing the individual stories. (As Vaillant notes, "The Old Testament isn't around today because it was full of useful statistics.") While Vaillant's writing is dense with correlations, it's also filled with compelling case studies. In these miniature biographies the sweep of the Grant Study becomes clear. "I've come to know these men," Vaillant says. "I've eaten at their tables. I've met their kids. I've been asking them questions for forty years. And you know what? They're still surprising me."

Consider the sad tale of Oliver Kane, a subject in the Grant Study. Kane's childhood was framed by loss. His father died when he was one, followed by the death of his mother fourteen years later. Nevertheless, Kane relied on his unusual intelligence—Vaillant describes him as "perhaps the most intelligent man in the study"—to succeed at Harvard and embark on a lucrative career as a management consultant. (In the early 1960s, Kane was making more than $70,000 a year, which is equivalent to more than half a million dollars today.) But the money proved meaningless.[129] Instead of buying a home, Kane chose to live in residential hotels, using a men's club as his mailing address. He traveled constantly for work—his final interview with Vaillant took place in the Admirals lounge at O'Hare Airport—and he made few lasting relationships.[130] "I came to see him as a man who tried to live without love," Vaillant says. "Whether that was because of his shitty childhood, or because he just didn't want to be bothered, I don't know. But he was very much an experiment."

The experiment had a terrible ending. What Kane learned—a lesson that came too late—is that success means nothing if it's not shared. When he was fifty years old, Kane flew his small plane into a mountain. The authorities couldn't say for certain if it was suicide, but Vaillant notes that Kane had spent the days before the crash revising his will. And then there's his last note to the Grant Study, written a year before Kane's death. The words are steeped in despair: "Ironically, as I have acquired more external success, I have more and more doubts that I have chosen a way of life that really means anything."[131]

In his writings, Vaillant counterposes the tragic life of Oliver Kane with the story of Anna, a woman in the "Genetic Studies of Genius." Begun in 1921 by the psychologist Lewis Terman, the study attempted to track the impact of intelligence in the classroom. It focused on outliers and included 1,528 children who scored in the top few percent on the IQ test. Although the initial plan was to end the longitudinal project after a few years, Terman's subjects enthralled him, and he continued to follow them for the rest of his life.

When the "Termites" were in their late seventies, Vaillant asked for permission to interview ninety of the women. He wanted to see if the patterns he'd observed among the Harvard men applied to both genders. That's when he met Anna, a woman with "short gray hair, dimming vision, too much weight, and arthritic hands."[132] Born into a poor family in rural Colorado, Anna spent her career as a math teacher in a public high school. She enjoyed teaching, but struggled to balance the demands of her job with the needs of her four children. (Anna's husband had been incapacitated by recurrent bouts of illness, which meant that the family largely relied on her income.) Most evenings, Anna would put the kids to bed, make a big pot of coffee, and then grade geometry papers until her eyes gave out. When Vaillant interviewed Anna, she was living alone in a small apartment; her husband had died a few years before. "You might look at her and think, 'She's had a rough go of it,'" Vaillant says.

But Anna was not sad or defined by her regrets. She insisted on telling Vaillant the happy story of her forty-year marriage, which had only grown "closer and closer" over time. She talked about the consolations of faith and the pleasures of driving her bright yellow Volkswagen Rabbit to the grocery store. She kept circling back to her children and grandchildren, pointing to their framed pictures. She bragged about their accomplishments before catching herself: "That's pride. And the church says we're not supposed to be proud." But then, Vaillant writes, "she would go right back to being proud."[133]

What can be learned from all these archived lives? When asked to describe the single most important finding of his longitudinal study, Vaillant focuses on the crucial importance of our closest relationships.[134] To make his case, Vaillant then describes a study he oversaw on the relative happiness of lottery winners and paraplegics. The newly rich, it turned out, weren't any happier than the paralyzed. Everyone eventually habituated to their condition; money was the most fleeting reward.

Instead, Vaillant found that as the Grant subjects entered their late eighties—nearly half of them were still alive—only one variable predicted their life satisfaction: *the capacity for loving relationships*. "I wrote once that when we are old our lives become the sum of everyone we have loved," Vaillant says. "That's still true. I believe it more than ever."

Vaillant struggled to live out that belief. After having four children with his first wife, Vaillant filed for divorce in 1970. He soon married again, had another child, and then, twenty years later, left his second wife for a colleague. Five years later, Vaillant asked his second wife to take him back. She did, but it didn't work out. Vaillant has since married for the fifth time, to the psychiatrist Diane Highum. In old interviews, Vaillant compared himself to King Lear, a distant father at the head of a dysfunctional family.[135] (Several of his children have been estranged from him for long periods.) While Vaillant's personal difficulties could be seen as undermining his scientific message—how can he preach about the importance of love when he can't even stay married?—I've come to believe that, in a strange way, his flaws have drawn him even deeper into the work. He studied the Grant men to see where he's been, but also to know where he's going; to understand what he has, and also what he lacks. "Use this gently," he tells me. "But I've often thought that writing *Adaptation* [*Adaptation to Life* was Vaillant's first book about the Grant subjects] was a plea for help. That I was saying, 'Won't someone please be attached to me?' I guess you could say that I learned about the importance of attachment in my own life by watching it unfold in my subjects."

It's such a melancholy thought—that this affirming research has been a cry for closeness, that Vaillant only discovered the importance of love from afar, as a statistical proof,

distilled from the lives of other people. And now the Grant
men are dying and will soon all be gone. I wonder what Vaillant
will do then. It must have been hard to lead a study when the
results put your own life in such stark relief, when the wisdom
you speak is what you've always sought, but never found.

At least, never found until he neared the end of his life.
Two years after our first interview, I contacted Vaillant again. I
wanted to make sure I'd got things right. He read a draft of this
chapter and said he had a "critical coda" to add to my description of his life and work. Over the last few years, Vaillant's wife
had "befriended" all of his children and helped him reconnect
with them. The man who had once compared himself to Lear
was now the patriarch of a "solid family unit." To celebrate
Vaillant's eightieth birthday, the entire extended family—all
fifteen of them, including his kids, grandkids, first wife, current wife, and stepdaughter—went on a five-day cruise to Ber-
muda. I ask Vaillant what it feels like to have finally repaired
his closest relationships. "I find the language of attachment
theory to be quite apt," he says. "It provides me with a sense of
security. Tranquillity. Peace, even."

As Vaillant notes, this unexpected turn is echoed in the
lives of some of his scientific subjects. In his final account of
the Grant men, Vaillant describes a number of them who were
saved by their later marriages. These men had struggled, like
Vaillant, to form lasting relationships with family and friends;
they had wrestled with intimacy and lost. But then, often because they found a stubborn partner, a wife who refused to
accept their failings, they discovered in old age the pleasures
of secure attachment. "She [Diane, his wife] has made this possible," Vaillant says. "Her kindness, her unconditional positive
regard. It's because of her."

Such is the nature of human salvation. Vaillant always knew the correlations. He has written so eloquently about the sway of love. But the words were never enough; the numbers didn't change his life. It took another person to do that.

Our last conversation is brief; Vaillant seems eager to get off the phone. I'm happy for his happiness, even if it's arrived in his last act. Because it's never too late—love never loses the capacity to transform what it touches. The most recent data from the Grant study makes this clear. Among the men who never formed intimate relationships, roughly 13 percent have survived into their late eighties and early nineties. However, among subjects who were better at attachment, the survival rate is closer to 40 percent.[136] "The capacity for love turns out to be a great predictor of mortality," Vaillant tells me. "I cannot tell you why that is. I can only tell you that it's so."

And so the science has come full circle: the feeling that once seemed so immeasurable has, in the lives of all these old men, become the only thing worth measuring.

Even John Watson would come to understand the power of love. In 1935, Watson's young wife, Rosalie, died of pneumonia. The loss devastated Watson. As his son James would remember, Watson spent the night weeping; it was the only time his children ever saw him cry.[137] Although he couldn't bear to tell his sons about their mother—they learned she was dead from the cook—Watson stood in the doorway and put his arms lightly around their shoulders. "That moment was the one occasion in which Watson's children experienced a genuine expression of intimacy and affection from their father," writes Kerry Buckley, Watson's biographer.[138]

After Rosalie's death, Watson began drinking heavily, consuming a quart of whiskey every day according to a friend. He worked as an advertising executive for another decade— he never lost his talent for sales—before moving to a vast estate in the hills of western Connecticut. He took care of the apple trees and the dogs, but rarely took visitors. He refused to talk about his dead wife, not even with his sons.[139]

In 1957, the American Psychological Association chose to honor Watson at its annual meeting for sparking a "revolution in psychological thought." Although Watson hadn't worked in a science lab in decades, his theories remained influential. (Bowlby was still little known outside the field of child psychiatry.) Watson had driven down to New York City to receive the award, but at the last minute refused to enter the ballroom. He was afraid that he would cry onstage, that the "apostle of behavior control" would not be able to handle his own feelings.[140]

The following year, Watson's health began to deteriorate. In the days before his death, Watson gathered his strength for one final act. He collected all of his papers—a lifetime of manuscripts, letters, and research notes—and carried them to the fireplace, where he began throwing them into the flames. His secretary asked him what he was doing. Watson's reply was cryptic: "When you're dead, you're all dead." And then he turned back to the fire and watched his work burn.[141]

INTERLUDE:

Limerence

IT'S the most influential love scene ever written. A boy goes to a party. He sees her through the crowd. He sees her and he *knows*. He walks over and, in a most reckless act, an act that if it happened to you would be a little creepy, touches her hand and starts reciting poetry. She touches him back. They talk. They flirt. Then, just before he leaves, he leans in and presses his lips against hers. His name is Romeo. Her name is Juliet.

Shakespeare wrote *Romeo and Juliet* in the early 1590s. Before long, the star-crossed couple became the archetype for lovers; we measured our own feelings against the ferocity of theirs. We looked at sweaty Romeo, obsessed with this pretty stranger, and we thought, *That's it, right? That's love?*

Such encounters have come to define popular descriptions of love. In general, we still assume that our immediate reaction to a potential partner—what we feel at first sight—will help us predict the long-term outcome. These stories of instant love are at the center of nearly all romance novels, from *Fifty Shades of Grey* to Danielle Steel; they are the inciting incidents in most romantic movies and the crucial plot twist in soap operas and Disney cartoons. In one analysis of American pop music from the late 1970s, 45 percent of songs on the radio were about intense feelings of erotic attraction.[1]

The technical term for this mental state—the condition of Romeo and Juliet—is *limerence*. As described by the psychologist Dorothy Tennov, limerence is an extremely common condition. The state occurs when people develop an all-consuming infatuation for another person, typically after a brief meeting. Their pupils dilate and their blood pressure spikes; their thoughts of the limerent object are intrusive and constant, a recurring loop of erotic hopes and insecurities. When their beloved withdraws, their hearts literally ache; when he or she reciprocates, they experience a sensation of "buoyancy," which Tennov describes as a "feeling of walking on air."[2] It's as if we know we are in love before we even know our lover.

Consider a middle-aged man Tennov refers to as Dr. Vesteroy.[3] At first glance, he seems like a levelheaded fellow: a professor, he has been married for nearly twenty years. However, his staid exterior conceals a roiling inner life, as Dr. Vesteroy is secretly limerent for a colleague, Dr. Ashton. Dr. Vesteroy remembers the moment his feelings began. A faculty meeting had just ended in his office; the other professors were gathering up their things and getting ready to leave. Dr. Ashton, however, was still taking notes. "Suddenly," he remembers, "Dr. Ashton—Elena her name is—looked up and seemed startled to find herself the only leftover from the meeting. She flushed a bit and gathered her things saying that she hoped she had not kept me. Then just before she went out, she looked at me and smiled! It was that smile and that look that started the whole thing off."[4] For the next year, Dr. Vesteroy was preoccupied by his illicit passion. He couldn't stop thinking about Dr. Ashton's beauty, her smile, her radiant eyes. "I became—there's no other way to put it—lovesick!" he told Tennov. "My mind was filled with her, my knees trembled when I saw her."[5] Although the professor realized that his obsession was irrational, he "could not shake off the feeling."

Alas, limerence is almost always an illusion; the ardor is not to be believed. Based on Tennov's detailed interviews with more than five hundred ordinary Americans who had experienced limerence, she concluded that the swoon was an inherently "unstable state," bound to quickly fall apart. Limerence is such an unreliable indicator of long-term attachment that even "limerent-limerent" couples—those seemingly perfect pairings in which both partners are fixated on the other— rarely last for more than a few years. As Tennov writes, "Limerence is a distinct state that creates that 'feeling of being in love'—that state which Hollywood loves to portray as 'love.' . . . [But] limerence is really as far from the genuine article as a zircon is from a true diamond."[6]

Why is limerence so dangerous? Because it feels so true, even when it's based on virtually nothing. (As Tennov wrote, "Limerence can live a long life sustained by crumbs. Indeed, overfeeding is perhaps the best way to end it.")[*7] In the midst of limerence, when our pulse is racing and our face is flush, it's

---

[*]Tennov then goes on to compare limerence to the manic behavior of lab rats and pigeons, who will keep on pressing a bar for food even as the probability of a reward is gradually diminished. As she notes, many animals will keep pressing the bar even as the odds of payoff are one in several thousand.

hard to remember that our feeling is flimsy, a chemical fiction rooted in little actual experience.

Shakespeare knew this. Even as he invented our romantic tropes, he insisted on complicating them, layering his drama with doubts. While the randy teenagers are frantically celebrating their feelings—"Oh, that I were a glove upon that hand, / That I might touch that cheek!"—Shakespeare suggests that Romeo and Juliet are getting carried away, that what they think is true love is actually just its fickle precursor. Here is the Friar, cautioning the couple on their wedding day:

> *These violent delights have violent ends*
> *And in their triumph die, like fire and powder,*
> *Which as they kiss consume. The sweetest honey*
> *Is loathsome in his own deliciousness.*

It's a simple warning. The Friar is telling the teenagers that their passion will burn itself out, another pleasure ruined by habituation. Time will destroy it soon enough.

2

THE
ABRAHAM PRINCIPLE

i carry your heart (i carry it in my heart)

—E. E. CUMMINGS

THE INVENTION OF love is not a human story. Or rather, it is not *only* a human story. Like every emotion, love has its origins in other species—nothing is uniquely ours. Elephants mourn their dead; emperor penguins pair-bond for a season; dogs are loyal to their owners. Jane Goodall once described an infant chimpanzee named Mel, whose mother had recently died in a pneumonia epidemic. Goodall assumed Mel would soon die, too. But then she watched as the helpless baby was adopted by a teenage male named Spindle, who had also lost his mother to the outbreak.[1] "Spindle let little Mel ride on his back," Goodall remembered in a recent interview. "If it was cold or Mel was frightened, he let him cling to his belly as a mother would. If Mel crept up to his nest at night and made whimpering sounds, Spindle reached out and drew him in."[2] The chimps slept together in a nest, curled into each other; Spindle shared his food, letting Mel eat first; Spindle protected the baby from the alpha males, even if it meant that he got beaten instead. Spindle's devotion to Mel was so complete that it could only have been for love. Why else would he sacrifice his own body? Why else would he risk his life? "Let us not forget," Goodall writes, "that human love and compassion are equally deeply rooted in our primate heritage."[3]

And it's not just primates. The instincts underlying love extend throughout the animal kingdom. In the early 1930s, Konrad Lorenz began conducting experiments on baby geese.[4] He was interested in a peculiar habit of goslings born in a lab, which is that they "imprinted" on the first moving object they encountered after birth. (Harry Harlow would later study similar instincts among his monkeys, as they clung to those soft rags.) In natural settings, such imprinting led the birds to attach themselves to their mother. Lorenz, however, demonstrated that this same instinct could easily be manipulated, so that the baby geese would imprint on model trains, dolls, and even Lorenz himself. These attachments were not about food, at least not directly, as the goslings imprinted *before* they were fed. Rather, they were about the desire for security and affection, the same needs that inspire attachment in human beings.

For John Bowlby, Lorenz's research on baby birds was a revelation and led Bowlby to explore the broader implications of his work on those children in hospitals.[*][5] "Whether it is a brood

---

[*]Not all of Bowlby's colleagues agreed that Lorenz's ethology research had anything to do with children. As one fellow psychiatrist remarked, "What's the use to analyze a goose?"

of ducklings on a pond, twin lambs in a meadow, or a human toddler around the house, the young are quickly distressed if they get lost," Bowlby wrote, "and scamper to get close to their mothers as soon as anything happens which frightens them."[6] Bowlby believed that these experiments were proof that love had deep biological underpinnings.[7] Animals craved closeness. It was part of being an animal.

Yet, Bowlby also knew that something about the human child was unique, that people required a kind of relationship unknown in the animal kingdom. Even if other creatures experienced intense attachments, only humans have made those attachments an inescapable need from "the cradle to the grave." Somehow, for some reason, this invisible feeling—a bond we can't touch or weigh or see—has become a main motive of our lives. Jane Goodall has spent decades documenting the astonishing mental talents of chimps, how they fish for termites and tickle each other for fun. But even she knows that the attachments of *Homo sapiens sapiens* are unique in scale and scope: "Human love at its best, the ecstasy deriving from the perfect union of mind and body, leads to heights of passion, tenderness and understanding that chimpanzees"—our closest biological relatives—"cannot experience."[8]

Why is love so important to us? How did we become the most romantic species? Our evolutionary history will always be shrouded in mystery. We can only speculate about the distant past. Nevertheless, we have hints of an answer, or at least a compelling hypothesis. The speculation begins with the extravagant expansion of the human brain, starting around 2 million years ago. This swollen cortex came with obvious intellectual advantages, but it also caused a bottleneck in the female birth canal. (Biologists refer to this as the "obstetrical dilemma.")[9]

Natural selection solved this dilemma in typically ingenious fashion: it had human babies enter the world before they were ready, when the immature central nervous system was still unable to control the body. (As David Bjorklund notes, if human infants "were born with the same degree of neurological maturity as our ape relatives, pregnancy would last for 21 months.")[10] The good news is that, according to some scientists, such premature births reduced the risk to the mother and the child. The bad news is that it means our offspring require constant care for more than a decade, which is roughly twice as long as for any other primate.

Such care is grueling. There's no use pretending otherwise. Hillard Kaplan, an anthropologist at the University of New Mexico, estimates that it takes approximately 13 million calories to raise human children from birth to independence.[11] (That's a lot of food and a lot of diapers.) What's worse, these years of nonstop child care are hard on parents. We lose precious hours of sleep; we have far less time to spend with our own friends, which helps explain why 58 percent of new mothers report feelings of loneliness:[12] the vast majority of spouses will report a "small to medium" decline in "relationship functioning."[13] Perhaps the bleakest news, however, concerns the moment-by-moment experiences of parents. According to a 2004 study that tracked the moods and activities of 909 working American women, taking care of the kids ranked twelfth out of sixteen possible activities, proving less pleasurable than eating, cooking, shopping, napping, exercising, and talking on the phone.[14] This unsettling finding has since been replicated numerous times, as nearly every kind of parent—from stay-at-home dads to single moms, British couples to spouses in Columbus, Ohio—seems happier with fewer children. And the happiest people of all are those with no children at home. "The only symptom of empty nest syndrome," said the Harvard psychologist Daniel Gilbert in a 2012 lecture, "is nonstop smiling."[15]

The burden of child care poses a thorny evolutionary problem. If children make us so unhappy, then why do parents put up with them? What keeps us from running away after a wicked tantrum, or from giving up when children refuse to let us sleep? What binds us to these difficult little people?

Love is the answer to these questions. Because human babies are so needy for so long, natural selection was forced to evolve a new category of relationship. We required a bond strong enough to keep us tied to our children, even as they tested our patience and consumed our scarce resources. The result was the most durable emotional attachment ever created, a feeling sturdy enough to transcend all the frustrations of caring for a person who takes years and years to develop.

There is a larger lesson in these evolutionary theories. They teach us that the hard work of parenting is also the reason attachment exists. Although we associate the pleasures of parenthood with those moments that feel effortless—the rare days when the baby is delightful and the teenager isn't surly—the logic of biology suggests that our affection depends on the struggle. We don't love our kids despite their demands; we love them *because* of them. Caregiving makes us care.

This is an ancient truth, reflected in our oldest languages. In Hebrew, the word for "sacrifice" (*korban*) shares a root with the verb "to draw close." As David Wolpe, the rabbi of Sinai Temple in Los Angeles, points out, the first mention of love in the Old Testament occurs during an unspeakably awful scene, in which God demands that Abraham sacrifice his only son, Isaac, "whom you love."[16] Wolpe argues that the timing is not an accident. Abraham only learns how much he loves his son when God asks for him. So the request becomes a lesson: Abraham is learning what love requires, that attachment and sacrifice are hopelessly intertwined.

There is a wonderful passage in Henry David Thoreau's *Walden*, a memoir of his time alone in the woods.[17] The text is dense with meditations on classical literature and the virtues of solitude, but my favorite chapter is "The Bean-Field," a detailed accounting of Thoreau's struggles to grow common white bush beans. (The biographer Bradley Dean estimates that Thoreau planted nearly twenty-five thousand bean vines on his two-and-a-half-acre plot.)[18] The transcendentalist must have been so tired of eating beans, so sick of bean soup and bean stew and baked beans. Yet he never let the plants wither, cursing the worms and woodchucks that stole his harvest. Although Thoreau's chapter on farming is full of wry, self-satirizing humor, he is serious about the lessons of this "small Herculean labor." The plants have taught him the lesson of Abraham: "I came to love my rows, my beans," Thoreau writes. "I cherish them, I hoe them, early and late I have an eye to them; and this is my day's work."[19]

Moments of Attunement

Here is something I'm ashamed of: for the first sixteen months of my daughter's life, I never put her to sleep. Not once. Not even close. Not even for naps.

I made jokes about this. I pretended that my kid was just a quirky sleeper, that because I still changed the occasional diaper, I was an acceptable parent. And when that excuse failed—when it became clear that I didn't know how to care for her because I was never there—I told myself that it didn't matter anyway, since she wouldn't remember my failings. I would get better later, when I had the time.

This was a terrible mistake. The first reason it was a mistake is that fathers play an important role even for newborns and infants.[20] In one study of cesarean births, researchers found that infants placed on the chest of their father were far less likely to cry in their first hours than those placed near their parents in a cot. They also fell asleep in about half the time.[21] Other studies have found that the extent of paternal involvement in early child care—Does he change diapers? Feed with a bottle? Put the baby to bed?—is closely associated with cognitive development, as babies with more present fathers babbled and played with toys at an earlier age.[22] These gains are long lasting: one study found that children with highly involved biological fathers are 43 percent more likely to get mostly A's in school.*[23]

The second reason is more personal. After I lost my job, when I was home with nothing to do, I was forced to confront the consequences of my absence. The sad truth is that I did not know how to be alone with my daughter, and she did not

---

*The importance of paternal caregiving has also been confirmed by careful anthropological studies of hunter-gatherer societies. Barry Hewlett has, for instance, shown that among the Aka foragers in Central Africa, fathers spend 51 percent of their time in camp "within arm's reach" of their infants. While Aka fathers are unusually engaged with offspring, the anthropologist Sarah Blaffer Hrdy notes that "almost invariably, fathers in hunter-gatherer societies spend more time with infants than fathers in most Western societies do." Barry Hewlett, "Cultural diversity among African pygmies," ed. Susan Kent, in *Cultural Diversity Among Twentieth-Century Foragers: An African Perspective* (Cambridge: Cambridge University Press, 1996), 240.

want to be alone with me. One night when my wife had to work late, I had to put my child to bed by myself. I said it would be fine, not a problem. I knew what to do. Although I carefully repeated her bedtime ritual—*Sesame Street* and a glass of milk, followed by a long procession of books in bed—nothing worked. I begged and pleaded; I tried to explain the situation, how her mom would soon be home. But she wasn't listening. Why would she? Then, when I felt anger welling up inside me, I exiled myself to the hallway. I sat down outside her door and listened to my daughter cry herself to sleep. She was crying because she wasn't attached to me. Because I provided no comfort at all. That's when I started crying, too.

These are the moments that test us, the conditions that force us to admit the difficulty of unconditional love. I wanted to be a good father. I wanted to be a good father right away. Instead, I was confronted by a stubborn gap between the attachment with my daughter that I hoped for and the one we had.

Change happens slowly. As a parent, I desperately needed practice. But the challenge of child care is that the practice is also the performance; every one of my mistakes was noticed and felt. It didn't help that two-year-olds tell the truth: my daughter wasn't afraid of pointing out my errors. My stories were boring and I'd take forever to install the car seat. I'd leave the snacks at home and forget the one stuffed animal that she wanted on the swing. When she cried because I was doing it wrong—because I let the sunblock get in her eye or left the crust on her sandwich—I would lose my patience. I would raise my voice. She probably thought I was mad at her. I wasn't. I was furious at myself.

But children are forgiving. They are the most forgiving people in the world. I first noticed the change in our relationship in little ways. When we'd go to the local park, she started keeping track of where I was. When she encountered something unsettling, she'd look back at me, checking to make sure I was paying attention. (To borrow the language of attachment theory, I was finally becoming a "secure base.") We gradually found new books to read; my voices were usually acceptable. We bonded over her favorite television shows; when the shows were over, she listened attentively as I spun out sequels to Elmo skits and *My Little Pony*. I learned how to make her laugh without tickling her; how she squirmed when she had to pee; the most efficient way to ease her out of a tantrum. It sounds so silly when you write it down, but this intimate knowledge is what makes parenting possible. You either know it or you don't, and I was beginning to know.

The technical name for this process, the education that occurs when we spend endless hours with our children, is *attunement*. A classic set of experiments was begun in the late 1970s by the psychologist Ed Tronick and colleagues to better understand these interactions of parents and children. Although most researchers assumed these interactions were transactional—children made bids for attention and parents responded—Tronick believed that something far more subtle and interesting was going on. In one study, Tronick had mothers interact with their babies while seated in a chair. The mothers made the usual patter of *parentese*, those singsong sentences full of glissando variations. The babies would point at objects beyond their reach, and their mothers would follow along, attentive to whatever their kids were looking at. Tronick then instructed the mother to make a "still face." No matter what the baby did, she had to remain totally unresponsive. The effect was immediate. The children began by increasing the urgency of their own expressions, smiling and giggling and pointing with even more excitement.[24] When that strategy failed, the kids attempted to reach out and touch their mothers. And then, often within a minute of the first appearance of the still face, the babies were unraveled by stress. They lost control of their posture and started flailing. Who was this person? Where had their mother gone?[25]

The psychiatrist Daniel Stern, in *The Interpersonal World of the Infant*, describes another example of attunement and its disruption. A nine-month-old crawls away from his mother and toward a new toy. He plays with it excitedly. The mother then approaches the baby from behind and, in an affectionate gesture, pats his bottom several times. But these were not random pats. Stern describes how the intensity of the mother's "jiggles" mirrored the infant's own movements, thus establishing the moment of attunement.[26]

Now comes the "perturbation." The mother was told to intentionally misjudge her baby's level of activity, patting his bottom either too fast or too slow. The effects of this perturbation were immediate. Once the mother began her awkward jiggling, the infant stopped playing with the toy. He looked back with a worried expression, confused by her behavior. Only when the mother once again demonstrated her attunement— patting his bottom at the exact right rhythm—did he feel confident enough to resume his playing.[27]

What makes attunement so astonishing is that it's almost entirely automatic. A mother doesn't need to be told to adjust the tenor of her pats or to follow her baby's gaze; these acts of affection are like reflexes. And the child isn't aware of his expectation for perfectly timed touches or facial expressions. He only looked up when something went amiss. *He took it for granted.* According to Tronick, these interactions reveal the elaborate cross-talk constantly taking place between parent and child. What looks, at first glance, like mere play is actually an exquisite discourse, a wordless script of coos, touches, and glances.

The psychiatrists Thomas Lewis, Fari Amini, and Richard Lannon refer to attunement as an example of "limbic resonance," noting all the ways in which humans learn to synchronize their feelings with loved ones.[28] Although we tend to think of the human body as a closed-loop system, able to regulate its own autonomic needs, the intricacies of attunement reveal that we're actually open loops, designed to be influenced by the emotions of others. When we are attuned with someone else, our bodies come to mirror each other, with heartbeat, breathing rate, and even blood chemistry all converging on a similar, shared state. Children are an extreme example of this open-loop system, which is why *not* experiencing attunement in the first few years of life can be so crippling.

You can measure the impact of these intimate interactions on the young brain. In a recent paper published in *Psychological Science*, a team of researchers led by Dylan Gee, Laurel Gabard-Durnam, and Nim Tottenham put fifty-three children and teenagers into an fMRI scanner. (To help the younger kids acclimate to the confined space, the scientists had them participate in a mock session before the experiment. They also padded their head with air pillows.) While in the scanner, the children were shown a series of photographs. Some of the pictures were of their parent, while other pictures were of an "ethnicity matched" stranger. The subjects were instructed to press a button whenever they saw a smiling face, regardless of who it was.

When analyzing the fMRI data, the scientists focused on the connection between the right hemisphere's amygdala and the medial prefrontal cortex (mPFC). Both of these are promiscuous brain areas, "lighting up" in all sorts of studies and all kinds of tasks. However, the scientists point out that the right amygdala is generally activated by stress and threats; it's a warehouse of negative emotion. The mPFC, in contrast, helps to modulate these unfortunate feelings, allowing us to calm ourselves down when necessary. Unfortunately for parents, the frontal cortex is one of the last brain areas to develop fully, which means that the urges of the amygdala often dominate. When a toddler dissolves into a tantrum because she doesn't want to wear shoes or go to bed or eat her broccoli, you can blame her immature frontal lobes. Kids are mostly *id*; this is why.

For children older than ten, no significant differences occurred in right amygdala/mPFC activity when they were flashed pictures of their parent versus those of a stranger. For younger children, however, the photos of the mother made a big difference; the children exhibited the same inverse connection between the amygdala and the mPFC that is generally the sign of a more developed mind. Furthermore, these shifts in brain activity were influenced by the parent-child relationship. Children with more secure attachments to their parent were more likely to exhibit mature emotional regulation when looking at his or her picture. The scientists argue that these changes are evidence of "parental buffering," as the presence of a loving parent can markedly alter the ways in which children deal with their feelings.

The child psychiatrist Donald Winnicott, in his essay "The Capacity to Be Alone," observed that the goal of a parent should be to raise a child capable of being alone in the parent's presence. That might seem like a contradiction, but Winnicott was pointing out that one of the greatest gifts of love is the ability to take it for granted, to trust that it is always there, even when it goes unacknowledged. In Winnicott's view, maturity is the process of internalizing our attachments, so that the child can "forgo the *actual* presence of a mother or mother-figure."[29] Winnicott knew, of course, that learning how to be alone requires endless amounts of togetherness. The child only takes the "mother-figure" for granted because she is so often there, attuned to his feelings, soothing his amygdala, literally making the world a less scary place.

I realize I'm making this process sound practical, as if attunement were just another technique to calm a whiny toddler or boost her emotional intelligence or fast-forward his neural development. But attunement is much more profound than that. When we develop an attuned relationship with an attachment figure, we learn how to break down the distance between minds, how to listen so carefully and look so closely at someone else that our bodies blur together.[30] It's empathy at its most intense. As the psychiatrist Daniel Stern writes, "What is at stake here is nothing less than the shape of and extent of the shareable inner universe."[31]

Besides, there is no other way to interact with young children. We can't engage them in long conversations or reason our way through a disagreement. In a famous monologue, the comedian Louis C.K. announces that he has a four-year-old daughter, who is "also a fucking asshole." The audience bursts out laughing. He tells a story about trying to get out of the house and repeatedly telling his daughter to put on her shoes. She doesn't listen. "Seriously, if you're with a group of people that are trying to go somewhere, and you can't go . . . because a member of your party just refuses to put their shoes on? That person is a fucking asshole, okay?"

Such parenting frustrations are rooted in one of the defining mental quirks of children: they live almost exclusively in the present. For little kids, the future is a meaningless abstraction, which is why they often act like such reckless hedonists. Although this tendency has a clear neurological explanation—those frontal lobes are still immature—it's responsible for many of the most maddening moments of child care, those meaningless fights over cookies and bedtime and shoes. (One recent study found that mothers and toddlers had "conflict interactions" every two and a half minutes.)[32]

Attunement turns the immediacy of children into a virtue. It allows us to appreciate the intensity of their attention, how they aren't worried about e-mails or bank balances or being a few minutes late to the dentist. Instead, all they care about is the rhythm of our patting and the quality of our gaze and maybe that pile of Play-Doh, which feels so nice smashed between the fingers and the carpet. It can be hard to slow down, forget the clock, see the world as a child sees it, but that's when we notice all the important things, such as the marching ants, the sheen of oil on a wet street, and the fun of a whirring salad spinner. In this sense, scenes of attunement are a brief vacation from the stresses of adulthood, a chance to lose ourselves in the most visceral delights of life. We are finally present in the moment, which is where we should have been all along.

When I was first trying to care for my daughter, I kept searching for the shortcuts. I assumed I must be able to learn my daughter in punctuated bursts, or while watching her watch television. But such shortcuts don't exist, or at least I haven't found them. For me, learning how to be attuned has mostly just required time with my children. Time and vast amounts of effort.* A famous Zen tale speaks to this simple lesson. The story, as recounted in *The Three Pillars of Zen*, goes like this:

> One day, a man of the people said to Zen master Ikkyu: "Master, will you write down for me some maxims of the highest wisdom?"
>
> Ikkyu immediately took his brush and wrote the word "Attention."
>
> "Is that all?" asked the man. "Will you not add something more?"
>
> Ikkyu then wrote twice running: "Attention. Attention."
>
> "Well," remarked the man rather irritably, "I really don't see much depth or sublety in what you have just written."
>
> Then Ikkyu wrote the same word three times running: "Attention. Attention. Attention."
>
> Half angered, the man demanded: "What does that word 'Attention' mean anyway?"
>
> And Ikkyu answered gently: "Attention means attention."[33]

---

* For parenting to have an impact on young children, quality matters much more than quantity. According to a 2015 study by Melissa Milkie et al., the amount of time spent with kids by their parents had little to no impact on their academic achievement and emotional well-being. Instead, Milkie et al., like so many researchers before them, stress the importance of sensitive and attuned caregiving, even if it's only for a few hours every week. (The exception to this rule is in adolescence, when quantity does seem to matter.) My problem was that I'd never put in enough time as a father, which meant I didn't even know *how* to be a quality parent. Melissa A. Milkie, Kei M. Nomaguchi, and Kathleen E. Denny, "Does the Amount of Time Mothers Spend with Children or Adolescents Matter?," *Journal of Marriage and Family* 77.2 (2015): 355–72.

The necessity of attention returns us to the paradox of parental love. In the beginning, when I was just starting to be with my daughter every day, the sacrifices felt like sacrifices. I tried to hide my boredom; I saw the days as something to endure; I resented the carpet stains and all those LEGO pieces I stepped on in the dark. Although I told myself that parenthood could be my consolation, on some days my incompetence made me feel even worse. I left her jacket at the grocery store and lost a shoe at the park. She refused the nap and swallowed a penny, which I then had to spend the next week searching for in her diapers.

But I had nowhere else to go. So I kept showing up. I kept trying to master all those verbs of parenthood—comfort, play, feed, sleep—that can seem easy when you're not the one doing them. Then, as the months piled up, as I learned my daughter and she learned me, I started to realize how much fun it could be. I got glimpses of attunement, those precious hours when I could disappear into the rhythms of her world. That it was a world of playgrounds and organic cheese puffs only made it more comforting, further removed from my own troubles.

One of the first games we learned to play together was doctor. At the time, my daughter was deep into *Doc McStuffins*, a Disney show about a little girl who tends to her sick toys. In our version, I was the toy. My daughter would begin by asking me to list all of my wounds. She would pore over my limbs, asking for a history of every scar and bruise. That was where I cut my knee and got stitches. That was where I banged my shin into the car door. I fell off my bike here and broke this finger, which is why it's still crooked. Then she would get out her doctor kit and, with a patience I didn't know she had, tend to every injury with a magic purple stethoscope and some gentle touches. At the end of a session, I'd find myself covered in Band-Aids, gauze, and Scotch tape.

And so went our days. I thought I was taking care of my child. Only later did I realize that she was taking care of me.

Ambivalence

In 1963, when Sharon Roszia was pregnant with her first child, she was greeted at the front door by a pair of FBI agents. They were there to deliver some heartbreaking news: Sharon's husband was a con man. He was living under a false name. He was wanted in seven other states for embezzlement and fraud. She was not his only wife.

Sharon was devastated. Her family pressured her to give the baby up for adoption. They said it was best to make a clean break from the past. But Sharon refused. Although she was only twenty-one years old, with no income and few resources, she insisted on keeping the child.

The next few years were brutal. Sharon filed for divorce, declared bankruptcy, and got a job to support herself and her baby daughter. She would eventually remarry and move to Orange County, where she got a job as a social worker, specializing in adoption. But the memory of her ex-husband's sudden disappearance marked her forever. "I know what I speak of when I talk about how loss has reverberations in people's lives," she said in a 1995 interview. "I know that everything I teach and work with . . . is all a direct reflection of what I've had to do on my own journey."[34]

Sharon Roszia is now one of the world's leading experts on adoption. She has written influential books, received numerous awards, and counseled hundreds of families on adoption. But she's perhaps best known for the honesty of her advocacy, her willingness to talk openly about the difficulties of parenting. (As she puts it, "Even the easy ones are so hard.") In the mid-1980s, Sharon published an influential model of adoption, referring to it as an "institution based on loss." Along with Deborah Silverstein, she identified seven primal issues typically triggered by adoption, including feelings of rejection and fears of intimacy. While her model was not without its critics— many adoption organizations criticized her for "pathologizing" adoption and discouraging potential parents—Sharon insisted she was simply telling the truth, and that it was irresponsible to leave out the hardest parts. "I'm not a salesman," Sharon says. "I'm there to help people, to make sure they know what parenthood is going to be like."

Sharon speaks from experience, her wisdom hard-won. After she remarried, and when her biological daughter was six years old, Sharon adopted a brother and a sister. Their young lives were haunted: their mother had died of a drug overdose, and their father was gone. The boy had a severe stutter, and the girl was terrified of men. The children might have been given drugs as pacifiers, and the girl might have witnessed her mother's death. "I specialized in counseling adoptive parents where the kids had tough backgrounds, so I thought I could handle it," Sharon told me. "Besides, these kids had no other options. I knew it would be hard, but I thought I was prepared."[35]

She was wrong: Sharon was soon overwhelmed. The tantrums and outbursts were constant. The kids rejected her attempts to reach out, and Sharon struggled to satisfy their emotional needs. "Looking back, I can see that I was parenting them all wrong. It's taken me a long time to forgive myself for that." Sharon tells me a story about the time her adopted son broke her nose with a Tonka truck. "He'd only been living with us for a few months. And it had been a wonderful day—he'd let me hold him and rock him. So we're playing with his toys and I'm feeling good about everything, like maybe this will work out, and he goes off for a moment to the bathroom. When he gets back, he says, 'Mom,' so I look up. That's when he swings this metal truck through the air and hits me in the face. He knocked me out."

Sharon was furious. "I probably yelled at him and took something away. That became the cycle: they would do something bad, and I would get livid and send them to their room. What I should have been doing instead is reaching out, not pushing them away." But Sharon's nose had been broken by that toy truck. How do you reach out when blood is streaming down your face? "You tell the child honestly how you're feeling. You say, 'I'm angry and I'm hurt, but I'm not going to hurt you.' Get small with your anger. Get down on their level. They're probably scared, too. They don't know how to be attached, so you have to show them what attachment means."

This is what Sharon knows now. At the time, though, she was just trying to hold it together, to not let her anger take over. "One day, I just broke down at my friend's house. I said I felt like a fake, and that I didn't love all my kids the same way. I said I loved my own daughter more. And I said all this as an adoption expert, which made it so much worse." Sharon's friend listened and gave her a hug, then told Sharon that every parent struggled with the same issues. "I'll never forget her words. She said, 'I don't love all my kids the same way either. And some days I don't like any of them.'"

Sharon's private struggles led her to rethink the language

of adoption. While counselors routinely told prospective parents that their adopted child would feel just like a biological child, especially if he or she was adopted at birth, Sharon's experience had convinced her that it was time for more candor. "It can be hard when your kid doesn't look like you. It can be hard when they go to the bathroom and they don't smell like you. Or when they don't like your family recipes. Maybe it sounds silly, but that stuff can be really hard to deal with." While every child is distinct from his or her parents, adoption forces us to grapple with those differences on an entirely different scale. "I like to say that being an adoptive parent is like parenting in Technicolor: everything is just a little more intense. This means the highs can be really high"—when attunement finally comes, it can feel like a miracle—"but it also means that the lows are going to be really low. You have to prepare yourself."

Along with her second husband, Sharon went on to take care of twelve children in the foster system, ranging in age from toddlers to teenagers. "We had kids of every race, creed, and religion. Black, Vietnamese, you name it." Sharon doesn't elide the challenges. She describes how she'd dread Mother's Day because it brought up so many fraught issues: the way her kids fought over every toy in the house, how she struggled with feelings of doubt and resentment. "You have to measure things differently [in an adoptive family]. If the child has two tantrums instead of ten, that's a day to celebrate. If you made it through the holidays, then congratulations." It's a cliché, says Sharon, but it's especially true for adoptive parents. They have to find pleasure in the little things because the big pleasures take years. They are the work of a lifetime.

What makes Sharon such an effective counselor for parents

is that she's willing to talk about these complicated feelings, how the love is mingled with guilt and anger and regret. She doesn't pretend that taking care of kids is always fun or full of Instagram-worthy moments or that darker emotions aren't also part of attachment. *Hate* is a strong word, Sharon says, but at moments raising a child will make parents jittery with rage. "One time, my daughter got into my jewelry box and tied all the necklaces in knots. I saw her doing this, and then I looked in the mirror and I saw my face. I'll never forget what I saw because I looked like I was ready to strangle her. I mean, you could just see the rage. But that's part of parenting. That's part of what you have to deal with, particularly when children have early trauma."

Freud wrote extensively about these conflicted feelings. Although parents tried to hide their dark impulses, Freud insisted that they were a necessary part of child care. "It might be said that we owe the fairest flowering of our love to the reaction against the hostile impulse which we sense within us," he wrote. "Nature, by making use of this pair of opposites [love and hate], contrives to keep love ever vigilant and fresh."[36]

John Bowlby would later extend Freud's argument, insisting that every mother experienced negative feelings about her children. (Such feelings were a natural consequence of caring for a little person who couldn't stop crying.) Bowlby suggested that it might even be useful for parents to lose their temper on occasion, so that the young child could understand that adults also struggle with difficult emotions.[37] We also get angry and upset and frightened. We're all only human.

In the right dose, this ambivalence can even become an essential part of the parent-child relationship. Because we experience such an extreme range of emotions toward our kids—what parents haven't cursed their crying children in the middle of the night, only to be overcome a few minutes later by the sight of their still, sleeping faces?—we are motivated to try to understand our kids better. "The suffering of ambivalence can promote thought," writes Rozsika Parker, a feminist and psychotherapist, in her insightful book *Mother Love, Mother Hate*. "And the capacity to think about the baby and child is arguably the single most important aspect of mothering."[38] To illustrate her point, Parker imagines a hypothetical mother who only knows "untroubled love." Why would she bother to reflect on her parenting? What would motivate her to think about how to do it better, or what she might be missing? According to Parker, the ambivalence of our attachments is what propels them. We think about what's broken because we want to fix it; we focus on our differences because we want to bridge them. And even if these complicated feelings never go away—ambivalence is not an illness to be cured—that's okay because it keeps us focused on those we love.

I think here of *Where the Wild Things Are*, Maurice Sendak's masterwork.[39] It's a book about many things: the unruly imagination, nightmares, punishment. But it's also a portrait of parental ambivalence. The story begins with anger from the unseen mother: she calls her son a "wild thing." He responds with more anger—"I'll eat you up!"—and is sent to bed without supper. The bedroom then becomes a forest, and Max discovers a tribe of big monsters with terrible teeth who like to dance in the moonlight. The story ends with Max's return to his bedroom, where his dinner awaits.

That's the power of Sendak's story: it shows us our wild things—look at what they make us do!—and ends with forgiveness and a warm meal. It's a reassuring tale about monsters because it reminds us that we all have them inside. And that we still love each other anyway.

It's an uplifting moral. It's also a children's book. Real life tends to be messier, more complicated, the lessons more confused. That is what I've learned from Sharon's story. When Sharon talks about the first pair of siblings she adopted—that boy and girl whose mother died of a drug overdose—her voice quivers with sadness: "I failed to help them. They have repeated the experience of their birth parents." When her daughter was seventeen years old, she ran away from home; she has been on the streets ever since, addicted to drugs and in and out of jail for prostitution. Sharon's son hasn't fared much better, and she hasn't spoken to him in years. When I ask Sharon if she ever regrets these adoptions, she doesn't hesitate. "No, I don't regret them at all. It has not gone the way I ever wanted, but I tried my best with the knowledge I had." And then she tells me about her grandchildren.

The story begins in 1994, when Sharon was giving a lecture on open adoptions in Boise. She knew that her daughter had two girls, and that she'd given them up because of her addictions. A few years before, Sharon had heard that the girls were living in a foster home in Idaho. After Sharon's lecture, when she was casually chatting with the director of the state foster system, she asked if the director had heard of her granddaughters. The director said yes, and that the social worker responsible for the children was sitting nearby.

Six months later the phone rings. It's a social worker: Sharon's granddaughters want to meet. Sharon's first reaction is fear: "What if they didn't like me? What if the family wanted me to take over raising the children or needed money?" But then Sharon worked up the nerve and dialed the number she'd been given. The older one answered. She sounded just like Sharon's daughter. Same voice, same attitude, same blunt manner. "I said my name was Sharon and she called out, 'Grandma Sharon from California is finally on the phone!'"

That call was the start of a lasting relationship. Sharon traveled to Idaho and was welcomed into the girls' foster family. After many difficult conversations—the younger granddaughter wanted to know about her mother, and why Sharon couldn't save her—they formed a strong connection. Their differences are obvious, but the women have learned to bond over them. "I'm Jewish and my granddaughters are conservative Baptists," Sharon says. "I'm a social worker and they think that social workers are the meddlers of the world. I guess you could say we have conflicting worldviews. But you know what? That makes our visits much more interesting." Her granddaughters have taken Sharon "mudding" in the back of a truck and got her drunk on their favorite cocktail of tomato juice and dark beer. Severe arthritis has limited Sharon's travel, but the three still skype every week. "The reunion has taught me, again, that adoptions make strange relationships," Sharon wrote in a recent essay about her grandchildren. "That adapting is part of adopting and reunions. That genetics are very powerful. That we benefit from relationships no matter the packaging. That there are so many different life styles and they are all rich in their particular way and we have much to learn from each other."[40]

When our interview is over, Sharon gives me a tour of her apartment, which is really a tour of her family pictures. The assortment of smiling faces is astonishing; I have a tough time keeping track of them all. But that, I soon realize, is the point.

Sharon's life is a model of what she calls "expanded kinship," in which our kin are defined less by blood and more by the give-and-take of close relationships. "Kinship is ultimately about the obligations we have to each other," she says. Because what Sharon has discovered, after a lifetime of work and learning, is that she loves these people more than anything else, and that the sacrifices of family are all mixed up with the pleasures. There will be moments of ambivalence; there will be seasons of regret; we'll call our kids wild things and worse. But what matters most is never in doubt.

The morning I met with her, Sharon's phone kept ringing and beeping. Her biological daughter called to talk about a dying cat. Then one of her granddaughters from Boise left a message. A niece texted. "There were days when I didn't think I'd ever say this, but as I get older, I find that I prefer the company of my children and grandchildren to everyone else," Sharon says. "They've become my spiritual teachers; I'm an entirely different human being because of them. As painful as the journey has been, I wouldn't trade it for anything. My family is the biggest gift of my life."

Parenting Lessons

Love requires no theory. It governs our existence regardless of what we know about it. Yet, the struggles of parents such as Sharon—and what parent doesn't struggle?—suggest that there is a good reason to study the feeling. The simple hope is that if we can learn a little about love, then we might learn how to love a little *better*. The only way to avoid heartbreak is to figure out how the heart works.

Such learning is not straightforward. It's messy and uncertain and full of confounding variables; the science of love might always be defined by its limitations, by all the ways it's not a science at all. Nevertheless, as the data slowly accumulates, an intimate knowledge begins to emerge. It's not a how-to manual, and it never will be, but the research has given me a little clarity on what parenthood is all about.

One of the long-standing controversies of attachment theory concerns those babies who do not cry, at least during the Strange Situation task. The mothers leave the room, but the children remain stoic, unperturbed. Then, when the mothers return, the babies show far less interest in the reunion. They seem content to play by themselves.

John Watson regarded such babies as the ideal. They were already independent! How precocious! Mary Ainsworth, however, saw this behavior as a form of attachment insecurity, which she labeled "avoidant." She insisted that a healthy ten-month-old should experience intense separation anxiety. If the baby didn't cry after the mother's sudden departure, then something was wrong. Ainsworth was drawing the clearest possible distinction between the advice of attachment theorists and the claims of scientists such as Watson, who believed that good parenting was about teaching children how *not* to be vulnerable. Self-soothing was the ideal.

This distinction might seem like a technical disagreement—the scientists were arguing about how to explain a sliver of a data set—but it has serious practical consequences. At its core, the debate was about the independence of human beings. If we are here for ourselves—if dependence is just weakness in disguise—then kids must learn how to be alone. They should find a way to cope, even as infants. However, if we are designed to depend on others, then babies must learn how to reach out. They need to know how to call for help, even if all they can do is cry.

The controversy came to a head in the 1980s when Jerome Kagan, an influential developmental psychologist at Harvard, pushed back against the growing acceptance of attachment theory. Like Watson, he argued that the stoicism of these "avoidant" infants was actually an advantage. "A child whose mother has been otherwise attentive and loving, but has successfully encouraged self-reliance and control of fear, is less likely to cry when the mother leaves," he wrote in his treatise *The Nature of the Child*. "Although some psychologists [such as Ainsworth] might regard these latter mothers as less nurturant, the mothers may have behaved as they did because they valued control of fear and sturdy self-reliance in their children. It may have been no accident that these infants were better able to cope with uncertainty when their mothers left them alone."[41] In other words, where Ainsworth saw a failure of parenting, Kagan saw a success. He didn't want mothers to feel as if they could never leave their child alone, or that a lack of crying was always a sign of insecure attachment.

How to settle this intellectual argument? One of the first attempts to resolve the dispute began in Bielefeld, an industrial city in northern Germany. In 1976, the husband-wife team of Klaus and Karin Grossmann started following the development of forty-nine babies born to married couples in the industrial city. (The study literally began at birth—Karin made her first observations in a hospital delivery room.) While the Grossmanns initially conceived of their longitudinal project as a straightforward replication of Ainsworth's research, important differences existed. When the German babies were measured on the Strange Situation task, the Grossmanns observed a strikingly distinct distribution of attachment styles. In most studies of American children, about two-thirds are classified as secure, with the remainder split between avoidant and re- sistant. But the Grossmanns found the inverse, with two-thirds of West German babies showing signs of insecure attachment. What's more, this increase was mostly caused by a sharp rise in the percentage of children who refused to cry when their mothers left the room. Nearly half of the German sample was classified as avoidant, a rate two and a half times higher than in similar studies conducted with babies from middle-class American households.[42]

Kagan saw this data as compelling evidence that avoidance was not a bad thing. "Should we conclude from these data that many more German than American children are 'insecurely attached'?" he asked. "Or, rather, that the German children were taught to control their fear?"[43] The implied answer was that learning to control fear was useful. The Grossmanns ini- tially agreed, arguing that the high incidence of avoidance was merely a by-product of Germanic parenting habits. Because German mothers prized early "self-reliance," they were less responsive to a child's cries, especially when they perceived no obvious cause. One could "imagine a whole culture functioning on the avoidant principle," said Karin Grossmann in an inter- view with the psychologist Robert Karen for his book *Becoming Attached*. "In old Prussia I think it would have been a high ideal to keep a stiff upper lip and never bother anybody else with your problems."[44]

However, as the subjects got older, the Grossmanns began to revise their beliefs. They concluded that the stoicism of the Bielefeld infants actually came with disadvantages. When the German children were five years old, those with secure attach- ments seemed to be better off. They showed higher levels of concentration when playing, were better at dealing with conflicts with their friends, and were more likely to seek out comfort when sad or upset. (Avoidant children, in contrast, still relied on self-reliance, even when someone else could have helped them.) These behavioral patterns persisted into adolescence and early adulthood. At the age of sixteen, the avoidant children had a tougher time forming close friendships. When they were twenty-two, the avoidant infants were significantly less likely to have experienced a secure romantic attachment. In the end, the Grossmanns concluded that Bowlby was right: there is a "strong causal relationship between an individual's experience with his parents and his later capacity to make affectional bonds."[45]

What explains these differences? According to the Grossmanns, they were rooted in the larger question of how the children handled adversity. When the German children were in their late teens, the scientists interviewed them about their closest relationships and most trying experiences. Then, the Grossmanns analyzed the transcripts in terms of the hierarchy of psychological adaptations outlined by George Vaillant in his work on the Grant subjects. The Grossmanns found that, many years after being tested with the Strange Situation task, those children rated as securely attached were far more likely to cope with their struggles in a healthy manner, which included seeking support from loved ones.[46] They had stronger relationships because they weren't afraid of showing weakness.

While the Grossmanns initially argued that the high prevalence of avoidant attachments was merely a by-product of "German cultural demands," they discovered that it was actually triggered by less effective caregiving techniques. After observing the children in their homes, the researchers concluded that,

in many instances, their avoidant attachments were characterized by "less tender body contact, less responsiveness to crying,
more abrupt and interfering pick-up episodes and less sensitive
as well as less cooperative mothers."[47] This wasn't just a cultural
norm—it was a cultural *shortcoming*, a collective tendency that
led to worse outcomes.[48] "We fight the notion that crying doesn't
matter, that it strengthens the lungs," Klaus Grossmann told
Robert Karen. "We fight the notion that independence has to be
trained, or that you must punish a child by withdrawal of availability of love. We've explained over and over again that those
children who get the most sensitive responsiveness on the part of
the mothers are the ones who will be least clinging."[49]

The upside is that our culture seems to be trending in this
direction. It's easy to lose sight of progress, especially when it
unfolds in private spaces, but the evidence suggests that parents are getting better; our human attachments are becoming
more secure. The first sign of progress is the amount of time
American parents spend with their children. In 1965, the typical mother spent 10.2 hours every week on child care; by 2008,
that figure had risen to 13.9 hours. Fathers, meanwhile, went
from spending 2.5 hours per week on child care in the 1960s—
that's twenty-one minutes per day—to 7.8 hours, which is more
than a threefold increase.[50]

What's more, this extra attention seems to have lasting
benefits. To understand why, it helps to know about a classic experiment from Michael Meaney's lab in which rats
were put through a difficult water maze.[51] (This is a standard measure of rodent intelligence.) While scientists had
long assumed that those rats that performed better on the
maze were blessed with better genes—they were innately
smarter—Meaney and colleagues noticed that they also had

more attentive mothers, who engaged in far more licking and grooming. In contrast, those rat pups with less attentive mothers tended to perform poorly. To test the power of parenting, the scientists then "cross-fostered" a new generation of pups shortly after birth. They took baby rats born to less nurturing mothers and had them raised by mothers that spent more time comforting their pups. If performance in the maze test was determined by genetics, this switch shouldn't matter. The rats should perform the same regardless of how they were raised.

But that's not what Meaney's lab found. Instead, the scientists discovered that the pups raised by attentive mothers now performed well on the maze test, even though they were born to less "smart" parents. (The pups also showed elevated levels of NMDA receptors associated with learning and memory.) When it comes to various cognitive abilities, parental sensitivity can play a big role, especially when it's directed at those pups at highest risk.

What does the nurturing of rat pups have to do with human beings? The Flynn effect refers to the steady increase in human IQ scores, by about three points a decade, since the 1940s. (The effect is particularly pronounced at the low end of the bell curve, which means that fewer people now score in the "deficient" range.) If a person born in the middle of the twentieth century had an IQ of 100, their grandchildren should have an IQ around 118, more than a full standard deviation higher.

The Flynn effect has no single explanation. Researchers speculate that everything from improved education to better nutrition might play a role. However, as Meaney's research demonstrates, the quality of parenting can have a dramatic impact on measured intelligence, with more nurturing leading to higher scores. According to James Flynn (the Flynn effect is named after him), the decrease in average family size over the twentieth century has meant that parents are able to devote more attention to their young children and are better able to practice "liberal parenting" techniques, such as engaging in lengthy conversations and taking "their children's 'hypothetical' questions seriously."[52] This speculative theory is supported by data showing that measures of infant mental development are also increasing rapidly, suggesting that the Flynn effect begins early in life, when parents exert their strongest influence.[53] (If the jump in IQ scores was driven by educational changes, it probably wouldn't be evident in babies.) Perhaps our children are getting smarter because we are getting better at caring for them.

This doesn't mean all this extra parental attention is spent in rapturous attunement. Far from it. Nevertheless, it does seem to reflect a shifting of priorities, as parents increasingly realize that there is no substitute for time spent with their children, and that the closeness of our attachments have far-reaching implications. Jennifer Senior, in her book, *All Joy and No Fun*, quotes a sociologist who describes the history of American childhood as an arc away from useful labor. Kids used to help the family make a living. Today, they are "economically worthless but emotionally priceless."*[54]

---

*In many societies and cultures families can't afford the luxury of "economically worthless" children. In his fascinating book *The Anthropology of Childhood*, David Lancy observes that most human children grow up not as "cherubs"—the Western ideal that views little kids as angelic beings—but as "chattel" (items of property) or "changelings" (unwanted burdens). As a result, their childhoods are marked by very different kinds of mother-child interactions, with far less playing, questioning, or positive exchanging. (In Fiji, for instance, children are not supposed to make eye contact with

And isn't that as it should be? If our children aren't emotionally priceless, what in the world is? One of the virtues of longitudinal projects such as the Grant Study is the way they expose the very modernity of the modern family, how the duties and anxieties we take for granted are often recent cultural trends. To read about the childhoods of the men in the Grant Study—raised in mostly upper-class households in the 1920s and 1930s—is to encounter a litany of neglected attachments. It's to enter a world of parents trying to follow the "scientific" advice of John Watson, determined not to spoil their kids with too much affection. For too long, love wasn't taken seriously by science, and the result was bad policy and wretched advice. "I think a lot of heartbreak could have been prevented if we'd had more sophisticated ideas about attachment," says Sharon Roszia, the adoption expert. "Not all of it, but a lot of it."

That was John Bowlby's noble goal: the prevention of heartbreak. While he wanted to understand the nature of love, he was most interested in its clinical applications. Unfortunately, it took nearly half a century before the concept of attachment became a therapeutic tool, able to help those parents and children most in need. One early intervention was led by Dymphna van den Boom at the University of Leiden.[55] She focused on one hundred "highly irritable" infants born to low-income mothers. (The ratings of irritability were based on the frequency and intensity of crying.) Previous research had demonstrated that such children were at particular risk for attachment problems,

---

adults.) Nevertheless, as Lancy notes, almost all of these children turn out just fine, which suggests that many ways exist to raise and love a child and form a sturdy attachment. And that we definitely don't have to pretend they're always little angels.

as their parents often lacked the resources and support to cope with the incessant crying.

Van den Boom's experiment was simple. She randomly divided the babies into an intervention group and a control group. The intervention group received six hours of counseling in attachment parenting, which was focused on "enhancing maternal sensitive responsiveness." Over three short sessions, the mothers were taught how to problem-solve the cause of the crying and to find reliable soothing techniques. (Van den Boom described one mother who turned up the radio to drown out her child's wails; during the counseling session, she learned how to comfort the baby.)[56] In addition, the mothers were encouraged to develop fun routines with their children, so that their interactions were not all about tears and burps and dirty diapers. ("Techniques used here included asking the mother to play with toys and play infant games.") The mothers and babies were then followed for a year, as van den Boom measured their relationship with a variety of attachment tests.[57]

The results were stunning. In the control group—those who had received no counseling—only 28 percent of infants were securely attached at the age of twelve months. However, in the treatment group that number more than doubled, with 63 percent of children showing a secure connection to their mother.[58] This result wasn't just about passing the Strange Situation test. Van den Boom also found a wide range of parenting improvements. According to her data, mothers in the intervention group became more responsive and tender, and their babies were better at dealing with adversity and playing with new toys. The fussiness still wasn't fun, but a few hours of counseling had minimized the effects of the babies' temperaments.

In recent years, many other researchers have demonstrated the surprising power of therapies rooted in attachment theory. Dante Cicchetti, a psychologist at the University of Minnesota, has pioneered a form of family counseling known as child-parent psychotherapy (CPP). The premise of the therapy is that poor parenting isn't caused by a lack of knowledge or bad intentions. (Almost all parents know what they should do, and almost all parents want to do it.) Instead, the problems begin when parents are undermined by their own attachment insecurities, which "evolved in response to [their] experiences in childhood." So the failures of love get repeated in a new generation. It's a tragic inheritance.

The goal of the child-parent psychotherapy is to help parents get past their own past, and to become increasingly aware of the ways in which their personal history shapes their caregiving behavior. Coupling this self-awareness with new techniques, such as teaching the parents how to listen closely to their children, helps to improve the parent-child relationship. "In CPP," Cicchetti writes, "the patient is not the mother or the infant, but rather it is the relationship between the mother and her baby."[59]

This simple clinical intervention has undergone numerous controlled trials. The results have been consistently impressive. If we had pills that triggered the same outcomes, every at-risk parent would have a prescription. For instance, a 2006 trial led by Cicchetti looked at 137 infants living in families with a known history of abuse. (This abuse usually took the form of neglect, which the scientists define as the "failure to provide for the child's basic physical needs for adequate food, clothing, shelter, and medical treatment.") The attachments of these children reflected their tragic circumstances, as only a *single child* in the abused group showed a secure attachment to the mother.[60] The families were then randomly assigned to either a treatment condition, in which they were given weekly sessions of CPP, or a control condition, in which they "received services that were typically available to maltreating families in the community." In addition, a second control group consisted of nonabused children from the same socioeconomic background.

A year of CPP led to profound changes. While 61 percent of abused children given therapy now had a secure attachment to their mother—a figure nearly double that of their demographically matched peers—less than 2 percent of children in the control group had a secure bond.[61] Although these children had experienced the hardest kinds of childhood, Cicchetti showed that their closest relationships could still be fixed, provided the parents received a little training.* These parental improvements come with vast societal benefits. According to a 2013 study by Richard Reeves and Kimberly Howard, if the

---

*Another trial, led by Sheree Toth at the University of Rochester, looked at 130 mothers of toddlers who had experienced a major depressive disorder since the birth of their child. (It's long been recognized that maternal depression is a significant risk factor for young kids, leading to more fussiness, higher levels of stress, and significant developmental delays.) As expected, the children of depressed mothers were significantly more likely to have an insecure attachment, at least as measured on the Strange Situation task. However, after a year of child-parent psychotherapy, the results were reversed. The children of depressed mothers actually showed higher percentages of secure attachments than a control group.

"emotional support skills" of the weakest parents are merely boosted to an average level—and current interventions can accomplish that—the result would be a 12.5 percent decrease in teen pregnancy, a 4.3 percent increase in high school graduation rates, and an 8.3 percent decrease in criminal convictions before the age of nineteen.[62] Other research suggests that adverse childhood experiences, such as emotional abuse and emotional neglect, are highly correlated with drug and alcohol addiction later in life.[63] According to scientists at the Centers for Disease Control, adverse childhood experiences "account for one half to two thirds of serious problems with drug use."[64] As a result, the scientists recommend that parenting interventions become a core part of the war on drugs. Emerson was right: "Souls are not saved in bundles."[65] The hope of attachment therapy is to change the world one soul at a time.

The success of these therapies doesn't mean the science is perfect or settled; any attempt to parse human relationships into discrete categories will have some large error bars. And it doesn't mean we've solved the problem of parenting or know how to heal every broken bond. To raise a child is ultimately humbling—it's to learn how little we know, and how useless all knowledge tends to be when the baby won't stop crying. At such moments, we're not interested in Bowlby's theoretical insights or the results of some longitudinal study of German infants. We're just trying to hold it together.

So the science isn't a practical guide. It doesn't help me get my fussy son to nap or give me tips on persuading my daughter to brush her teeth. Nevertheless, the success of these attachment therapies has provided me with a better sense of what matters, a dose of clarity amid the helter-skelter of family life. So much about our kids we can't change: the constraints of genetics are real. Nevertheless, a child's working model of attachment—one of the most important variables of life—is largely under our control, for we can try to become more sensitive and more attuned.* We can try to love our children better.

Try is the key word in that sentence. I wish I could write that I've mastered the art of parenting, that I no longer lose my patience at bedtime or clench my jaw when my kid throws a tantrum over some plastic toy. I wish I could say that I rely less on the iPad to get me through moody afternoons. I wish I could say that I was better at simply *being* with my kids, and that I didn't feel as if I deserved praise for spending the afternoon with them.

I can't say any of those things. But that's okay, because I've learned an obvious truth: parenting isn't about perfection. What the science reveals, to the extent that the science reveals anything useful, is that the work of parenting is the work of attachment. The rest is mostly noise.** After all, our kids will

---

*According to a highly cited twin study, the "shared home environment" established by parents accounts for more than half of the variance in infant behavior on the Strange Situation task. The remaining variance was explained by "unique environmental factors," with the researchers concluding that "the role of genetic factors in attachment disorganization and attachment security was negligible." Caroline Bokhorst, et al., "The importance of shared environment in mother–infant attachment security: A behavioral genetic study," *Child Development* 74.6 (2003): 1769–82.

**Consider one question my wife and I have struggled with: day care. Is it okay? Will it damage the attachment bond to have our young child spend so many hours away? One of the best and most cited studies on the subject was done by scientists at the National Institute of Child Health and Human Development (NICHD). The study began in 1991 and tracked more than one thousand randomly selected American children for the next fifteen years. The researchers set out to study the long-term impact of day care. Since the average American child spends twenty-seven hours a week in nonmaternal care over his or her first four and a half years, this scientific mystery has huge practical implications.

learn most things on their own. What they need us for is an education in love and its requirements: we have to show them how to get close, even when the closeness feels like a sacrifice. We have to teach them what it takes, even when it takes everything we've got.

Love, the poet Randall Jarrell once wrote, "removes none of the contradictions of our lives but, by adding one more, induces us to accept them all."[66] And so it is with kids. They are such a pain. They take and take and take. They leave us exhausted and disappointed; their crying makes us cry; caring for them is an endless work.

We love them best of all.

The results were reassuring, even as they confirmed the crucial importance of the parent-child relationship. When it came to the strength of that attachment, the amount of time spent with a nonparental caregiver didn't really matter. No reliable differences were observed between children cared for by a nanny and those in day care, those who started nonmaternal care at six weeks of age and those who started when they were three years old. Instead, the researchers found that the only variable significantly correlated with levels of attachment—and thus with the raft of benefits associated with *secure* attachment—was the sensitivity of the parents, how well they responded to a child's state of mind. The data is clear: if we love our kids, and if we can find a way to manifest that love, they will be okay. We don't always have to be there. We just have to be present when we are. NICHD, "The effects of infant child care on infant-mother attachment security: Results of the NICHD Study of Early Child Care," *Child Development* (1997): 860–79.

3

THE MARRIAGE PLOT

I have no notion of loving people by halves; it is not my nature. My attachments are always excessively strong.

—JANE AUSTEN, *Northanger Abbey*

IN JULY 1838, Charles Darwin considered the possibility of marriage while scribbling in pencil on the back of a letter. His thoughts took the shape of a list, a balance sheet of reasons to "marry" and "not marry." (As Darwin noted at the top of the page, "This is the question.") The pros of wedlock were straightforward: Darwin cited the possibility of children ("if it please God"), the health benefits of attachment, the perks of a cleaner house, and the pleasure of having a "constant companion, (& friend in old age)." A wife, he wrote, was probably "better than a dog anyhow."[1]

The list of cons, however, was more convincing. After five years spent exploring the world on the *Beagle*, Darwin was accustomed to his freedom. He chafed at being tied down.

According to Darwin, the benefits of bachelordom included "Freedom to go where one liked," the ability to read in the evenings, less "anxiety and responsibility," and, more generally, the ability to live a life unconstrained by the shackles of commitment. On the back of his marriage balance sheet, Darwin made his true feelings plain: "How should I manage all my business if I were obliged to go every day walking with my wife. —Eheu!! I never should know French,—or see the Continent—or go to America, or go up in a Balloon, or take solitary trip in Wales."[2] As Darwin noted, the best one could hope for in wedlock was to emulate the life of a "happy slave," resigned to his chains.

Yet here's the thing: *Darwin still got married.* A few months after composing his list of reasons for and against marriage, he proposed to his first cousin Emma Wedgwood. Although the proposal surprised Emma—she wrote to her aunt that she was "too much bewildered all day to feel my happiness"—she immediately accepted, which surprised Darwin even more. (Their families were far less startled; Charles's sister had married Emma's brother the year before.)

Why did Darwin do it? Why did he propose when he had so many good reasons to stay single? Nobody knows. Perhaps Darwin himself didn't know. But maybe the young scientist realized that the steep cost of commitment—"an infinity of trouble & expense"—is also inseparable from the benefits of a lasting love, which he imagined as having a "nice soft wife on a sofa with good fire, & books & music perhaps." His audacious gamble was that the risk of marriage was worth it, and that the compromises of intimacy remained our best hope for "good pure happiness."

Was he right?

Friends with Benefits

Let's begin with an unexpected truth: long-term romantic relationships have never been more important. This might seem like a strange claim in the era of no-fault divorce, Tinder, and drunken hookups, but it's true. And it's true for a simple reason—our social networks outside of these committed relationships keep shrinking. (That this contraction is taking place even as people accumulate "friends" on Facebook tells us something depressing about our online lives.) Miller McPherson, a sociologist at the University of Arizona and Duke University, has been studying these changing social habits for years.[3] One of his studies attempted to replicate a face-to-face survey of 1,531 American adults conducted in 1985 that featured the following question: "From time to time, most people discuss *important matters* with other *people*. Looking back over the last six months, who are the people with whom you discussed matters important to you?"

In 2004, McPherson and his colleagues followed up with a new sample of adults, asking them the same question. The results were stark: in nearly every category of relationship, people reported having fewer confidants. While 26.1 percent of respondents in 1985 reported discussing important matters with a "comember of a group," such as a church congregant, only 11.8 percent of people did the same in 2004. In 1985, 18.5 percent of subjects had important conversations with their neighbors. That number shrank to 7.9 percent two decades later. Even friendship appeared to be in steep decline, as the percentage of Americans who regularly confided to their friends fell by nearly 23 percentage points.* Other studies have reached similar conclusions. The sociologist Robert Putnam, for instance, uses the DDB Needham Life Style Surveys to show that the average married couple entertained friends at home approximately fifteen times per year in the 1970s. By the late 1990s, that number was down to eight, "a decline of 45 percent in barely two decades."[4]

How are we coping with this shrinking circle of friends? By relying more than ever on our romantic partner. Although Americans reported spending far less time talking about life issues with their friends, colleagues, siblings, parents, and community members, they reported spending *more* time talking with their spouse. (The percentage of Americans who said their spouse was their "only confidant" nearly doubled between 1985 and 2004.) The sociologists say we are increasingly dependent on our lover for support and counsel; our "core discussion network" is often a network of one.

Such a winnowed social network poses an obvious risk, as it means we are utterly dependent on a single human being for affection and support. Given the high American divorce rate—it has hovered between 35 and 45 percent for the last thirty years[5]—such dependence can seem rather reckless. Isn't it safer to live alone? To learn the habits of self-reliance? Montaigne once compared marriage to a cage: "The birds outside

---

*According to the scientists, a number of factors caused this decline in friendship, such as the entry of women into the workforce, which leaves less time to participate in volunteer, community, or civic activities. They also blame the Internet: "While these technologies allow a [social] network to spread out across geographic space, they seem, however, to lower the probability of having face-to-face visits with family, neighbors, or friends in one's home."

despair of getting in, and those inside are equally anxious to get out."[6]

But this dependency also has an upside, since it means that those surviving couples are closer than couples have ever before been. Somehow, their love endures: they get to have regular sex with their best friend. (As Montaigne would later admit, "If you form it [marriage] well, and take it rightly, there is no finer relationship in our society.")[7] While it's not easy to estimate the exact percentage of truly happy marriages—one recent study concluded that 40 percent of those married more than ten years were still "very intensely in love"[8]—these lasting relationships clearly represent an unprecedented kind of human union. In a recent meta-analysis of ninety-three studies, the psychologist Christine Proulx at the University of Missouri found that the rewards of a good marriage have increased in recent decades, with the most loving couples providing a bigger lift to the "personal well-being" of the partners.[9] The influence of a good marriage on overall levels of life satisfaction has doubled since the late 1970s.[10] Romantic love remains a gamble, a crazy wager, but when the gamble pays off, there's nothing better.

On July 26, 1985, the psychologists Cindy Hazan and Phillip Shaver, then at the University of Denver, published a series of questions in the *Rocky Mountain News* that would reshape the way scientists conceived of romantic love.[11] The lengthy survey included ninety-five questions, focused on a person's "most important" relationship. While many of the questions asked for intimate details—Were you sexually attracted to your lover? How often did you experience strong feelings of jealousy?—the most important part of the survey asked subjects to identify which of the following statements best described their attitudes about love:

1. I find it relatively easy to get close to others and am comfortable depending on them and having them depend on me. I don't often worry about being abandoned or about someone getting too close to me.
2. I am somewhat uncomfortable being close to others; I find it difficult to trust them completely, difficult to allow myself to depend on them. I am nervous when anyone gets too close, and often, love partners want me to be more intimate than I feel comfortable being.
3. I find that others are reluctant to get as close as I would like. I often worry that my partner doesn't really love me or won't want to stay with me. I want to merge completely with another person, and this desire sometimes scares people away.

These simple questions concealed a radical hypothesis: Hazan and Shaver wanted to redefine adult relationships in terms of attachment. When the scientists asked the newspaper readers to pick one of those statements, they were actually asking them to choose an attachment style, slotting them into the categories first used to define twelve-month-old infants. (The first statement represented a secure attachment; the second was avoidant; the third was resistant, or what Hazan and Shaver called "anxious/ambivalent.") After analyzing 620 responses, Hazan and Shaver discovered that the distribution of adult attachment styles was roughly equivalent to the infant distributions first observed by Ainsworth. In both the infant and adult samples, just over half of subjects were securely attached, with the remainder divided between avoidance and anxiety. And this result wasn't a statistical accident. Hazan and Shaver argued that the categories reflected a natural variation in close human relationships, which seemed always to be defined by the same basic tensions and tendencies. Most couples stressed the benefits of their love, how their partner put them at ease and helped them cope with stressful situations. (This was usually a sign of secure attachment.) Other subjects said they avoided intimacy and ran away whenever anyone got too close. (Avoidance 101.) And then some couldn't abide any separation at all; they were jealous and clingy, always worried that their partner was about to leave them. (Such are the symptoms of anxious or resistant attachment. In general, women are slightly more likely to have an anxious attachment style.)[12] These predicaments always feel so unique, a symptom of the particular history of our relationship, but attachment theory revealed their underlying causes. When it came to love, adults were babies with language and credit cards.

Once you begin looking at romantic relationships through the prism of attachment theory, the parallels can seem obvious, inescapable. Like a parent bonding with a young child, new lovers also spend hours engaged in constant physical contact, cooing and cuddling in isolation. (Bowlby referred to this as "proximity seeking"; adults call it dating.) They hold hands, stare into each other's eyes, and rely on childish diminutives, such as *sweetie pie* and *baby*. Even the chemistry overlaps: oxytocin, a hormone associated with intimacy and pair-bonding, is released in large quantities in the brain during breast-feeding *and* when couples have sex.

The most convincing evidence, however, came when Shaver and colleagues looked at how these attachment categories shaped the actual romantic relationship. The effects were sweeping, as secure people in relationships consistently reported having more satisfying marriages.[13] As a result, their relationships tended to last longer—they averaged ten years, versus 4.9 to 6 years for insecure couples—and they experienced far lower divorce rates.[14] They felt closer to each other, had more sex, and were much less likely to break up during moments of "relationship distress."[15]

In the years since, scientists have begun to dissect the mechanisms that make securely attached couples happier and more likely to stay together. The psychologists Jeffry Simpson, William Rholes, and Julia Nelligan led a study of eighty-three couples, dating for an average of eighteen months.[16] After giving the couples a modified and expanded version of the questionnaire first developed by Hazan and Shaver, each woman was escorted to a waiting room. An experimenter feigned taking a blood pressure reading, to raise the woman's anxiety level, and explained what was going to happen next. Here is the script:

"In the next few minutes, you are going to be exposed to a situation and set of experimental procedures that arouse considerable anxiety and distress in most people. Due to the nature of these procedures, I cannot tell you any more at the moment."

The scientist then led the woman down the hall to a heavy door. Behind the door was a dark, windowless room, resembling an "isolation chamber." The room contained a mass of technical equipment that, the scientist said, would be used to measure her stress levels during the experiment. However, the machines weren't quite ready yet, so the scientist led the woman back to the original room, where her partner was waiting.

The point of the study was whatever happened next. As the couple sat by themselves, Simpson and colleagues secretly videotaped their conversation. The scientists wanted to see how each woman dealt with her anxiety. Did she tell her partner about the scary machine? Was she able to share her fears and vulnerabilities? And how did her partner respond? Did he try to comfort her?

In many respects, this experiment is an adult version of the Strange Situation task.[17] It also attempts to measure the strength of a relationship by exposing it to stress. As expected, the results demonstrated that the attachment style of each partner was correlated with his or her behavior. Women who were more securely attached were far more open about their anxieties—they might describe, for instance, what they'd seen down the hall and what might happen to them—and the securely attached men responded with reassuring words and touches, which helped to calm their distressed partners. In contrast, those women with insecure avoidant attachments were much more likely to suppress their fears and not share information with their partner. The more anxious they were, the *less* they sought support.

Over time, these everyday interactions can add up, settling into patterns of behavior that define the relationship. When partners successfully support each other through times of crisis, the relationship can grow closer and become stronger. But when that same support is lacking, it tends to wither. As Bowlby wrote, "All of us, from the cradle to the grave, are happiest when life is organized as a series of excursions, long or short, from the secure base provided by our attachment figure(s)."[18]

This is a strange way of thinking about adult love affairs. When most people think about romantic love—when we sing along to the chorus of a country-western song or read a romance novel or even reflect on our own marriage—we tend to think of it as far removed from the needs of early childhood. Kids require comfort and caregiving; adults crave seduction and desire. We want to fall in love and then keep falling, to find a passionate love in which the passion never disappears.

But the dismal truth is, the passion will disappear. It will fade. Passion *always* fades. Here, for instance, is a chart from Hazan and Shaver, which attempts to summarize the course of an ordinary adult attachment relationship over time[19]:

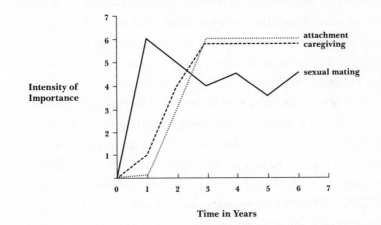

Time in Years

Notice the fickleness of desire, the sheer unsteadiness of its strength. In a typical relationship, sexual passion spikes at the start—if romantic love were a physics equation, it would provide the initial momentum—but then it starts to flicker. We gain weight, sprout hair in the wrong places, stop trying to hold in our farts; the body parts that once drove us mad are now merely entertaining, and that's when we're in the mood. As Hazan and Shaver drily note, "If sexual passion is indeed the initial motivating force in the formation of many adult pair bonds, a decline in satisfaction is inevitable."[20]

This decline has an obvious cause: habituation. (Even carnal pleasures get boring.) The search for new sex positions might delay this boredom for a little while, but we'll eventually run out of variations. There is only so much skin to explore. This is why, if the relationship is going to survive, the steady diminishment of lust and passion has to be countered by a gradual rise in what's known as "companionate love." [21] First defined by the psychologists Elaine Hatfield and William Walster, companionate love is "the affection we feel for those with whom our lives are deeply intertwined."[22] While passionate love often precedes companionate love—attachments often start with an intense emotional rush—the two states remain distinct psychological processes. The passion makes us fall. Companionship is what we fall *into*.

This process is extraordinarily complex; companionate love remains one of the grand mysteries of human nature. Nevertheless, we can see its underpinnings with carefully done fMRI studies of the brain. In a recent experiment led by Bianca Acevedo at Stony Brook University, seventeen individuals in the midst of a "long-term intense" love affair—they'd been happily married for an average of 21.4 years—were shown pictures of their partners, close friends, and acquaintances while they were stuck in a brain scanner. The most revealing results were those unique to companionate love, as the scientists observed a spike in brain activity in parts of the brain, such as the globus pallidus and substantia nigra, that have also been associated with maternal attachment. What makes this pattern of activity surprising is that the subjects were looking at pictures of their lover, not their mother.[23] According to the scientists, this finding suggests that "there is an underlying 'attachment system' which coordinates proximity seeking, and that it shares common biological substrates for pair-bonds and parent-infant bonds." All lasting love is made of the same nerves and wires.

It also leads to the same intimate union. Parents and children in a state of attunement become porous beings, their bodies blurring together when they play. A similar process occurs with adults in long-term relationships. In one recent study, married couples had immune systems that bore a striking resemblance to each other, featuring 50 percent less cellular variation than strangers drawn from the same demographic.[24] This might seem surprising—love alters our very fabric!—until you realize that a ten-second kiss leads to a swapping of somewhere between 10 million and 1 billion bacteria from 278 different species.[25] (The variability is, presumably, related to the amount of tongue involved.) Over time, all those kisses add up, turning the loving couple into an island of being and biology that they share with no one else, only each other.

Here's the bad news: staying in love on this island isn't easy. Long-term couplings don't avoid the trap of habituation by chance or by dint of some mental loophole—the attachment persists because the partners *make* it persist. (It's not an accident that the word *wedlock* is derived from the Old English words for "pledge" [*wedd*] and "activity" [*lac*]. To marry, then, is to commit to constant activity.) As Erich Fromm warns his reader at the start of *The Art of Loving*, "The reading of this book would be a disappointing experience for anyone who expects easy instruction."[26] He lists all the attributes that love requires: "discipline, concentration, patience, faith, and the overcoming of narcissism." Fromm says love "isn't a feeling, it is a practice."[27]

So what must we practice? A million little things. Sometimes, love demands that spouses touch their partner in an affectionate way or say something nice. (Happily married couples average five positive interactions—a quick kiss or a random compliment, for instance—for every negative interaction. The ratio is closer to one-to-one in couples headed for divorce.)[28] Sometimes, love means that we share the chores, equitably dividing up the housework. (When women feel responsible for the majority of domestic chores, they are less satisfied with their marriage and more prone to depression.)[29] It can require that, in the midst of a heated argument, we take a moment to turn toward our spouse, orienting our body so that we are face-to-face. (A study that tracked married couples for six years found that those who stayed together were two and a half times more likely to turn toward each other during conflict conversations than couples who separated; the body positions helped to de-escalate the fight.)[30] And sometimes love means that we make time for intimacy, that we insist we are not too busy for a sit-down dinner or a long walk or pillow talk. (According to a 2008 longitudinal study by researchers at the University of Massachusetts at Amherst, the marital satisfaction of couples is closely linked to their amount of "shared leisure time.")[31]

These can seem like such minor acts, such trite habits, social science at its most obvious. Nevertheless, these everyday behaviors represent the essence of adult attachment, the hard work that's required if you want a relationship to last. As the therapist Daniel Wile writes, "Choosing a partner is choosing a set of problems."[32] Wile's point is that most marriages revolve around a set of fundamental disagreements that never get resolved. (According to one study of marital disputes, less than a third of them had practical solutions. The remaining 69 percent of problems had to do with "differences in personality or needs that were fundamental to their core definition of self.")[33] Yet, despite this Sisyphean struggle—you will never win the fight!—the couple cannot give up. They need to keep loving their problems, just as they promised they would.

Sex

The language of attachment theory is not romantic; it obeys none of our time-tested clichés. When scientists recast adult love in terms of attachments, passion seems to become little more than a prelude; the sensuality is gone, replaced by talk of "proximity seeking" and "separation distress." This is not the wild lust of a Hollywood movie or the fated coupling of a Nicholas Sparks novel. This is love as function. More flannel pajamas, less frilly lingerie.

But the clinical language is misleading. The power of attachment theory is that, even as it addresses our need for safety and comfort, it also helps us understand the persistence of desire. The explanation is rooted in a paradox, which was first noticed by Bowlby: children who are securely attached are also far more willing to explore the world, take risks, and enjoy novelty. When we have a secure base, we are better at dealing with our feelings of *in*security.

What's more surprising, perhaps, is that this principle also seems to apply to adults. If we are securely attached, we're better able to explore alongside our partners, trusting them to take us to new places. Maybe we tag along to a ballroom-dancing class or try a new food they've cooked for dinner or listen to them explain the joys of Marvel comic books. The details don't matter. What does matter is that our attachment is also a source of surprise, that we use its safety to try things that we've never before tried.

This pattern is even apparent in the bedroom, as studies show that people who are securely attached tend to spend far less time fretting about sex and much more time enjoying it. In an unpublished 1994 survey, Hazan and colleagues found that

measures of attachment were "systematically and strongly related to the kinds of intimate sexual activities a person enjoys,
with secure individuals enjoying a wider range of sexual activities."[34] When people in a relationship were securely attached to
each other, they were more willing to experiment with novelty
and kink; the bed had become a playground. More recently, a
2012 review of fifteen published studies found that securely attached partners reported having sex more frequently and were
more satisfied with their sex life.[35] Other studies have found
that avoidant individuals have less sex (but masturbate more),
while insecurely attached women are far less likely to report
"orgasmic experiences."[36]

What accounts for these differences? Unless spouses feel
confident in their love, they won't be able to enjoy all the delights afforded by the body. Instead, they'll be too wrapped up
in the usual anxieties of nakedness. *How do I look in this light? Am
I taking too long? Not long enough? Where should I put my hand? There?
Is that okay?* As Phillip Shaver and Mario Mikulincer write,
"These positive mental representations allow secure adults to
relax their defenses and be less preoccupied with sexual performance, which, when combined with enjoyment of closeness,
is conducive to 'letting go' sexually and experiencing maximal
sexual pleasure."[37] Too often we think of sex as a purely physical act, a performance of nerves and friction, like the scratch-
ing of an itch. But desire is so much more complicated than
that—it is always tangled up with our deepest needs and associations. We never actually fuck our brains out.

The emotional entanglement of sex also helps explain why
simply having more sex doesn't solve any of our relationship
issues. Researchers at Carnegie Mellon recently conducted a
study that makes this clear.[38] Sixty-four married heterosexual

couples had been randomly assigned to one of two groups. The first group received no instructions or advice on their sex life. The second group was instructed to double the frequency of their sex acts. Unfortunately, this extra copulating didn't improve their marital happiness. If anything, it was associated with a slight *decrease* in sexual desire, sexual enjoyment, and overall happiness levels.

This failed intervention contradicts the long-standing link between sexual activity and life satisfaction. (One study concluded that having sex once a week, as opposed to once a month, provided a boost of happiness equivalent to having an extra $50,000 in savings.)[39] However, these correlations are often misleading, as they don't account for the real reason sex makes us happy. It's not about the orgasm, which we are perfectly capable of accomplishing on our own. It's about what the sex means to our relationship, how it triggers feelings way below the skin.

The mingling of fleshy pleasure and emotional intimacy helps explain another reason securely attached couples have better sex: they're more willing to please each other. That's the conclusion, at least, of a 2013 study led by the psychologist Amy Muise at the University of Toronto of forty-four long-term couples. After closely tracking their bedroom experiences for three weeks—the partners were asked to rate their enjoyment after every sexual activity—the scientists found that the best predictor of desire and "sexual benefits for the self" was whether spouses felt motivated to meet their partner's sexual needs.[40] (The researchers refer to this tendency as "sexual communal strength.") This tendency might seem like an obvious contradiction—people feel more desire when they try to satisfy the desires of another person?—but it reflects the intense give-and-take that makes lasting love possible. The best sex is not about sex. It is about getting as close as we can, in the most literal sense, to another human being.*

Secure attachments lead to better sex. But the converse is true, too: when our attachments wither, the passion tends to disappear. As the couples therapist Sue Johnson notes, sexual issues are often the "canary in the mine" of a relationship, a tangible symbol of an emotional loss. (Happy spouses attribute only 15 to 20 percent of their contentment to their sex life; unhappy spouses, in contrast, say that 50 to 70 percent of their problems are rooted in sexual issues.)[41] While many of Johnson's patients insist that a lack of sex is a primary cause of their relationship issues, she sees sexual issues as mostly a side effect, triggered by larger attachment insecurities. "What's really happening is that a couple is losing connection," Johnson writes. "The partners don't feel emotionally safe with each other."[42] Over time, this situation creates a dangerous feedback loop, as a lack of attachment leads to a slackening of desire, which only leads to less attachment and even less desire.

To stop this spiral, Johnson has pioneered, along with Les Greenberg, a form of couples therapy known as emotionally focused therapy, or EFT. The therapy is founded on the principles of adult attachment; it assumes, Johnson writes, that people "are emotionally attached to and dependent on your

---

*Consider an unpublished study led by Bernie Zilbergeld of one hundred married couples. He found that variation in "sexual technique"—what couples actually did in bed, from oral sex to foreplay techniques—explained little of the variation in sexual satisfaction for husband and wife. Instead, Zilbergeld found that the most important factor by far was the maintenance of a close friendship. John Gottman, *What Makes Love Last* (New York: Simon & Schuster, 2012), 177.

partner in much the same way that a child is on a parent for nurturing, soothing, and protection." While earlier forms of marital counseling treated marriage as a rational bargain— the couples were taught how to become better negotiators— Johnson's insight was that you can't bargain over the basic human need for love. Her EFT sessions focus on revealing and strengthening the attachment bond, teaching partners to be sensitive and attuned to each other, just like a good parent. Instead of pretending we don't need comfort, Johnson tries to create "hold me tight" moments, when people discuss their fears and admit their need for connection. (EFT sessions, Johnson says, do not include "learning how to argue better, analyzing your early childhood, making grand romantic gestures, or experimenting with new sexual positions.") The goal is to create a more secure connection.[43]

That sounds nice, but is it effective? The initial evidence suggests it is: in randomized, controlled trials, approximately 90 percent of couples show significant improvements after undergoing eight to twenty EFT sessions. What's more, these improvements appear to be long lasting. When Johnson and her colleagues followed up with patients several months after the end of their therapy, they found that the percentage of people saying their relationship had "recovered" or was in "recovery" continued to increase.

This doesn't mean good sex is just a side effect of security, or that every person you're closely attached to knows how to make you climax. Desire is a cipher, and it takes time to crack the code. While couples therapists are currently debating the importance of treating sexual problems directly, and not as a by-product of underlying relationship issues, most everyone agrees on the importance of candor and honesty about the bedroom.[44] Sex gives rise to feelings for which there are no words, just awkward sounds. But we're more likely to get those feelings when we use our words to say what exactly we want.

Love is a labor. Even good sex takes work. When a relationship endures, it is not because the flame never burns out. It is because the flame is always being relit.

The Arrangement

Before Farahad and Sameera Zama got married, on New Year's Eve in 1989 in the southeastern Indian city of Visakhapatnam, they'd spent a total of forty-five minutes together. They'd never kissed or hugged or talked by themselves. Since they knew almost nothing about each other, it's easier to list what they *did* know: Sameera was the niece of Farahad's parents' next-door neighbor. She had a pretty face and made a delicious *halwa*. Farahad worked in Mumbai, doing something with computers. They both spoke English. The rest was mystery.[45]

Nevertheless, Farahad and Sameera committed to a life together in front of hundreds of people, participants in the ancient ritual of arranged marriage. "I went in [to marriage] with very limited expectations," Sameera says. "I trusted that he was a good man, and that our families had made a good match. But that was about it." Notice the modesty of this story: There is no star-crossed narrative, no fanciful account of their first date. They don't talk about sudden swells of love or the machinations of fate. Instead, Farahad and Sameera speak in pragmatic terms, focusing on the factors that led their families to pair them. Sameera was getting old—"I was twenty, which meant that I was considered past my sell-by date," she jokes—while Farahad's mother insisted that he marry a local girl, so that he wouldn't have to spend half of his vacation time in a different city. When I ask about their first days together—What was it like living with a stranger?—they brush the question aside. Instead, they begin recounting all the ritual obligations of newlyweds, how they had to entertain dozens of relatives for weeks. "You don't have time to worry," Sameera says. "You are too busy feeding people."

Once upon a time, Farahad and Sameera's setup was the standard: matrimony was less about love and more about economics. "Marriage had as much to do with getting good in-laws and increasing one's family labor force as it did with finding a lifetime companion," writes the historian Stephanie Coontz in *Marriage, a History*.[46] The idea of marrying for love, she says, was "considered a serious threat to social order." Not until the 1760s did European couples begin thinking of romance as a primary motive for wedlock, or what the French called "marriage by fascination."[47]

In the twenty-first century, the idea of marrying *without* love seems absurd, at least for most people in the developed world. Farahad and Sameera seem far stranger to us than the crazy-in-love couple who run away to Vegas after a few ecstatic dates. That's why I was surprised by the numbers: arranged marriages remain an extremely popular form of matchmaking, with roughly 80 percent of nations outside the Western Hemisphere practicing some form of an arranged marriage system.[48] (In some countries, such as India, more than 90 percent of marriages are still arranged, and many young adults are satisfied with this setup.[49]) While I flippantly concluded that arranged relationships must be a relic of the past, modern marriage remains a strikingly diverse institution.

However, the more I talked with Farahad and Sameera, the

less I thought about how their relationship began. (If anything, their easy banter and constant teasing reminded me of my parents.) "I never worried about Farahad being the man of my dreams, because dreams are very generic and not very interesting," she says. "What we've got is much better than that." Like every other lasting attachment, the story they tell is of love growing over time, a tale of endless rewards and endless work. I asked Sameera how long it took before she felt that she really knew Farahad. "I don't know," she said. "I never really thought about it." Six months? A year? Five years? "It's not a very good question," Sameera finally told me, as politely as possible. "You see, I never thought I would one day feel like I knew him. Even then I knew that I would always be getting to know him."

It's such a subtle linguistic turn that it's easy to overlook. I didn't notice it until later, when I was reviewing the notes from our conversation. But what Sameera has done is transform my question of the past tense—"When did you finally know him?"—into an answer of the present tense. That turn is telling. Because arranged marriages begin with so little—the spouses have no shared history, no base of intimacy, no inciting passion—the pair are forced to see their relationship as a never-ending process. Their love is not something that happened. It's something that *keeps* happening.

I don't want to romanticize this attitude. Throwing two strangers together into a house and telling them they can't leave sounds more like a bad reality-television show than a recipe for lasting love. Nevertheless, the evidence is solid that the romantic attitude associated with arranged marriage often comes with real benefits. While it's difficult to make cross-cultural comparisons of marital satisfaction, researchers have repeatedly and consistently found that couples in arranged marriages are just as happy, if not happier, than those in "free choice" marriages.[*50] Furthermore, the trend tends to increase over time. In one study led by Usha Gupta and Pushpa Singh at the University of Rajasthan, and cited by the psychologist Robert Epstein, couples in arranged marriages showed lower average levels of love at the start of their marriage when compared to free-choice marriages. (This finding was not unexpected, since the arranged couples barely knew each other.) However, the pattern reversed after ten years, so that those in arranged marriages scored nearly twice as high on the Rubin Love Scale as couples in "love marriages."[**51] This phenomenon was most recently replicated in a 2012 study led by Pamela Regan, a psychologist at Cal State Los Angeles. In her comparative survey of free-choice and arranged marriages among Indians living in the United States, Regan found that couples chosen largely at the behest of their families were just as likely to have loving relationships as those who chose each other.[52]

---

[*]The same pattern even applies to "institutional marriages" in the United States. These traditional couples embrace a "norm of marital permanency," in contrast to the more prevalent "soul mate" model of marriage. (In other words, they believe passionate love is a less important motive for wedlock than child care.) According to a survey of 1,414 married men and women in Louisiana, these institutional marriages typically lead to high levels of marital stability and satisfaction, provided the spouses are "embedded" in large social networks. W. Bradford Wilcox and Jeffrey Dew, "Is love a flimsy foundation? Soulmate versus institutional models of marriage," *Social Science Research* 39.5 (2010): 687–99.

[**]The Rubin Love Scale was pioneered by the Harvard psychologist Zick Rubin. It asks people to rate, on a scale of 1 to 9, whether they agree with thirteen statements designed to assess the intensity of their emotional attachment. Sample statements include "If my partner were feeling badly, my first duty would be to cheer him or her up" and "If I could never be with my partner, I would feel miserable."

What accounts for the startling success of arranged marriages, at least compared to all those "love" marriages that end in divorce? To answer this question, the psychologist Robert Epstein interviewed couples from nine different countries and five different religions. He concluded that eleven factors accounted for the "excessive" stability and satisfaction of arranged marriages, at least when compared to Western "love" marriages. Two of these factors strike me as particularly important. The first is a sense of "unwavering commitment," both to the partner and to the relationship. (As Sameera notes, couples in arranged marriages tend to treat divorce as taboo, since it's seen as bringing shame to the entire family.) The second factor is a willingness to engage in "accommodation," which Epstein defines as the "voluntary altering of [one's] behavior to meet the other person's needs."[53] These couples do not expect their marriage to take care of itself. They understand, like Farahad and Sameera, that attachments only emerge over time, and that they take endless work. Incessant repair. Constant compromise. The advantage of spouses in arranged marriages is that they know this from the start.

At one point in our conversation, Sameera seems a little worried that she's making their marriage sound *too* practical, as if their relationship were merely an exercise in duty and commitment. "Just because you begin with very limited expectations, doesn't mean you never expect more," she says. "I think everybody wants to experience a love marriage, not only people who fall in love before they have the wedding." She describes the fun of slowly discovering your spouse, unraveling the mystery that's another person. "Every now and then, I see something he's said or done and I become very grateful for him. I know this sounds corny, but I fall in love all over again."

I first learned about Farahad through his fiction. His debut novel, *The Marriage Bureau for Rich People*, tells the story of Mr. Hyder Ali, a former government clerk living in Visakhapatnam, or Vizag. The book begins with his retirement, which soon dissolves into boredom. Ali's wife says he's like "an unemployed barber who shaves his cat for want of anything better to do." To pass the time, Ali decides to become a matchmaker. He soon hires a pretty young assistant, Aruna, who is full of marital advice even though her family won't let her get married. Not surprisingly, the novel ends with a grand wedding—Aruna is the happy bride—and with a rekindling of affection between Mr. and Mrs. Ali.

Why did Farahad decide to write novels? And why did he choose matchmaking as his subject? He was inspired, he says, by the interest of his British friends, who constantly peppered him with questions about what it was like to get married to a woman he didn't know. "They'd act very surprised that ours was not a quote-unquote 'love' marriage," Farahad says. "I guess because we seem happy together? Or because she is not silent and we laugh at each other's jokes? Eventually I thought maybe I should write a book about it."

That's how Farahad became a gentle advocate for arranged marriage. It's not that he thinks the custom is right for everyone, or that it should necessarily persist into the twenty-first century. (Like Mr. Ali, Farahad espouses plenty of liberal views, especially on the subject of female emancipation.) Rather, it's that his own marriage has shown him the virtues of the tradition, how it inspires a set of realistic attitudes about love that help the love persist. "Our marriage, arranged with other considerations in mind, took us from acquaintance to love and kept us together," Farahad wrote in a 2009 essay. "Now we consider ourselves absolutely perfect for each other. Somewhere in that is a lesson, I am sure."[54]

It's very much like Farahad not to spell out the particular lesson, lest he overgeneralize from his own life. ("I put my trust in statistics," he says. "I don't know how much one can learn from our little story.") Furthermore, as Farahad and Sameera point out, not every arranged marriage is as successful and modern as theirs. In many instances, the tradition is still tangled up with the subjugation of women. In Bangladesh, for instance, approximately 25 percent of females enter into a forced marriage before the age of fifteen. Meanwhile, the United Nations estimates that tens of thousands of Pakistani girls are still used each year as bargaining chips, pushed into wedlock to resolve family debts.

But these tragic examples obscure a more common situation, in which the couple are brought together by relatives after extensive research. "It's like when you hire someone for a job," Sameera says. "You check their references first." Once the match is approved by both families, the couple are introduced to each other. Sometimes, this meeting consists of a short date—Farahad and Sameera had tea and sweets in the company of her uncle—while other traditions encourage the couple to spend a weekend together. The marriage can only proceed with the consent of both partners, which is what separates an arranged marriage from a criminal forced marriage. "You must have a chance to say no," Sameera says. "Just because it is arranged doesn't mean you can't refuse."

Farahad and Sameera now live in South London. He works as an IT manager at an investment bank and writes popular novels during his spare time, which mostly means on the train into work and when Sameera is watching television. As in all happy marriages, their days are filled with small squabbles. They bicker over his slovenly habits—Farahad admits that he doesn't care much about "dirty socks and strewn cushions"— and continue to disagree about what to eat for dinner. (He likes sushi, while she favors long-simmered fish curries.) They have two teenage boys, both of whom insist they will choose their own brides someday. "I ask them if I can pick their wives, and they just laugh," Sameera says. "They see us as very old-fashioned."

Yet, even if their children reject arranged marriage, Farahad and Sameera hope that their sons will learn from their parents' relationship. "I hope they'll realize that passionate love is very nice, but that it has a shelf life," Sameera says.

"I hope they'll learn how to compromise with each other," Farahad says.

His wife jumps in, pointing out that compromise doesn't sound very exciting. "I wish there was a better word, because it's a very important quality."

"How about *change?*"

"That's better."

"Then I hope they'll learn how to change for each other."

Matchmaking

Romantic love exists at the intersection of biology and culture.[*55] It is a primal need influenced by the rhymes of poets

---

*According to a team of anthropologists, "clear evidence" of romantic love has been found in 147 of 166 studied cultures, from the Bushmen of the Kalahari to the Song Dynasty of China. Most of the exceptions are due to the absence of reliable anthropological evidence, which is quite different from having evidence of an actual absence.

and the clichés of screenwriters. As a result, the story of our own love is interwoven with the stories of other lovers. We steal their lines, we borrow their rituals, we act out their moves. It's all been done before.

That's why, if you want to understand the modern reality of love, you have to revisit its cultural history. A good place to start is with *The Symposium*, written by Plato between 385 and 360 BC. *The Symposium* tells the story of a drunken dinner party featuring various Greek intellectuals pontificating on the nature of love. The most memorable speech comes in the middle of the party, when the guests are at peak levels of intoxication. Plato turns over the lectern to Aristophanes, the comic playwright. As expected, Aristophanes fills his talk with jokes, mingling serious insights with silly punch lines. In the beginning, he says, every human being was doubled up, with four arms and four legs and one head with two faces. Unfortunately, these composite beings were so nimble that they began scheming against the Gods. Zeus took offense and decided, after much consideration, to cut these beings in half, sliced down the middle.

According to Aristophanes, the memory of this catastrophic split remains. He describes human beings as defined by incompleteness, which is why we spend the rest of our lives searching for our missing half. Love is simply "the desire and pursuit of the whole," a desperate attempt to undo the punishment of the Gods.[56] When we meet our other half, we are overwhelmed by the bliss of finding the person we've always been looking for. These new lovers forget to eat and drink; their world shrinks to the circumference of their bodies. (In his final laugh line, Aristophanes points out that sex is only possible because Zeus kindly arranged our private parts "around to the front." When we were doubles, we had to spread our seed on the ground, "like grasshoppers.")

It's a ridiculous tale, a philosophical joke. Nevertheless, Aristophanes's parable continues to define our romantic lives. In particular, it has shaped the way we think about the start of love. Romeo meets Juliet and craves a fusion—"Oh, that I were a glove upon that hand, / That I might touch that cheek!" he sighs—while Freud described our "oceanic feelings," arguing that our desire for union represented a regression to the infant stage of development. You can even hear echoes of *The Symposium* in pop music, as Plato's version of love has shaped the ways singers croon about their beloved.

Alas, these philosophies and pop songs have led us astray; the model of romantic love they've inspired is founded upon a series of illusions. The first illusion is that love requires soul mates, and that soul mates are the scarcest of properties. If we are going to live happily ever after, Aristophanes suggests, we need to find that one person who is perfect for us.*

But true love isn't so rare. While scientists have attempted, probably in vain, to estimate the precise odds of finding a suitable long-term partner—the mathematician Peter Backus adapted the Drake equation to prove that London would pro-

---

*These clichés appear to be largely Western constructions. The late psychiatrist Stephen Mitchell tells a story about the anthropologist Audrey Richards, who studied the Bemba people of Northern Rhodesia. One day, Richards was telling a group of the Bemba "an English folk fable about a young prince who climbed glass mountains, crossed chasms, and fought dragons, all to obtain the hand of a maiden he loved. The Bemba were plainly bewildered, but remained silent. Finally an old chief spoke up, voicing the feelings of all present in the simplest of questions: 'Why not take another girl?'" Stephen Mitchell. *Can Love Last? The Fate of Romance over Time* (New York: W. W. Norton, 2003), 99.

vide only twenty-six women he could happily be in a serious relationship with[57]—the success of arranged marriages suggests
that we can form a secure attachment to a relatively wide range
of people. What's more, a study by Raymond Knee has shown
that a strong belief in the soul mate model can decrease our
chances of finding love, since we assume that every hiccup in
the relationship is proof that it wasn't meant to be.[58] For Aristophanes, love was all about the search, that desperate hunt
for a doppelgänger. But the reality of love is that the perfect
lover does not exist. The sooner we give up looking for him or
her, the sooner we can find someone who might actually make
us happy.[*59]

Aristophanes's model of love has another problem. When
the playwright framed love in terms of missing halves, he inspired people to seek out partners who were just like them,
with similar interests, backgrounds, and preferences. (If we
are cleaved from the same soul, then shouldn't we like the
same things?) The result, writes the marriage counselor Harville Hendrix, is that most people associate attraction with
the "phenomenon of recognition," in which the partners think
to themselves, "I know we've just met, but somehow I feel as
though I already know you."[60] We already know them *because we
are the same person*.

But this search for similarity is often a mistake. When we
look for instant recognition, we end up privileging the wrong
aspects of personality. A 2011 study by Paul Eastwick, Eli Finkel, and Alice Eagly showed that people with strong prefer-

---

*Two years after Peter Backus wrote that paper explaining why he would
never find a suitable partner, he fell in love and got married. She was a
friend of a friend.

ences for a specific partner characteristic do not "experience greater desire for their current partner to the degree that he or she possesses these characteristics."[61] Another recent paper summarized the results of 313 separate studies, concluding that the similarity of personality and preferences—such as, the scientists say, "matching people who prefer Judd Apatow's movies to Woody Allen's with people who feel the same way"— had no effect on relationship well-being.[62] Meanwhile, a 2010 study of twenty-three thousand married couples found that the similarity of spouses accounted for less than 0.5 percent of spousal satisfaction.[63] In short, what we think we want in a spouse—someone who is just like us and likes all the same things—and what we want in real life are fundamentally mismatched.

This problem is best demonstrated by the recent rise of dating websites, as 38 percent of people who consider themselves "single and looking" now use the Internet as a matchmaker.[64] For the first time in human history, we can browse for life partners the same way that we browse for a book to read or a movie to watch. Instead of trusting in the advice of family and friends, we rely on algorithms that suggest the most compatible partners.

At first glance, this advance seems unqualified. Big Data will solve the mysteries of matchmaking! True love will become an app! However, we have little reason to believe that these digital tools are improving dating outcomes. They might even be making things worse, at least according to a recent analysis by a team of psychologists from five universities.[65] In their paper "Online dating: A critical analysis from the perspective of psychological science," the scientists focus on the matchmaking strategies of most dating websites, which assume that similarity and complementarity are the keys to marital bliss. Chemistry.com, for instance, promises to pair people based on overlap of their neurochemical profiles—are you the serotonin type? Or tilted more toward testosterone?—while eHarmony .com attempts to measure applicants on twenty-nine dimensions of personality, from "spirituality" to "artistic passion."

Alas, such information tends to be useless. As the scientists noted in a follow-up essay, "The available evidence suggests that the mathematical algorithms at matching sites are negligibly better than matching people at random."[66] Although we continue to believe in the power of similarity, study after study has demonstrated that Aristophanes was wrong. We don't want to love a copy of ourselves.

Similarity isn't a useful metric for evaluating potential partners because, simply, people change. Even those preferences that seem so steady and stable—our favorite ice cream flavor, weekend hobbies, the shows on our DVR—are in constant flux; we shed our selves like skin. The psychologists Jordi Quoidbach, Daniel Gilbert, and Timothy Wilson refer to this as the "end of history illusion," noting that people continually underestimate the ways in which their values, pursuits, and predilections will evolve over time.[67] As the scientists write, "People, it seems, regard the present as a watershed moment at which they have finally become the person they will be for the rest of their lives." But no such watershed moment exists. Unless our relationship is based on something deeper than superficial similarity, we might find ourselves stuck with the wrong partner. We will change. And our partner will change. But we won't want to change together.

So whom should we be searching for? How can we ever find true love?

Nearly every Jane Austen novel has the same plot.* A young daughter—always pretty, always clever—leads a quiet life in a quaint rural town. At first, not much happens. There are dances, parties, letters, excursions to London. But then a handsome man in possession of a good fortune (but never in possession of a wife) appears, disturbing the peace with new possibilities. Misunderstanding is inevitable—pride is confused with prejudice, say—and the woman and the bachelor must confront their errors in judgment. The ending is always a wedding.

This crude outline is accurate enough, but it's also accurate to describe *Hamlet* as the tale of an indecisive prince, or to summarize *Lolita* as a love story and a road trip. Austen realized that her greatest talents were as a precise portraitist of human nature, focusing on "the little bit (two inches wide) of ivory on which I work with so fine a brush."[68] If she always wrote about marriage, it was because choosing a spouse was a choice with existential stakes, a moment when the questions of psychology overlapped with the problems of daily life. In nineteenth-century England, marriage was forever. To be wrong about a husband was to ruin a life.

Emma, Austen's fourth novel, takes these concerns to their logical extreme: it is entirely about matchmaking. Our protagonist is described as "handsome, clever and rich," which is another way of saying that she has nothing to do but think about romance. But here's the twist: Emma herself is not interested in marriage. Like Darwin, she is exquisitely aware

---

* *Mansfield Park* is the notable exception.

of the drawbacks of wedlock. "If I know myself," Emma tells Harriet, "mine is an active, busy mind, with a great many independent resources." Besides, Emma declares, "I never have been in love; it is not my way, or my nature; and I do not think I ever shall."[69]

The arc of Emma's story is toward her self-understanding: the moment she says, at the beginning of the novel, that she's never going to fall in love is the moment we know that she will. Unfortunately for Emma, this understanding doesn't come easily. Rather, it emerges out of the litter of her matchmaking mistakes, which serve as the narrative spine of the book. First, there is her misread of Mr. Elton, the crafty village vicar. Emma insists that her friend Harriet is a perfect match for Mr. Elton and convinces Harriet to turn down the proposal of a kind farmer. But the match falls apart as Mr. Elton is revealed to be a cad interested mostly in money. Emma's next mistake, which takes up the second volume of the novel, is her interest in Frank Churchill, a foppish young man who thinks little of dashing off to the big city for a haircut. Emma is charmed by his wit and humor and convinces herself that "if she *were* to marry, he was the person to suit her in age, character and condition."[70] But this desire turns out to be disaster, as Frank is secretly engaged to another woman. Emma's last mistake has a better ending. Although she never considered the older Mr. Knightley a potential partner—he seems more like a cranky uncle, always proffering advice—she finally sees that she's in love with him and has been all along. "The more she contemplated it [the possibility of marrying Knightley], the more pleasing it became," Austen writes. "Mr. Knightley, always so kind, so feeling, so truly considerate for every body, would never deserve to be less worshipped than now."[71]

But *Emma* is not just the tale of an immature rich girl forced to reckon with her foolishness. Austen is making a larger point about the difficulty of knowing *anyone*. We do not grasp people at the start—we can only know them slowly, as we attempt to translate the vagaries of emotion into glimpses of understanding. While the difficulty of knowing others is a theme in all of Austen's novels, it's most clearly stated in *Emma*, as Austen demonstrates, again and again, how our initial judgments of others are clouded by our own prejudices and preconceptions. Previous romances had celebrated love at first sight—think of Romeo and Juliet, or Tristan and Isolde—but Austen mocks the possibilities of instant recognition. No sudden swells of dopamine and adrenaline occur in her novels. Or rather, these infatuations happen but are never to be trusted.

Such skepticism raises a conundrum: If people cannot be understood from the outside, then how can we ever find a suitable spouse? Is there any escape from the trap of human opaqueness? Austen is cautiously optimistic. In her novels, she suggests that the only quality that counts is the way in which people manage their feelings, a feature she usually referred to as temperament. Austen foreshadows this wisdom as she almost always introduces her characters in terms of their emotional habits. Emma has a "happy disposition," marred only by the "power of having rather too much her own way," while Harriet had a "sweet, docile, grateful disposition,"[72] with an extreme "mildness of her temper."[73] Emma's father was a "nervous man, easily depressed," Frank Churchill displayed a "restlessness of temper," and Knightley proves to be "sensible" and "intimate," with a "cheerful manner." As the plot progresses and Emma begins to gain a little wisdom, these emotional tendencies—and not the more shallow variables that Emma obsesses over—clearly emerge as the crucial ingredients of matchmaking. It's not that sense is better than sensibility, or that nerves are always a bad thing; Austen rejects such easy dichotomies. She knows that there is no single recipe for character. However, she does suggest that similar tempers belong together, and that we need a partner who can understand our emotional habits. As one of the sisters observes in *Sense and Sensibility*, "It is not time or opportunity that is to determine intimacy—it is disposition alone."[74]

The lesson is most obvious in the pairing of Emma and Knightley. At first, the two seem to be poles apart—she is flighty and youthful, while he is a grumpy old man. However, as Emma learns from her misjudgments, and as Knightley comes to terms with his repressed emotions (there's a reason he's a middle-aged bachelor), we begin to realize that the young woman and the landowner share a set of "natural dispositions." In particular, they both tend to keep their feelings on a leash, hiding away those fears and affections they'd rather not confront. Avoiding emotion is generally not the healthiest behavior, but it works for Emma and Knightley. Because they share a temperament, they can deal with their faults. Emma learns this as she's exploring Donwell Abbey, Knightley's vast estate. For the first time in the novel, she's willing to engage in careful study, "eager to refresh and correct her memory with more particular observation, more exact understanding."[75] Emma discovers that the Abbey isn't perfect—she finds the layout "rambling and irregular"—but that these blemishes allow for a more comfortable set of living rooms. Here is a house in which she finally feels at home.[76]

In a letter to her beloved niece, Fanny Knight, Austen dispenses advice that echoes the lessons of *Emma*. Fanny, in the midst of a romantic crisis, had to decide whether to marry John Plumptre. Though a good man, he was also a little too devout; he didn't make Fanny twitchy with desire. Austen's letter reads like something straight out of her fiction, at least if a wise old aunt were giving advice.

> Oh! My dear Fanny, the more I write about him [Plumptre], the warmer my feelings become, the more strongly I feel the sterling worth of such a young Man & the desireableness of your growing in love with him again. I recommend this most thoroughly.—There are such beings in the World perhaps, one in a Thousand, as the Creature You & I should think perfection, where Grace & Spirit are united to Worth, where the Manners are equal to the Heart & Understanding; but such a person many not come in your way.

As the literary critic William Deresiewicz writes, the gist of Austen's counsel is that "the most important thing is character."[77] Grace and good manners are lovely, but what matters even more is a quality of mind that allows affection to grow over time. Because Plumptre possessed such a quality, Austen assured Fanny that she "would soon love him enough for the happiness of both." He might exhibit a few "deficiencies of Manner" and follow "the precepts of the New Testament" a little too strictly, but their shared dispositions meant that their marriage would work out, provided that young Fanny was ready to settle down.

Austen was not a hypocrite. She dispensed the same matchmaking advice to her family that she did to her characters. ("She put her money where her mouth was," Deresiewicz writes, in a discussion of the Fanny letters.)[78] It was easy to get swept up in the mythologies of love, but Austen wanted to write a different kind of story, in which our attachments were based on something deep and true and lasting. Instead of lingering on the surfaces of people, Austen tried to reveal their hidden interiors, which is precisely why her writing is so dense with references to temperament and its synonyms.*

The larger theme here is Austen's refutation of Aristophanes's model of love, in which we can identify our lover at first sight. As she reminds us again and again in her novels, our first reactions tend to be wrong. Human beings are complicated. It takes time to figure someone out.

Feelings about Feelings

Jane Austen never got married. She came close, though. In December 1802, Harris Bigg-Wither, the younger brother of one of her close friends, proposed to Austen in a private room at the Manydown House in Hampshire. Not much is known about Harris—Claire Tomalin, an Austen biographer, notes that he had a bad stammer—but the marriage would have made Austen the mistress of a large estate and helped "ensure the comfort of her parents to the end of their days." She immediately accepted. The evening ended with toasts and dancing.

The very next morning, Austen changed her mind and told Harris she could not marry him. What happened? Nobody

---

*Emma, for instance, is filled with references to *temper* (the word is used forty-seven times), *character* (forty-six times), and *disposition* (twenty-five times). Compare that to Thomas Hardy's *Jude the Obscure*. Although Hardy's novel is significantly longer, it only uses *temper* or *temperament* twenty-two times, *character* twenty-two times, and *disposition* once.

knows. In letters, even her family members disagree, with some insisting that she didn't love Harris—"[he] was very plain in person—awkward, and even uncouth in manner," wrote Austen's niece—while others believed it was a noble match and that Austen had made a grave mistake.[79] The most convincing answer, at least according to Tomalin, is that Austen was too in love with writing to settle down. Although the security of marriage must have been tempting, she was determined to finish her novels. In 1803, shortly after she turned down Bigg-Wither, Austen received word that *Susan*, her first major completed work, had been accepted for publication. The payment was ten pounds.[*]

So Austen wrote about marriage like an anthropologist from Mars, chronicling the pitfalls and pleasures of an institution she never experienced herself. Perhaps this distance accounts for her startling insights, which remain as wise and trenchant as ever. In recent years, scientists have confirmed Austen's focus on the temper when it comes to a good match. They have come up with a new name for the variable of character Austen focused on in her fiction: *meta-emotion*.[80] Although everyone experiences a similar range of feelings, from anguish to joy, we reliably differ in how we *feel* about our feelings. Do we like to talk about our moods? How do we react to praise and criticism? When stressed, do we seek out comfort or solitude? While our hobbies and preferences are fleeting—that's why they're not useful in matchmaking—meta-emotional tendencies are extremely stable, reflecting those habits of the adult

---

[*]The bookseller, Crosby & Co., would later change its mind and not publish *Susan*. The novel wasn't published until after Austen's death, when it was retitled *Northanger Abbey*.

self that stay mostly the same. (The meta-emotions of children remain malleable and are strongly influenced by parents.)

John Gottman, an influential marriage psychologist at the University of Washington, has pioneered the study of meta-emotions. His interest in the subject was inspired by his clinical experience, as he tried (often unsuccessfully) to heal the breaches in troubled relationships. "I kept on butting up against the fact that partners had different reactions to their own emotions," he says. "That meant they couldn't understand or empathize with each other."[81] Gottman tells me a story about a couple he'd spent years trying to help: "The wife had been sexually abused by her grandfather when she was eight years old. And so she was living with lots of anger. But she didn't see this anger as a bad thing; it felt to her like a source of strength, a way to crusade for justice." The husband, in contrast, was terrified of anger. He told Gottman about the screaming matches of his parents; their loud voices would keep him awake at night. "And so this couple is talking about some issue and he keeps on telling her, 'Stop yelling at me, stop yelling.' And she says, 'I'm not yelling. I'm telling you what's wrong. When do I ever yell?' And he says, *'You're yelling right now.'* And that's when I realized that the real problem was that they had these different philosophies on how to deal with and express their feelings."

To better understand the impact of these contrasting philosophies, Gottman developed an interview technique capable of measuring meta-emotions. The interview begins with a simple question: "How do you feel about surprise?" "The reason I start with that question is that it seems pretty harmless," Gottman says. "I mean, I'm not asking about anger or depression. And yet, people often have strong feelings about surprises. Some people love them. They'll tell stories about how they often surprise their spouse by picking up a favorite chicken dinner at the store, while other people say, 'I hate surprises. I was so miserable at my surprise birthday party.' It gets the conversation going."

Gottman then works his way through the other human emotions, from anger to sexual desire. He asks subjects to describe what they look like when they feel sad, and how they react when their child starts to cry. He interrogates them about their favorite and least favorite feelings and tries to understand how they get over their negative moods.[82] "Things can get pretty intense," Gottman says. "You ask someone about their temper and they might start talking about their dad, who was an alcoholic and would get violent when he was drunk."

When the interviews are over, a trained scientist analyzes the couple's answers, focusing on the metaphors and adjectives each of them uses to describe his or her feelings. The goal is to slot every subject into one of three basic meta-emotional categories: "Those in favor of emotional expression, those opposed to it, and those advocating finding a balance between positive and negative emotions."[83]

After validating this measurement of meta-emotion, Gottman set up an ambitious longitudinal project, featuring several dozen couples. Every spouse received a complete meta-emotional workup. Based on the interview transcripts, the spouses were placed into one of those fundamental categories of temperament. "These categories aren't perfect," Gottman admits. "I mean, human personality is always going to be a little fuzzy, but that doesn't mean these categories don't reflect something important about us." Gottman then tracked these relationships for eight years, measuring their ups and downs, their problems and pleasures.

Gottman discovered that meta-emotional compatibility—
whether we share a temperament with our partner—is a crucial predictor of marital satisfaction, able to forecast "divorce
with 80 percent accuracy."[84] (It is, he wrote with Lynn Fainsilber Katz and Carole Hooven, *the fundamental dynamic that oper-
ates to either make marriages work, or not.*)[85] While there is no ideal
meta-emotional style—all temperaments can lead to happiness and attachment—Gottman insists that it's important to
seek out partners who share our basic emotional philosophy.

Why is meta-emotion the "fundamental dynamic" of marriage? The answer is obvious: people are different. Aristophanes argued that love arose from the *absence* of difference—a
soul mate was just a long-lost twin—but the Greek playwright
was wrong. Austen recognized this fallacy and turned those
same differences into comic plots. What makes her couples so
interesting is that they begin as such unlikely pairs.* In *Pride
and Prejudice*, Elizabeth Bennet and Fitzwilliam Darcy start out
as foes; the only thing they have in common is their mutual
disdain. He refuses to dance, likes to use four-syllable words
in his letters, and talks in a meandering, abstract tone. Elizabeth, meanwhile, loves her country dances and speaks in short,
cheeky, and direct sentences.

But Austen insists that these surface distinctions are not a
problem. Although Darcy and Elizabeth seem like opposites,
they slowly realize that they share an underlying temperament.
They discover that the superficial distinctions of class—those
differences that led to their initial spats—hid their inner like-

---

*The glaring exception to this rule is Jane Bennet and Charles Bingley of
Pride and Prejudice, who are basically mirror images; no wonder their relationship is so dull.

ness. Austen reflects this transformation in their conversations, as Darcy and Elizabeth slowly come to speak in a strikingly similar manner, or what the critic Patricia Meyer Spacks refers to as "a shared linguistic register."[86] (Spacks helpfully points out that this new grammatical style is essentially the style of the narrator; to be in love is to talk the way Austen writes.) Darcy gives up his pretentious vocabulary and shortens his clauses, while Elizabeth relinquishes the certitude of her earlier observations.

This convergence of speech represents a literary model of companionate love. While Austen never shows us these marriages in middle age—she writes of courtship and flirtation, not domestic squabbles—the empathy demonstrated by all her lovers suggests they won't be undone by the disagreements that remain.* Because there will be disagreements. (One can easily imagine Elizabeth and Darcy, or Emma and Knightley, bickering in old age; none of these characters are pushovers.) "Every couple is going to have fights," Gottman says. "Every couple is going to have those moments where they just want to scream, 'Fuck you, asshole!' But the question is what happens next. Do they understand, at some basic level, what their partner is feeling and why they are feeling it?"

Much of Gottman's research has been devoted to the pro-

---

*In one of the last chapters of *Emma*, Austen shows us how Emma and Knightley have learned to make sense of each other. Because they share an emotional philosophy, they don't even need words. "Time passed on," Austen begins, before launching into a detailed description of a fairly ordinary conversation between the couple:

"I have something to tell you, Emma," Knightley says.

Emma asks if it's good news or bad news. But then she looks at Knightley's face and discerns the answer before he even has a chance to speak.

"Oh! Good I am sure," she says. "I see it in your countenance. You are trying not to smile."

cess by which we understand our partners. One of his studies, done in collaboration with the mathematician James Murray, used "nonlinear difference equations" to predict the likelihood that a given couple will divorce. While the equations are rather complicated—they were initially designed to explain the actions of rival countries during an arms race—they give us some insights into the crucial variables of marriage.[87] In particular, the equations reveal an important and unexpected component of marital understanding: *frequent complaining*, or what Gottman refers to as a "low negativity threshold." According to the scientists, spouses who complain to each other the most, and complain about the least important things, end up having more lasting relationships. In contrast, couples with high negativity thresholds—they only complain about serious problems—are much more likely to get divorced.

What explains this finding? The virtue of complaining, say the scientists, is that it keeps resentments from accumulating; problems are solved before they fester. (The geopolitical equivalent would be two countries with diplomatic back channels—they're probably less likely to start a war.) So the next time your husband leaves his fingernail clippings on the couch, or your wife forgets to put her cereal bowl in the dishwasher, don't pretend you don't care. *Start kvetching*. Help the other person understand what's wrong. One day, your complaints might even become a compromise.

The bittersweet theme of this research is that the success of a marriage depends on how willing we are to deal with its failures, those nagging tensions that never go away. It's not about becoming the same person or fusing our souls together—it's about finding a way to cope with our differences. Because part of what you learn from an intimate relationship is that you are not nearly as easy to live with as you imagined. (The marriage becomes our most honest mirror, showing us parts of ourselves we overlooked when alone.) We also have petty moods and bad habits; we pick our nose in the car and clip our toenails on the couch. For the relationship to work, we must admit these flaws and use them to overcome our own.

In his talks, Gottman likes to tell a story from his own marriage that captures this concept: "One night, I really wanted to finish a mystery novel. I thought I knew who the killer was, but I was anxious to find out." But then, in the midst of reading, he had to go to the bathroom. As Gottman walked to the toilet, he saw his wife brushing her hair. It was part of her nighttime routine, a habit he could easily have overlooked. Yet, he noticed a glint of sadness in her eyes. "I had a choice. I could sneak out of the bathroom and think, 'I don't want to deal with her sadness tonight; I want to read my novel.' But instead . . . I decided to go [back] into the bathroom. I took the brush from her hand and asked, 'What's the matter, baby?' And she told me why she was sad."[88]

It's such a mundane moment—a short conversation at the bathroom sink—yet Gottman uses it to illustrate the necessity of empathy in every lasting relationship, even when the empathy feels like a sacrifice. Although Gottman wasn't sad, and had other things he wanted to do, he still noticed the melancholy of his wife. Because they share a meta-emotional style, he recognized her vulnerability and responded to it, easing her disquiet before bed. A good marriage, Gottman says, is a series of such moments. It's feeling the feelings of our partner, even when it conflicts with our own desires. Maybe we want to talk about it, or maybe we just want to watch a little television and fall asleep. Maybe we want to kiss, or maybe we just want you to take the kid so we can go to the gym. The particulars don't matter; the empathy does. Because even if we take issue with the complaints, we should still try to understand where they're coming from.

However, couples with clashing meta-emotional styles struggle to communicate. Instead of noticing each other's vulnerabilities, they tend to become preoccupied with their lingering differences; every distinction becomes an annoyance. Even the most minor arguments about household chores or child care can slip into screaming matches over deeper, darker issues. *Does he listen to me? Does she understand? Does he even care?* "Spouses who have different meta-emotion structures will have unstable marriages and their interaction will be characterized by disappointment, negativity, criticism, contempt, defensiveness and by eventual emotional withdrawal," Gottman writes with his coauthors. For couples caught in such downward spirals, divorce often becomes the least bad option. "What happens is that couples [with conflicting meta-emotional habits] have a really hard time getting over their 'Fuck you' fights," Gottman says. "The regrettable incidents turn into a state of gridlock."

This finding doesn't mean that meta-emotions are the secret to a happy marriage. No such secret exists. Besides, the world is filled with exceptions to the rule. Gottman knows that his study is merely a probability game, and that every relationship creates its own logic. As Emma reminds us, "Seldom, very seldom does complete truth belong to any human disclosure," especially when that truth is about a feeling as complicated as love.

If nothing else, this research should make us skeptical of any matchmaking "science." While dating websites hold out the promise of finding our soul mate with the help of algorithms, there still is no shortcut for the analog date. As the psychologist Eli Finkel writes, "Browsing profiles is virtually useless for discerning the sort of information that actually matters in a successful relationship. Curated text and a handful of pictures will never be able to tell you whether the first-date conversation will crackle or whether you'll feel a desire to discover what makes this person tick."[89] The best way to tell if we like someone, and the only way to figure out if we share a meta-emotional style, is to spend time together, to experience the world side by side.* Because only then might we learn those "little particulars," as Emma put it, that reveal the temperament.

Gottman tells a funny anecdote about a couple in a canoe: "One day, I'm kayaking down the river and I see this man and woman sharing a canoe. And I look at them and think, 'How nice, they share a hobby!' But then I get closer and I realize they're screaming at each other. He's a perfectionist and he's trying to show her how to do a correct J-stroke. And she's saying, 'What does it matter? It's so pretty here. Let's just go around in circles.' Which of course only makes him even angrier." The moral is that their shared interest in canoeing is totally irrelevant. "A website might put these two together

---

*Because time is revealing—we seem to have a natural ability to identify suitable partners. It's not about trusting our first instinct. It's about listening to those instincts that emerge over time, as we go on date after date. Research led by Justin Lavner at UCLA has, for instance, shown that women who experienced doubts about their relationship during the engagement— they had "cold feet," so to speak, just like Austen—were 2.5 times as likely to get divorced within four years. Such doubts are often subtle enough to ignore, but are a reliable indicator that our fiancé isn't an ideal match. Emma herself comes to learn this, saying, "I lay it down as a general rule that if a woman doubts as to whether she should accept a man or not, she certainly ought to refuse him. If she can hesitate as to 'Yes,' she ought to say 'No' directly."

because they both like water sports, but what really matters is
how they approach the activity, how they define fun," Gottman
says. "That's the important stuff, but you can't really find that
out until you're going down the river."

The Healthy Estate

Why do we still read Jane Austen? She is a writer of nineteenth-
century marriage plots, those fairy tales in which the entire
drama hinges on a wedding. Such tales are charming. They
also seem irrelevant, at least for modern couples. In a time of
sexual equality and same-sex marriage and no-fault divorce,
the relationship travails of Austen's heroines often feel quaint
and outdated. As Jeffrey Eugenides puts it, "What would it
matter whom Emma married if she could file for separation
later?"[90]

But the marriage plot endures; Austen's literature is more
popular than ever. While the details of her fiction might be
obsolete—we no longer flirt in ball gowns or believe that pre-
marital sex is the gravest mistake—the basic premise of her
art holds true, which is that nothing matters more than the
matters of the heart. Like Elizabeth and Emma and Fanny,
most of us remain convinced that the best lives are shared with
someone else, and that choosing a partner is one of the most
important choices we will ever make. "Anything is to be preferred or endured rather than marrying without Affection,"
Austen wrote in a letter to her niece, later noting that one
thing was worse: never knowing love at all.[91]

The latest data confirms the power of adult love. As Austen
might have said, the importance of a satisfying romantic attachment has become a truth universally acknowledged. The

first gleanings arrived a few decades after Austen's premature death. In 1839, William Farr, a physician, was put in charge of compiling "statistical abstracts" for the General Register Office, a British government bureaucracy established to keep track of property transfers among the landed gentry. But Farr was curious. Before long, he was using his access to government data to make sense of all sorts of long-standing mysteries, few of which had anything to do with the estates of rich men. For instance, Farr analyzed the mortality rates of different professions and showed that some led to far shorter lives. (On average, butchers died young, which Farr blamed on "the elements of decaying matter by which he is surrounded in his slaughter-house."[92]) However, Farr's most important contribution was his 1858 analysis of the health benefits of marriage. After reviewing the death statistics of French adults, Farr convincingly demonstrated that married people had a far lower mortality rate than those who were "celibate" or widowed. "Marriage is a healthy estate," wrote Farr. "The single individual is more likely to be wrecked on his voyage than the lives joined together in matrimony."[93]

Farr was prescient. In recent decades, dozens of epidemiological studies have demonstrated that married people are significantly less likely to suffer from cancer, viral infections, mental illness, pneumonia, and dementia. They have fewer surgeries, car accidents, and heart attacks.[94] The effects are even more profound when the attachment is secure. For instance, one recent study of men with congestive heart failure sorted their marriages into high- and low-quality brackets. The researchers concluded that marital quality was as predictive of survival as the severity of the illness, with people in poor marriages dying at much faster rates.[95]

A loving relationship can keep us alive because, not surprisingly, love makes us happier, better able to bear the struggles of life.[96] "Perhaps the single most robust fact about marriage across many surveys is that married people are happier than anyone else," writes the psychologist Martin Seligman. "This is true of every ethnic group studied, and it is true across the seventeen nations that psychologists have surveyed. Marriage is a more potent happiness factor than satisfaction with job, or finances, or community."[97] These benefits are most notable during the hardest years of life. Although scientists have long recognized that our happiness dips in middle age—that's when work and family are most stressful—those partners in happy marriages experienced the shallowest dips.[98]

The resiliency provided by love, the way a good romance can get us through the toughest time, is evident in the basic chemical rhythms of the body. In recent years, scientists have become increasingly interested in the fluctuations of cortisol, a hormone that has far-reaching effects on the body. Cortisol levels typically peak shortly after we wake up, then decrease steadily as the hours pass, reaching a low point before bedtime. While nearly everyone exhibits this basic hormonal arc, the slope of the change varies from person to person. Some people have steep slopes—they begin the day with higher initial levels of cortisol, leading to sharper declines during the day—while others have flatter slopes, characterized by lower cortisol levels in the morning and a smaller drop-off before sleep. In general, flatter slopes have been associated with serious health problems, including diabetes, depression, and heart disease.[99]

What determines the shape of our cortisol slope? According to a recent study by the psychologists Richard Slatcher, Emre Selcuk, and Anthony Ong, "perceived partner responsiveness" plays a significant role.[100] (Such responsiveness is defined as the "extent to which people believe that their partners understand, validate, and care for them.") The scientists demonstrated this by collecting relationship data from 1,078 adults at two time points, roughly a decade apart. They also collected cortisol samples, allowing them to look for correlations between the flux of hormone and the nature of these people's most intimate relationships.

Here's the punch line: more responsive partners led to steeper (and healthier) cortisol slopes. Furthermore, these changes in hormone production were correlated with a general decline in the amount of negative emotion experienced by the subjects. This study is only a first step and needs to be replicated with other populations, but it begins to define the virtuous cycle set in motion by loving relationships. When we have a more responsive partner, we get better at dealing with our most unpleasant feelings, which leads to lasting changes in the way we process cortisol and cope with stress. The result is a longer life.

The power of these romantic relationships can also be measured when they end. Consider the widower effect, which describes the elevated risk of mortality for recently widowed spouses. The term was first coined in the 1960s, but not until recently was the effect confirmed. The most convincing evidence comes from a team led by the Harvard physician Nicholas Christakis, who tracked 518,240 couples over the age of sixty-five for nine years. (He used Medicare records to monitor their health.) During that time, 252,557 husbands and 156,004 wives passed away. These deaths had dramatic medical consequences, as the surviving spouse's risk of mortality increased by 53 percent for men and 61 percent for women over the next thirty days. (Other studies estimate the "excess mortality" of widowhood to be between 30 and 90 percent in the first three months.) The causes of death were all over the place, as the loss of a spouse significantly increased the likelihood that the surviving partner would die of cancer, kidney disease, stroke, accidents, and infection. The widower effect also applied to the heart, with the surviving spouse suffering from many kinds of cardiac disease at extremely elevated rates. Their heartbreak, in other words, was literal.[101]

For Charles Darwin, marrying Emma was one of the great decisions of his life. Despite his initial skepticism, Charles embraced family life, fathering ten children in seventeen years; Down House was crowded with little ones. When Emma wasn't busy caring for the kids, she was often helping Charles with his work. She read his drafts, and when she skeptically scribbled "a great assumption" in the margin, Charles went back and rewrote the passage. (She also corrected his spelling and punctuation.) Perhaps most important, the Darwins shared a deep and abiding attachment, which helped them deal with their disagreements over God and the tragedies of their shared life. After Annie, their beloved ten-year-old daughter, died, Emma wrote a short note to Charles: "You must remember that you are my prime treasure (& always have been) my only hope of consolation is to have you safe home to weep together."[102]

As the years passed, Darwin would come to see that his rational analysis of marriage had missed the point. While the young Darwin listed time with the wife as a burden—it would leave less time for the "conversation of clever men at clubs"— he learned to relish the small rituals of their domestic life. One of these rituals was to read books to each other in the afternoon. Charles preferred stories with happy endings, which led him to read and reread the novels of Austen "till they could be read no more."[103]

Toward the end of his life, Darwin became obsessed with earthworms. The invertebrate inspired his final scientific treatise, entitled *The Formation of Vegetable Mould, through the Action of Worms, with Observations on Their Habits*. Much to her surprise, Emma found herself sharing her husband's interest. The old couple would sit in their garden together watching the worms in the dirt.[104]

In 1882, as Darwin was dying of heart failure, wracked with pain and dazed from the useless drugs prescribed by his doctors, he called out to Emma.[105] It's sometimes said that Darwin turned to God on his deathbed, that the specter of damnation led him to finally accept Emma's faith. That's not what happened. Instead, the great scientist saved his last breath for his wife. "I am not the least afraid of death," he told her. "Remember what a good wife you have been to me." Then, according to multiple biographical accounts, he looked at her and whispered, barely audibly, the simplest of truths: "My love, my precious love. Tell all my children to remember how good they have always been to me."[106]

INTERLUDE:

Divorce

All around us, we are outlasted.

—"Plumbing," JOHN UPDIKE[1]

THE Maples had talked and thought about separation so long it seemed it would never come."[2] So begins "Twin Beds in Rome," a John Updike short story about a couple on the verge of divorce. The title is literal: the story begins with Richard and Joan Maple entering a Roman hotel room only to discover that it has separate twin beds, and not a single double. For Richard, the setup is a dark omen, a reminder that the couple can't escape their disintegrating relationship.

Updike wrote the story shortly after taking his own family to Europe. The vacation was more like an exile: the Updikes left town after he got caught having an affair.[3] But Updike, as usual, couldn't resist turning his life into literature. He wrote what he knew, and what he knew above all were the travails of love and marriage in twentieth-century America.[4] So Updike describes that trip to Rome and the escape into adultery, the home improvements that improve nothing (the Maples build a tennis court in their backyard), and the tiny resentments that grow like cracks in a plaster wall. In one story, Joan and Richard are sharing a dinner out, talking about the impact of their troubled marriage on the children. Joan looks at her empty glass, then interrupts her husband: "Isn't it amazing how a full bottle of wine isn't enough for two people anymore?"

At times, Updike's honesty was too much. He would write a story only to realize it could not be published, at least not yet. (As Updike would later confess, he "drank up women's tears and spat them out / as 10-point Janson, Roman and *ital*.")[5] But mostly his candor gives his work an unsettling intimacy, as if we are eavesdropping on those moments of family life that no one else dared expose. The honesty is most haunting in "Separating," an account of the night the Maple children are told their parents' marriage is over. (According to Adam Begley's biography of the writer, Updike wrote the story "just a couple of weeks after the events it so faithfully describes. This is a true story about telling the truth—and concealing it.")[6] Although Richard and Joan decide to speak to the children one at a time, Richard can't stop crying during family dinner. His tears force Joan to share the terrible news. It does not go well. "What do you care about *us*?" one of the children asks. "We're just things you *had*."[7]

The hardest scene is the last one, when Richard talks to his oldest son about the divorce. "I hate this," Richard confesses. "*Hate* it. My father would have died before doing it to me."[8] At first, his son is reassuring—he seems to have taken the breakup in stride. But then, when Richard returns to his son's room to kiss him good-night, he realizes that the boy's cheeks are wet with tears. The last lines of dialogue are heartbreaking: "In his father's ear he moaned one word, the crucial, intelligent word: '*Why?*'" Richard has no answer.[9]

The power of the Maple stories is their unsparing ambivalence. The divorce is inevitable. The couple have been breaking up for years. But the loss of the marriage, when it is finally sealed, is still confusing and awful. In "Here Come the Maples," written eight weeks after his own divorce was finalized, Updike describes the awkward ceremony of the courtroom proceedings, how it's like a wedding in reverse. (The Updikes were granted one of the first no-fault divorces in Massachusetts.)[10] Instead of a priest and parents, there are judges and lawyers; instead of kisses and smiles, there is guilt and anger; the promise of love has given way to legal negotiations. And then there are the children: not all of them are all right.

At the time Updike was writing these stories, in the "post-pill paradise" of suburban Massachusetts,[11] the American divorce rate was undergoing a dramatic increase, more than doubling from 1960 to 1975.[12] While some of this increase can be attributed to the introduction of no-fault divorce laws—in 1969, Governor Ronald Reagan is credited with making California the first state to allow divorce based on "irreconcilable differences"—Updike's fiction also captures the cultural shifts that made marriage a more accommodating institution. These were the years of free love and cheap birth control; more women entered the workforce, and divorce lost some of its stigma of shame.

Behind these societal trends is the human fallout. While the Maple stories are themselves a kind of longitudinal study— we follow the fall of the family over time—Updike's literature also coincided with the first scientific investigations of divorce. In 1972, E. Mavis Hetherington at the University of Virginia began studying several hundred recently divorced families with young children. She tracked these subjects for several decades, making house visits, sending out surveys, and conducting lengthy interviews.

The resulting data was full of surprises. Hetherington found, for instance, that the women were more likely to have initiated divorce; a quarter of the men reported having "no idea their wife was thinking about leaving the marriage."[13] She discovered that, after the marriage was over, many men entered a "sexual smorgasbord" phase in which they sought out casual hookups and short flings.[14] After about a year, however, these affairs grew frustrating, and the men tended to seek out more serious attachments. She learned that most people rarely married the person they left the marriage for, and that the vast majority of divorced spouses—even those who said they were better off—still questioned the decision to end the marriage.[15]

The most notable results from Hetherington's longitudinal research concerned the children. According to her data, about 75 percent of kids successfully coped with the breakup of their parents.[16] "That's not to underplay that most children are distressed," Hetherington said in a 2000 interview. "Even at age twenty-four, the grown-up children of divorce still describe divorce as the most traumatic experience of their lives. But they aren't permanently damaged; they are resilient."[17]

The bad news is the remaining 25 percent of children. These kids struggled to get over the divorce: their grades dropped, they acted out, they reported serious emotional issues. And while some of these children eventually recovered, Hetherington studied many who did not. "After forty years of research,

I harbor no doubts about the ability of divorce to devastate," she wrote. "It can and does ruin lives."[18] For many kids in this cohort, the divorce of their parents created a domino effect of bad outcomes. They became far more likely to quit school, start smoking, and get divorced themselves.[19] Over time, these correlations can have severe consequences. The Terman Longitudinal Study, which has been studying more than fifteen hundred people with high IQs since the 1920s, has found that parental divorce during childhood is "the single strongest social predictor of early death" among its subjects.[20] On average, the children of divorced parents died nearly five years before those from intact families.

Similar themes emerge from other longitudinal studies. Judith Wallerstein, a psychologist who spent most of her career at UC Berkeley, followed 131 children from sixty divorced families in Marin County, California, for twenty-five years. According to her data, about a third of children fully recovered from the breakup and maintained positive relationships with both parents after divorce.[21] Another third of children seemed to be "significantly worse off than before" and showed signs of clinical depression.[22] The remaining third of kids were somewhere in between.* Most children said they

---

*What explains this variation in outcome? The science can only offer subtle correlations, mere statistical hints. According to Wallerstein, one of the main risk factors is the age of children during the divorce. Children whose parents separated when they were in early adolescence seemed to experience the most problems. "The young people [preteens and teens] told us time and again how much they needed a family structure, how much they wanted to be protected," Wallerstein wrote in her book *Second Chances*. But that's not what they got. Instead, these adolescents often felt abandoned, forced to learn about romantic love without an obvious model. This finding fits with the results of the Minnesota Longitudinal Study of Risk and Adaptation, which found that the primary attachment relationship becomes *more*

still wished their parents would get back together, even years after the divorce.

The science of divorce ends up in the same unsatisfying place as Updike's literature: there are no easy answers, just characters and correlations. We swear to have and hold each other forever, but American couples fail about 40 percent of the time. (Every wedding is basically a coin flip.) The story of modern romance is the slow acceptance of this uncertainty, an acknowledgment that even love is subject to the forces of entropy and corrosion. In *Marriage, a History*, Stephanie Coontz surveys the long evolution of marriage as an institution, from the ubiquity of domestic abuse in the medieval ages[23] to the growing recognition of same-sex marriage. In general, the arc she describes is toward liberalism, a version of wedlock that is more flexible and forgiving. While Coontz acknowledges the risks of this approach, she insists that the gains produced by these social changes outweigh the losses.

Divorce is failure, but it's also a second chance. George Vaillant, the psychiatrist who led the Grant Study for decades, initially assumed based on his interviews with the Harvard men that "divorce was a serious indicator of poor mental health."[24] It signaled an unwillingness to commit, or perhaps an inability to deal with intimacy. These marriages didn't fail because they were bad marriages. They failed because the men were bad partners.[*]

---

important during adolescence. When we are at the edge of independence, searching for our own version of intimacy, we most need the safe haven of our family. Divorce can take that away.

[*]According to the Grant Study, the single most common cause of divorce was alcoholism; 57 percent of the divorces "had occurred when at least one spouse was abusing alcohol" (Vaillant, *Triumphs of Experience* [Cambridge,

But time, like the low tide, is revealing. When the Grant subjects were in their seventies and eighties, Vaillant conducted extensive interviews with the men about their marriages. As expected, more than 90 percent of those in consistently happy first marriages were still happy.[25] The same pattern applied to those stuck in poor relationships. They were still miserable and should probably have got divorced. However, Vaillant was startled by what happened to those men who divorced and later remarried: roughly 85 percent of them said "their current marriages were happy—and had been for an average length of thirty-three years."[26] This data forced Vaillant to reconsider his beliefs about divorce. Instead of seeing marital failure as a character flaw, he came to believe that it was "often a symptom of something else," and that ending a marriage was sometimes the only way to find a new kind of happiness. (Vaillant himself has been married five times and only recently reconnected with his first four children.) "Divorce raises all kinds of personal anxieties about the safety of our relationships," Vaillant writes. "It violates our sense of family stability and ruptures religious vows. It rarely makes for happy children. Yet it can also be a breakout from outworn social codes, chronic spousal abuse, or simply a bad decision."[27]

And so we are left with a bitter trade-off: the strength of the modern marriage depends on its fragility. Because we are free to leave, it means more when we choose to stay, which is one of the reasons a good marriage can provide greater rewards

---

MA: Belknap Press, 2012],198). While it's unclear if these statistics are unique to the generation and the demographics of the Grant men, Vaillant argues that "alcoholism is still, arguably, the most ignored causal factor in modern social science," especially when it comes to the breakdown of relationships.

than ever before. No-fault divorce is ultimately an acknowledgment of human nature: we are fickle creatures, imperfect lovers, jealous and selfish and sinful. (Nobody is at fault because everyone is full of faults.) If nothing else, the sad prevalence of divorce is a reminder of just how hard love is, and how lucky we are when it endures.

This idea was one of Updike's great themes. He spent years sublimating his marriage into art, transmuting the relationship that fell apart into a form that would not. In "Plumbing," a short story about the repair of the rusted pipes underneath the Maples' house, a plumber tries to sell Richard a new water pump. The old one has worn out. The news makes Richard despair: "All around us, we are outlasted," he thinks.[28] Pipes leak; pumps break; marriages end. Nobody knows what will survive. All we can do is make the repairs and try to hold on.

4

MOMENTS OF GRACE

God is love. Whoever lives in love lives in God, and God in them.

—John 4:16

Faith sees best in the dark.

—SØREN KIERKEGAARD

T HE AMERICAN CIVIL WAR was not supposed to be a war. A battle, maybe. But not a war. The North and South were both convinced that the other side would soon surrender, that their enemy lacked the stomach for death. A senator from South Carolina swore to drink all the blood caused by secession—it would not be more than a "thimbleful," he said—while a Union general promised that the rebellion would be crushed in an afternoon at Bull Run.

They were all wrong. Between 1861 and 1865, America convulsed with killing, was overrun with dead young men.

Approximately 750,000 soldiers perished in combat and hospitals, from bullet wounds and dysentery, cannon blasts and bayonet stabs.[1] This sum is staggering, greater than the number of Americans killed in every other war combined. If a modern American war were to have the same rate of death as the Civil War—it claimed 2 percent of all Americans, and nearly 10 percent of young white men—more than 7 million lives would be lost.

As the historian Drew Gilpin Faust writes in *This Republic of Suffering*, her history of mortality and the Civil War, the scale of this slaughter reshaped America's rituals of death.[2] Many of these changes were practical: the federal government established a pension system for the widows of soldiers, while new transportation methods were invented to carry the corpses home. (One transportation company marketed a refrigerated coffin car.) There were new funeral fashions and poetic forms, new graveside songs and embalming techniques. But all these novel rituals, Gilpin Faust notes, could not obscure the central question asked by the survivors: "Where had all those young men gone?"[3]

At first glance, the answer was obvious: they'd all gone to heaven. The problem was that the conventional description of heaven was not appealing, as it consisted mainly of abstract generalities, flying angels, and Bible study. (As Emily Dickinson wrote, "I don't like Paradise— / Because it's Sunday—all the time—.") So, in the midst of the Civil War, the faithful began revising their vision of the afterlife. These revisions took place all over the country, unfolding in church sermons and biblical commentary, in private conversations and in the letters of priests and reverends. By reimagining heaven, by making it a less mysterious place full of loved ones, these religious leaders hoped to describe a paradise that provided a little more solace to those left behind.

Amid this chorus of religious voices, one voice stands out. When Elizabeth Stuart Phelps was eighteen years old, her fiancé died at the Battle of Antietam. Two years later, Phelps began working on her first novel, *The Gates Ajar*. She said she wrote it to comfort herself and all those other women "whose misery crowded the land."[4] The story takes the form of a diary written by a woman named Mary Cabot. The entries start soon after Mary learns that her brother has been killed in battle. She is wracked with pain; not even her pastor can help. But then, just as Mary starts to contemplate suicide, her widowed aunt, Winifred Forceythe, arrives for a visit. The rest of the novel is essentially a dialogue between the two women about heaven and the afterlife. Unlike the conventional vision of paradise—a place of ceaseless "harping and praying"[5]— Winifred describes heaven in domestic terms. Everything is essentially the same as life, she says—there are flowers and meals and books—except we are reunited with our lost loved ones. (Paradise was more like a family reunion than anything else.) This means that Mary's brother isn't gone—he is "only out of sight."

For a country sick with grief, Phelps's theory of heaven proved appealing.* Those soldiers hadn't been left on a battlefield, or buried in some anonymous grave—they were laughing

---

*As Gilpin Faust notes, these religious beliefs had a far more complex effect on soldiers. "The widespread existence of such beliefs made acceptance of the Civil War death tolls possible," she writes. It's possible that "confidence in immortality could encourage soldiers to risk annihilation." Drew Gilpin Faust, *This Republic of Suffering: Death and the American Civil War* (New York: Knopf, 2008), 175.

up in the sky with friends and family. The bonds of attachment endured, even if the body did not. *The Gates Ajar* went on to become the second-bestselling novel of the nineteenth century, trailing only *Uncle Tom's Cabin*.[6] Before long, its success inspired a host of imitators. According to the historian Phillip Shaw Paludan, in the decade after Phelps wrote *The Gates Ajar*, interest in life after death exploded, with nearly one hundred books about heaven appearing in print. "These books described in graphic detail what heaven looked like," Paludan writes. "And, predictably, heaven looked just like home."[7]

This portrait of heaven altered the ways in which many Americans thought about the afterlife. Gone was the dream of a heaven as a pious New Jerusalem, which Mary Cabot described as "glittering generalities, cold commonplace, vagueness, unreality, a God and a future in which I sat and shivered."[8] Instead, believers were reassured that death was just a temporary separation, a pause before we spent the rest of eternity together with those we loved the most.

Most of these nineteenth-century novels on heaven are pulp fiction, most useful as historical documents.* To read *The Gates Ajar* (not to mention its sequels, *Beyond the Gates* and *The Gates Between*) is to confront an old, weird America, in which people are preoccupied with the practical questions of whether their favorite clothes will be in heaven (yes) and if amputated limbs

---

*One of the many artists influenced by *The Gates Ajar* was Emily Dickinson. As Barton Levi St. Armand, a literature professor at Brown, notes in his book *Emily Dickinson and Her Culture*, Dickinson took great comfort in Phelps's fiction. While the poet certainly didn't embrace all of Phelps's ideas—as Dickinson reminded herself, "The only secret people keep / Is Immortality"—Armand convincingly argues that *The Gates Ajar* helped Dickinson "put into some kind of meaningful order the sentiments, symbolism, and philosophy" of her later poems.

are restored in the afterlife (probably). Yet, one shouldn't underestimate the consolations provided by these novels: they
are examples of culture tending to our collective wounds. For
post–Civil War America, these "spiritualist" narratives provided people with a deep measure of reassurance, a specific
vision of eternity that they could cling to in the face of so much
death. While the rupture of the Civil War ultimately inspired
a new kind of doubt—how could any decent God allow such
killing?—the losses also exposed a primary motive for faith.
They reveal the holy and the divine as entangled with our
dearest attachments, bound up with our need to love and be
loved.

The entanglement of love and religion is both a strange hypothesis and an old idea. It's there in the Song of Songs, the
Bible's great erotic poem, and forms the essential theme of
Dante's *Divine Comedy*, in which every human love points to the
love of God. For Dante, falling for another person is the best
way to grasp the sort of spiritual fulfillment that is also at the
center of belief. The same nerves come alive; the skin goes
electric; we know what it's like to feel a connection that cannot
be explained, only experienced.

The ultimate source of that experience will always be
shrouded in mystery. Nobody knows if God exists. Nobody
knows if heaven is real. Nobody knows which parts of the Bible
are true, or which bible. I have my own beliefs, and so do you.
But even if God remains unknowable, He is still a source of
profound comfort to many people. When they talk about their
faith, what they often end up talking about is how they love
God and how He loves them back.

Like every other love, this one can change lives.

Abnormal Psychical Visitations

In *The Varieties of Religious Experience*, William James, the philosopher and psychologist, sought to make sense of religion in America after the tumult of the Civil War. His book reflects the evangelical ferment of the time: it's filled with tales of sudden conversions and mystical revelations. People commune with the dead and channel the voice of their savior. Yet, James takes all of these stories seriously. He assumed that religious experience was simply part of human experience: "God is real," James wrote, "since he produces real effects."[9]

James wasn't endorsing miracles. Rather, he simply wanted to understand the natural motives at the center of supernatural belief. Consider the conversion tale of Charles Finney, a leader in the Second Great Awakening and the president of Oberlin College. In *Varieties*, James returns several times to Finney's writing, showing how his faith is rooted in mystical feelings of connectedness. "The Holy Spirit descended upon me in a manner that seemed to go through me, body and soul," Finney wrote. "Indeed, it seemed to come in waves and waves of liquid love. . . . No words can express the wonderful love that was shed abroad in my heart. I wept aloud with joy and love."[10] According to James, this same sense of love is a recurring theme in accounts of religious experience. In many respects, it is *the* theme, the only feeling that unites the varieties of belief. It is the cause of evangelical revivals and the inspiration for medieval nuns; it's why saints are willing to sacrifice their bodies and worried believers turn to prayer.*

---

*Perhaps the most famous conversion narrative occurs in the *Confessions*, as St. Augustine wrestles with what these intense feelings of religion actually

For James, these conversion narratives revealed the origins of faith. People did not reason their way to God. Rather, He came into their life because of a powerful and inchoate feeling. (What Keats said of philosophy is even more true of religious belief: it is "proved upon our pulses.") To have a spiritual experience, James wrote, is to be overwhelmed by a "shifting of the emotional centre towards loving and harmonious affections," a sense of "immense elation" that echoes the joy of a great romance.[11] In one of the most famous passages of *Varieties*, James insists that these uncanny emotions are "the deeper source of religion, and that philosophic and theological formulas are secondary products, like translations of a text into another tongue."[12]

James was prescient. In recent years, scientists have begun to confirm the wisdom of his psychology, showing how religious experience is often rooted in feelings of inexplicable attachment. God might be an abstract presence, but the faithful feel Him in the most intimate terms. ("The Lord loves each of us like an only child," wrote St. Augustine.) Lee Kirkpatrick, a psychologist at the College of William and Mary, has documented the parallels between the way we attach ourselves to people and the way we attach ourselves to God.[13] As Kirkpat-

---

mean. "When I love you [God]," he asks, "what do I love?" Augustine begins with a long list of what he is *not* loving: "It is not physical beauty nor temporal glory nor the brightness of light dear to earthly eyes." But then, just as the reader begins to worry that Augustine's love is entirely numinous, he recounts the particulars of his religious experience: "Yet there is a light I love . . . and a kind of embrace when I love my God—a light, voice, odour, food, embrace of my inner man, where my soul is floodlit by light which space cannot contain, where is sound that time cannot seize . . . and where there is a bond of union that no satiety can part. That is what I love when I love my God." St. Augustine, *Confessions*, trans. Henry Chadwick (Oxford: Oxford University Press, 2009), 183.

rick points out, our connections to the divine typically fulfill the five basic requirements of attachment theory. The first requirement is proximity seeking: people want to feel close to their God, which is why they pray and sing hymns and engage in religious rituals. The second requirement is that the attachment figure provides a sense of protection; the God of the Bible is often described as an exalted parent figure, keeping us safe from the vagaries of existence. Third, believers rely on God as a secure base, providing them with a sense of confidence and security for exploring the world. (As Kirkpatrick notes, scripture is full of references to God serving as a "shield," "rock," and "fortress.")[14] The fourth and fifth features of attachment relationships involve the specter of separation and loss, which provoke anxiety and grief. Kirkpatrick cites the accounts of many people who stopped believing in God— stories of "deconversion"—as evidence that the disappearance of faith can often be extremely painful and unsettling. Gordon Kaufman, a theologian at the Harvard Divinity School, put it this way: "The idea of God is the idea of an absolutely adequate attachment figure."[15]

Absolutely adequate. Kaufman was pointing out that part of God's appeal is the way He is always present, a parental figure who is "available to [His] children when they are in need."[16] This idea is not some casual metaphor. In daily life, believers turn to God in times of stress and strain, just as young children turn to their parents. It's almost like a reflex. In a study by the psychologists Andreas Birgegard and Pehr Granqvist, a group of religious Swedes were subliminally exposed to a computer screen flashing the attachment-related threat "Mother is gone."[17] The sentence was flashed on the screen too quickly for the students to consciously process; they knew they'd seen something, they just didn't know what. (A control group of believers was shown a neutral statement: "People are walking.") Then, the students were asked to complete a questionnaire that assessed their desire to get close to God and the extent to which they used God as an attachment figure. Did they turn to God for solace? Did they want to share their feelings with God? Those believers exposed to an attachment threat were significantly more interested in seeking out God than those in the control condition. Another study led by Granqvist showed that when children were told stories about a fictional child in need of comfort—because his dog died or she was sick in the hospital or he fell off a bike—they placed a God symbol closer to the picture of the child, at least when compared to neutral stories. (All of the stories were told using a felt board.) The effect was particularly strong when the children had a secure attachment representation, suggesting that our early views of God are shaped, in part, by the system that creates our closest human relationships.[18]

The same pattern appeared in a test of 110 religious Israeli Jewish students.[19] Each subject was subliminally shown one of three different words, or primes. (As before, these words appeared for only twenty milliseconds, which is too fast for conscious awareness.) The first word was neutral—the Hebrew word for "hat." The second was a "mild distress" condition, in which the students glimpsed the word *failure*. The last was the "severe distress" prime, and they were flashed *death*. Then, the subjects were asked to identify as quickly as possible whether a subsequent string of letters appearing on the screen was an actual word. Some of the words were random nouns—*notebook*, *window*, etc.—while others were directly related to God and religious belief, such as *prayer* and *salvation*. As expected, people exposed to distress primes reacted much more quickly to words involving thoughts of God, especially when they had a secure attachment orientation. This is evidence, write the scientists, that for believers God is "viewed implicitly as a safe haven," and that whenever we are worried we seek out His comfort. The mere feeling of distress can put us in a more religious state of mind.

This research clarifies part of God's appeal. Because He is everywhere, believing in Him means that we are never alone. And since loneliness feels awful, God can become a powerful source of solace. One recent study, led by Nicholas Epley at the University of Chicago, demonstrated that even fleeting feelings of loneliness make more people more likely to believe in "non-human agents," such as omnipotent Gods, sensitive pets, and sophisticated gadgets.[20] In John Milton's *Paradise Lost*, God creates Eve because Adam is in need of "collateral love." In his sly way, Milton suggests that Adam might believe in God to satisfy that same emotional desire.

The profound comfort of faith, especially in times of great difficulty, helps explain the changes in religious life during the Civil War. The war wrecked America; vast stretches of land stank of death; it was hard to find a family untouched by the slaughter. Given all the heartbreak, it shouldn't be too surprising that a grieving country might invent a new kind of afterlife, or that a region such as the American South—an area that had lost nearly 15 percent of men between the ages of 10 and 44—might experience a surge of interest in forms of Christianity that emphasized the personal experience of a loving God.[21] These people had lost so much, but He was still there, providing a collateral love.

It's easy to denigrate such belief, since it cures such an obvious ailment. Besides, if God is so unknowable, then how do we know that He loves us, or that heaven is just like home?

(St. Augustine wrote, "If you think you understand God, it is not God."[22]) Yet the ability to take comfort in a divinity remains a remarkable mental ability, a defining feature of human nature. These Gods don't talk back to us; they don't kiss us in the morning or argue with us at night. But many of us are still bound to them; they give our lives structure and support, consoling us in dark times. While our feelings for such abstractions are unquestionably distinct from our feelings for family and friends, they share a taproot. They emerge from the same nerves and serve the same needs. As William James insisted, whether these Gods are real is beside the point. They feel real, and that is reality enough.

The Compensation Hypothesis

Godfrey Minot Camille was born in 1919 in a wealthy Boston suburb. An only child, Camille was sent to the finest private schools and had a household staff tending to his whims and needs. But these advantages concealed a terrible curse: Camille never knew love. His mother was suspicious and cold. She forbade Camille from playing with the neighborhood kids. His father spent most of his life fretting about his place in Boston high society. (They were the type of people, Camille would later say, who kept a Steinway grand piano in the living room but never learned to play.) If it weren't for the maids who ate dinner with him, he would always have been alone at home.

The lack of love left scars. As a college junior, Camille was diagnosed by a psychiatrist as having an unstable personality. He complained of constant illness, but the medical evaluators disregarded his worries as nothing but intractable hypochondria, concluding that "this boy is turning into a regular psychoneurotic." Later that year, a social investigator advised him, "When you come to the end of your rope, tie a knot and hold on." Camille's response was ripe with despair and self-pity: "But the knot was tied so long ago, and I have been hanging on for such a long time."[23]

Then things got worse. Camille began having aggressive fantasies about other people, which led him to self-diagnose as a schizophrenic. He muddled his way through medical school, fought in World War II but stayed a private, and returned home only to break off his engagement. Shortly after he graduated from medical school, Camille attempted suicide. He was deemed "not fitted for the practice of medicine."[24] The next year, he contracted pulmonary tuberculosis and spent fourteen months in the hospital.[25]

But life is strange, full of unexpected twists. Only at his lowest moment—crippled by the sort of illness he'd always feared—did Camille experience the beginnings of a rebirth. It began with what he would later call a "spiritual awakening," complete with a vision of a loving Christ appearing in his hospital room.[26] In a letter written decades later, Camille described the moment: "In the stillness of twilight, there was suddenly a blinding light in the corner of the room, an indoor supernova. Instinctively, I climbed out of bed and onto my knees, sensing I was in the presence of the Holy, like some Old Testament character. I heard no voice, yet the injunction was plain: Follow Me. Limp and in tears, I slowly climbed back into bed." Camille explained the impact of this vision on his emotional life: "Someone with a capital 'S' cared about me," he wrote. "It made me feel that I was nutty for awhile, but in the Catholic Church it's known as Grace."[27]

The effects of the religious vision were immediate. Camille soon left the hospital—the medicine finally worked—and he slowly recovered from his lingering depression. He became a successful psychiatrist, specializing in the treatment of children with severe health issues. While Camille still had his ailments, he never stopped thinking of that spiritual awakening as the turning point of his story. "I had problems and went to others," Camille said. "And now I enjoy people coming to me."[28]

Godfrey Minot Camille was a subject in the Grant Study, the longitudinal project that has been tracking 268 Harvard undergraduates since 1938. Although Camille died more than a decade ago from a heart attack while hiking in the Alps, George Vaillant, the longtime director of the study, continues to mine Camille's life for wisdom. In particular, Vaillant remains interested in the effects of that religious apparition, how the sudden appearance of Jesus gave Camille his first glimmers of love. (The conversion experience was straight out of William James.) While Vaillant remains skeptical of the vision—"I myself (at forty) was more inclined to think that it was all the loving nursing care [that triggered Camille's recovery in the hospital]," he writes[29]—Vaillant also knows that such questions are largely irrelevant. "It took me many more years of prospective follow-up, and many more years of emotional growth, to learn to take love seriously," Vaillant writes. "What it looks like—God, a nurse, a child, a good Samaritan, or any of its other guises—is different for everybody. But love is love."[30]

Vaillant's larger point is that, even if one doubts the reality of Grace, there can be no doubting the power of its revelation. Sometimes that revelation can be a destructive force; history is pockmarked with holy wars. Nevertheless, as the Harvard case studies demonstrate, the feeling of connectedness inspired by faith can also become a powerful life motive. That moment in the hospital room not only helped Camille recover his health, but also helped him become a dedicated husband and father, focused on the most important relationships in his life. When Camille was seventy-two, he sent Vaillant a letter: "Before there were dysfunctional families, I came from one. Others may list accomplishments in the wider world, but it's the internal journey I savor and celebrate. My professional life hasn't been disappointing . . . but the truly gratifying unfolding has been into the person I've slowly become: comfortable, joyful, connected and effective." While Camille was no longer so sure about what had happened to him in the hospital, he still believed that his spiritual awakening had saved him, allowing him to get over the sadness of his childhood and become a more loving husband and father.[31] Vaillant wrote about what it was like to spend time with one of Camille's daughters: "I have interviewed many Grant Study children, but this woman's love for her father remains the most stunning that I have encountered among them."[32]

It all began with a fleeting sense of grace. For Camille, the hospital vision was an education in love, a way of experiencing those feelings of attachment the young man had never felt before.* Scientists refer to this as the "compensation hypothesis" of belief, as people use God to make up for

---

*Vaillant tells a story to illustrate the intertwined nature of human and holy love: "There was this charismatic Argentinean psychiatrist who once asked people to draw a picture of God. Of course, people say, 'I can't do that, I don't know what God looks like.' But eventually, because she kept insisting, they start to draw a picture. Then, when they're done drawing God, she asked them to draw their families. And what you discover is that the pictures overlap. The drawings look pretty much the same."

attachment traumas and failures elsewhere in their lives. Sometimes, death begins the process, which may be why many people become more religious after losing a loved one.[33] But mainly it seems to result from a chronic absence of attachment in early life. According to a recent meta-analysis by Pehr Granqvist and Lee Kirkpatrick of eleven different studies, an insecure-attachment history during childhood nearly doubles the probability of experiencing a sudden religious conversion as an adult.[*] Like Camille, these people come to know God as a "compensatory attachment relationship," which helps them "regulate distress and obtain felt security."[34] The result, say the scientists, is a "renewed confidence in the world, including increased self-esteem, an intense experience of elation, and a significant decrease in feelings of distress."[35]

This logic plays out in religious practice: every faith is built around rituals and ceremonies that help believers feel closer to their divine attachment figure. The Stanford anthropologist T. M. Luhrmann spent several years immersing herself in services at churches of the Vineyard Movement, a "charismatic" denomination in which members, writes Luhrmann, seek out "concrete experiences of God's realness." The fundamental assumption of Vineyard believers, Luhrmann writes, is that God wants to be our friend, and that if we develop a relationship with God through prayer, then "God will answer back,

---

[*] "Tongue-speakers" are people, typically in the Pentecostal tradition in America, who begin speaking in nonsense syllables, which they believe to be a sacred language from God. One study found that more than 85 percent of tongue-speakers "experienced a clearly defined anxiety crisis preceding their speaking in tongues," but that their newfound ability led them to feel more confident and secure. Lee A. Kirkpatrick, *Attachment, Evolution, and the Psychology of Religion* (New York: Guilford Press, 2005), 62.

through thoughts and mental images he places in your mind, and through sensations he causes in your body."[36] The challenge is not getting God to talk, for he is always talking. The hard part is learning how to listen, which Luhrmann compares to the training of a sonogram technician, who must figure out how to make sense of that "wavy green blur on the screen."[37]

In a 2013 experiment, Luhrmann and colleagues showed how this process unfolds.[38] She began by randomly dividing Christian students at Stanford into two groups. The first group were told to listen to lectures by the theologian Luke Timothy Johnson on the Gospels for thirty minutes six days a week. (The recordings were loaded onto iPods.) The second group were given recordings that encouraged the subjects to "feel God directly." Here, for instance, is what they heard in a meditation on the twenty-third psalm: "The Lord is my shepherd. . . . See the shepherd before you . . . see his face . . . the light that streams from him. . . . notice his gait. . . . see the hill over which he leads you . . . feel the breeze over the grass . . . smell its sweetness . . . listen to the birds as they sing. . . . notice what you feel as you follow this shepherd." These instructions were interspersed with long pauses, as the listener was encouraged to "carry on a personal dialogue" with Jesus.

The results were striking. After four weeks, Luhrmann found that those encouraged to feel God directly had developed a closer relationship with God. (Religious experience, she argues, is like anything else: practice makes perfect.) What's more, this newfound spirituality had tangible benefits: those students asked to imagine God reported significantly lower levels of stress, loneliness, and psychiatric symptoms, at least when compared to those exposed to theology lectures. Similar results emerged from research conducted by Lynn Underwood, as the more people affirmed the statement "I feel God's love for me, directly," the better their mental health. These effects are heightened in people undergoing difficult life circumstances. According to Underwood's data, frequent spiritual experiences were correlated with reduced feelings of depression among survivors of domestic violence, heart attack victims, and patients with chronic disease.[39] For these believers, God was not an explanation of the universe. He was a much needed attachment figure, a constant source of comfort and affection. Other work, by Lee Kirkpatrick and Phillip Shaver, showed a strong correlation between secure attachments to God and various measures of physical and mental health. In general, secure attachments were associated with lower levels of loneliness, depression, and psychosomatic symptoms and with higher levels of life satisfaction.[40] As Kirkpatrick notes, these results parallel the benefits of having a secure attachment in a human love relationship.[41]

These studies reveal the practical benefits of faith. But I think there is also a danger here, a risk that that science can be misinterpreted as explaining God away. It is all too easy to look at the data and conclude that He is merely a side effect of our wiring, an imaginary friend that some people never learn to live without. When we describe the utility of faith—how it staves off depression and soothes our nerves—it's possible to conclude that belief is *nothing but* these uses, that God is just another form of self-help.

This tension is not new. William James wrestled with that worry while writing *The Varieties of Religious Experience*. By the time he began working on the book, James was a lapsed believer: "I have no living sense of commerce with a God," he wrote in a letter. "I envy those who have." Nevertheless, James insisted that science needed to take religious experience seriously, and that it could not dismiss such a universal element of culture. (Too often, James said, scientists slipped into "medical materialism," which "finishes up Saint Paul by calling his vision on the road to Damascus a discharging lesion of the occipital cortex.") For James, human spirituality was a window into human nature, a glimpse into how we coped with our flaws and limits and loneliness. In a chapter in *Varieties* on the "sick soul," James tells the story of a "French correspondent" suffering from a "bad nervous condition." The young man describes himself as a "mass of quivering fear," besieged with a "sense of the insecurity of life that I never knew before."

But the man did not kill himself or sink into a deep depression. In the midst of the existential crisis, just when his "morbid feelings" couldn't get any worse, he explains how he found religion and was saved: "The fear was so invasive and powerful that if I had not clung to scripture-texts like 'The eternal God is my refuge,' etc. . . . I think I should have gone really insane."

In 1904, two years after *Varieties* was published, James's French translator wrote to request the original text of the letter from the student. James replied that he could not provide it, for he had made it up. The case was his own. Those were his feelings; he was the one held together by scripture. Even though James would continue to struggle with melancholia for the rest of his life, and even as his own faith ebbed away, he never forgot the lessons of that awful time. God matters because He changes lives. That sentence is true even if God does not exist.

A Higher Power

In the winter of 1934, a bankrupt Wall Street stockbroker named William Griffith Wilson was trying to avoid the delirium tremens as he drifted in and out of consciousness at a fancy Manhattan rehab center. Wilson was undergoing the so-called Belladonna cure, a detox program devised by Dr. Alexander Lambert, a professor of medicine at Cornell and the personal physician to Teddy Roosevelt. Lambert's cure was actually a poison, as it required regular injections of *Atropa belladonna*, or deadly nightshade, along with other "fluid extracts." While belladonna is fatal in large doses, even small amounts can trigger intense hallucinations.[42]

The toxin was coursing through Wilson's veins as he tried to survive his first days without alcohol. (Wilson had tried quitting drink many times before, but he'd always relapse, often falling into benders of juice and gin that nearly killed him.) Wilson knew withdrawal was brutal—a chemical cascade of tremors, fevers, nightmares, and seizures—but this time seemed particularly rough. Maybe it was the belladonna, or the sedatives that went along with it, but Wilson wasn't sure how much more he could take. If his brain didn't settle down soon, he'd need a shot just to stay alive.

On the second or third night of detox—the time of peak tremens—Wilson's "depression deepened unbearably"; he felt as though he were "at the bottom of the pit." But then, just as he slipped into utter despair, right before he was ready to relapse, he called out to the dark, "If there is a God, let Him show Himself! I am ready to do anything, anything!" Wilson described what happened next:

> Suddenly the room lit up with a great white light. I was caught up into an ecstasy which there are no words to describe. It seemed to me, in the mind's eye, that I was on a mountain and that a wind not of air but of spirit

was blowing. And then it burst upon me that I was a free man. Slowly the ecstasy subsided. I lay on the bed, but now for a time I was in another world, a new world of consciousness. All about me and through me there was a wonderful feeling of Presence, and I thought to myself, "So this is the God of the preachers!" A great peace stole over me and I thought, "No matter how wrong things seem to be, they are all right. Things are all right with God and His world."[43]

It's important to note that Wilson was not a devout person. At best, he saw himself as a polite agnostic, willing to entertain the possibility of a greater power but utterly contemptuous of organized religion. ("When they talked of a God personal to me . . . I became irritated and my mind snapped shut against such a theory," he said.)[44] Yet here he was, communing with God in a tiny hospital room.[45]

Wilson assumed he was going insane. He called out for his doctor and told him about the religious vision, if only because he worried it was a sign of brain damage caused by his drinking. His doctor was reassuring, telling Wilson that he had nothing to worry about; withdrawal did strange things to the head. However, as the doctor walked out of the room, he gave Wilson one last piece of advice: "Whatever it is you've got now, hang on to it. Hang on to it, boy."[46]

Wilson hung on. The next day, he began reading a book left behind by a friend.[47] Wilson's head was still a mess, and the text was full of strange words. But he read enough to get the point. This book was about how religious conversions were "almost like gifts from the blue." The book was by William James and it was called *The Varieties of Religious Experience*.

Reading James was one of the most important moments of
Wilson's life. Not only did these conversion tales convince him
that he wasn't crazy—even sober people sometimes had visions
of God—but they revealed a deeper pattern, which helped
him understand why the vision was so necessary. He began by
noting that nearly every story of religious awakening shared
"common denominators of pain, suffering, calamity." Like
Wilson, these people discovered God at their lowest moment.
"Complete hopelessness and deflation at depth were almost
always required to make the recipient ready," Wilson later
wrote. "The significance of all this burst upon me. Deflation
at depth—yes, that was it. Exactly that had happened to me.[48]

"Deflation at depth"—a fancy way of saying rock bottom.
It was excruciating, but Wilson was convinced there was no
shortcut. For an alcoholic, he said, it was necessary to feel
unlovable before one could experience the salvation of God's
love.[49] Of course, salvation is no cure—it's only the start of a
never-ending fight. Even after that initial encounter with God
in the hospital, Wilson continued to struggle with sobriety. The
struggle came to a climax on a business trip to Akron, a few
months after his belladonna treatment. Wilson was standing
in the hotel lobby when he began to panic. He heard the buzz
of voices from the bar and felt his dry mouth; he thought of
his loyal wife, who deserved better; he remembered his father,
who had left the family when Wilson was a little boy. These
sad thoughts became a recursive loop, a recording on repeat
that could only be stopped with a glug of whiskey. (At such
moments, alcohol can seem like the only cure for alcoholism.)
Wilson looked around the hotel. God wasn't here. So he did the
next best thing: he called a minister, who put him in touch with
a young woman named Henrietta Seiberling.

Seiberling understood the ravages of alcoholism. For the last few years, she had been trying to sober up Dr. Bob Smith, the husband of a close friend. Her efforts had failed—Smith was drinking more than ever—but now this stranger named Bill was on the telephone, asking to talk with other alcoholics. She called the Smiths and arranged a meeting for the following afternoon.

Wilson saw Smith and he knew: the doctor had it bad. Wilson saw the trembling hands, the sweaty upper lip, the pallid hungover complexion. Here was a man ruined by drink. Wilson took Smith to a side room and began telling the doctor his story. He told Smith about his childhood—Wilson was born, fittingly enough, in a small room behind a bar in East Dorset, Vermont—and what it felt like to lose all his money in the stock market crash of 1929. He talked about his failed attempts to quit drinking and how, in desperation, he turned to the Belladonna fix. He described his encounter with God. But then came the punch line, as Wilson made it clear that he wasn't here to save the doctor. He was here to save himself: "I called Henrietta because I needed another alcoholic. I needed you, Bob, probably a lot more than you'll ever need me. So, thanks a lot for hearing me out. I know now that I'm not going to take a drink, and I'm grateful to you."[50]

Alcoholics Anonymous was born from this desperate conversation. What Wilson realized in Akron was that faith is not enough, for it was only by helping others that he might help himself; sharing his weakness was his last source of strength. The following month, Wilson and Smith began spreading their gospel, tending to others in hospital wards and churches, street corners and hotel lobbies. A few years later, Wilson wrote up the twelve steps, which distilled his life story into a narrative of recovery. (The choice of twelve was not accidental—Wilson liked the echo of Jesus and his dozen apostles.) While the first step is the admission of powerlessness, six of the remaining steps were entangled with a higher power, or what Wilson referred to as "God, *as we understand Him*." The point of these steps was to hold on until the last one, in which the message of "spiritual awakening" was used to save other alcoholics. From drunkenness to clarity, despair to connection. This was the struggle of sobriety, Wilson said. It was also the struggle of life.

Since Bill Wilson first cobbled together his twelve steps, borrowing liberally from William James and the New Testament, his instructions have become the most popular form of addiction treatment in the world. Currently more than 2 million people attend one of Alcoholic Anonymous's 115,000 meeting groups in more than 170 different countries. These local meetings are self-run; the organization itself seems to consist of little more than a mission statement. It has no leaders or spokespeople, no fees or dues, few rules, and even less hierarchy. Despite this inchoate structure, the steps of AA have saved untold lives. While the program isn't effective for everyone, Bill Wilson's twelve steps can be a lifesaving treatment for alcoholics.[51]

Nevertheless, it's important to make clear that our knowledge of AA is bracketed by unknowns and uncertainties.[52] In part, this limit is because the strictly enforced anonymity of AA makes long-term scientific study extremely difficult. Membership is also famously fluid, as AA adherents are free to attend meetings "as needed." As a result, it's hard to find reliable estimates of recovery rates, or to figure out which aspects of

AA are most essential for recovery. It's also a reminder that far more research is needed, and that we should continue to experiment with a wide variety of rehab approaches, as the twelve steps certainly don't work for everyone.[*][53]

Despite these limitations, scientists have recently begun to measure, as best they can, the benefits of AA. One of the most widely cited studies tracked 628 members of AA for sixteen years. The researchers concluded that involvement with AA was significantly correlated with long-term abstinence.[54] While only 34 percent of drinkers not involved with AA in their first year of abstinence were able to quit drinking for good, 67 percent of individuals who participated in AA for six months or more stayed sober. This result is not an anomaly: another meta-analysis of seventy-four studies looking at AA found a correlation between attendance at meetings and sobriety.[55]

Why does AA work? What is it about Bill Wilson's twelve steps that makes them so effective, at least when compared to many alternative treatments? George Vaillant, the director of the Harvard Grant Study, has been a Class A (nonalcoholic) trustee of AA since 1998. His interest in alcoholism began with the Grant subjects, as he noticed that many of their closest relationships had been ravaged by problem drinking.[56] But the problem often came with a solution, with nearly half of the

---

[*]As critics have pointed out, the most glaring limitation of AA remains its antiquated approach to female members. Wilson's writing caters almost exclusively to men and only addresses women in his chapter "To Wives," which preaches patience for their addled husbands. What's more, the psychologist Charlotte Kasl speculates that the larger goal of AA's twelve steps—they are designed to reduce the "selfishness" and "narcissism" of alcoholics—might backfire for the female drinker, who already "self-blame for just about everything that goes wrong." Charlotte Davis Kasl, *Many Roads, One Journey: Moving beyond the Twelve Steps* (New York: HarperPerennial, 1992), 10.

subjects achieving abstinence with the help of AA or a similar twelve-step program. The men who were "stably abstinent" attended, on average, about twenty times as many AA meetings as those who continued to relapse.[57] Among Grant subjects who attended at least thirty AA meetings, more than 80 percent achieved sustained abstinence.[58] "Until you spend time there [at a meeting], it's convenient to think that AA is just a cult," Vaillant says. "But if it works, it works. I like things that work."

Vaillant believes that a significant part of AA's effectiveness depends on its spirituality. "In the treatment of addiction, Karl Marx's aphorism 'religion is the opiate of the masses' masks an enormously important therapeutic principle," Vaillant writes in *The Natural History of Alcoholism*, his survey of alcoholism among the Grant subjects and others.[59] "Religion may actually provide a relief that drug abuse only promises." This speculation is supported by a recent study led by J. Scott Tonigan, a professor of psychology at the University of New Mexico. After following 130 newly abstinent members of Alcoholics Anonymous for nine months, Tonigan and colleagues concluded that changes in spirituality predicted changes in drinking habits, as those who professed more belief in God were less likely to relapse.[60] Wilson himself would later attempt to explain why his religious conversion came with lasting benefits: "What I really meant was this. I was catapulted into a spiritual experience, which gave me the capability of feeling the presence of God, His love, and His omnipotence. And most of all, His personal availability to me."[61] Even at his worst moments Wilson never lost the love of God.[62]

But Vaillant also notes that religious belief is not enough. While faith in God might lift our spirits, most alcoholics need more than faith to stay sober.[63] Bill Wilson, after all, wasn't saved by the hospital vision; that was merely the first step. Rather, Wilson only found lasting sobriety after he confessed to Dr. Bob, forming a loving friendship with his fellow alcoholic.

These new relationships are an essential part of the recovery program. A recent study of 1,726 people enrolled in AA found that alcoholics who were determined to help others— typically by serving as a sponsor—were nearly twice as likely to stay sober.[64] "When you quit drinking, there's a sudden void in your life," Vaillant says. "These relationships help fill the void. They are, like every attachment relationship, about caring for someone else and having them care for you." AA tries to replace a chemical dependence with a human one.

David Foster Wallace once observed that the great challenge of writing about AA and other twelve-step programs was the inescapable clichés. (Wallace spent time in rehab for alcohol and drug abuse in his late twenties.) He's right: the writing of Wilson and his followers is full of childish theology and Hallmark aphorisms; if you're not ready to feel that higher power, the lines will probably feel like bullshit. ("An ironist in an . . . AA meeting is a witch in a church," Wallace wrote in *Infinite Jest*.)[65] But Wallace also realized that the banal language of recovery was beside the point. These are not ideas meant to be experienced alone. They are not designed for solitary criticism or Talmudic unpacking or close scrutiny. The steps are as simple and artless as they sound. But sometimes the words matter less than what is behind them. Wallace liked to quote a line he first heard in recovery, from a grizzled addict who'd been going to meetings for years: "It's not about whether or not you believe, asshole, it's about getting down and asking."[66]

The Tapping

The philosopher Simone Weil tells a story about two prisoners in solitary confinement, locked in adjoining cells. The men are separated by a wall. As the years pass, they learn to communicate with each other, tapping out words on the stone. "The wall is the thing which separates them but it is also their means of communication," Weil writes. "It is the same with us and God. Every separation is a link."[67]

I first encountered this parable in the writing of Christian Wiman.[68] A poet turned essayist, Wiman describes himself as deeply sympathetic to Weil's metaphor. He is drawn, he says, to its limited sense of salvation—there is hope here, but it's a "bare and lonely hope." (The taps of language let us talk, but we are still tapping against a wall.) The same bittersweet theme suffuses all of Wiman's work. Again and again, his writing returns to the image of a "bright abyss," a bottomless pit giving off a great light. Such is life. What a pit. What a light.

Wiman was born in Snyder, Texas, a "flat little sandblasted town" on the Western prairie. Raised a strict Southern Baptist, he grew up taking faith for granted; he didn't know anyone who didn't believe. Not until Wiman was a freshman at an East Coast college did he meet his first atheist, a "dauntingly hip" undergrad who announced his disbelief as if he were ordering a slice of pizza. Wiman assumed the young man would soon be struck down. When the lightning bolt failed to arrive, and when college filled his head with theories of science and skepticism, Wiman's own faith began to ebb. He fell hard for the modernists, began worshipping *The Waste Land*, and decided to become a poet himself. After twenty years of making poetry the center of his life, Wiman stopped writing verse. "Whatever connection I had long experienced between word and world . . . went dead," Wiman writes. "It felt like I was watching a movie of my life rather than living it, an old silent movie, no color, no sound, no one in the audience but me."[69]

Time passed. Although Wiman was no longer writing, he became the editor of *Poetry*, the most influential poetry magazine in the world. He was exhausted, unhappy, successful. But then, Wiman says, something astonishing happened: he fell in love. "I remember tiny Albert's Café on Elm Street in Chicago where we first met," Wiman writes about a date with his wife, Danielle. "A pastry case like a Pollock in the corner of my eye, sunlight suddenly more itself on an empty plate, a piece of silver." Wiman had never felt so alive, so "fully possessed by being itself." Instead of thinking about Weil's prisoners tapping on the wall, he thought of another Weil line: "Joy is the overflowing consciousness of reality." For the first time in his life, Wiman was overflowing.[70]

So Wiman got married. About eight months after the wedding,[71] on the afternoon of his thirty-ninth birthday, in a doctor's office, Wiman was given a devastating diagnosis. He had Waldenström's macroglobulinemia, an incurable cancer of the blood. The disease soon took over his life with bulging tumors, fat needles filled with chemo, and desperate bone marrow transplants. No doctor would say how many birthdays he had left.

How does one deal with such a blow? Poetry proved useless; the pain was too literal. Wiman wrote that being in love made his diagnosis that much harder: "If I had gotten the diagnosis some years earlier . . . I'm not sure I would have reacted very strongly. It would have seemed a fatalistic confirmation of everything I had always thought about existence, and my response, I think, would have been equally fatalistic."[72] But now his losses were palpable. He was mourning for himself, but also for his wife, for their unlived life, for all the happiness they would never know.

The joy and the grief, the love and the fear of its loss . . . these are the feelings that led Wiman back to God. One Sunday morning not long after his diagnosis, Wiman and his wife cast aside the newspaper and wandered into a church. It was a small sanctuary, filled with old German immigrants and young couples.[73] Wiman doesn't remember much about the service or the sermon, but he does recall the details of the walk home: the birdsong, the rumbling L train, the white blooms on the catalpa, "an iron sky and the lake so calm it seemed thickened."

It's a telling scene: Wiman reconnects with his faith, but not because of the church. *Because of the world*. Because of the city and the water and the metro. Because of the woman walking with him. Because of how she made him feel. In his essays and interviews, Wiman sources his belief not to cancer, but to falling in love, which had added to "the stock of his available reality." His spirit swelled; a veil had been lifted; he felt the sort of emotions that required, at least for him, the hypothesis of religion. "We tend to think of love as closing out the world and we can only see the face of the beloved," he said in a 2012 interview with Krista Tippett. "Everything else goes quiet or goes numb, but actually what I experienced was that—and I've experienced it again with my children—is that the love demanded to be something else. It demanded to be expressed beyond the expression of the participants. You know, it kept demanding more. That excess energy, I think, is God, and I think it's God in us trying to return to its source."[74]

Excess energy. That's the poet's way of giving a name to the mystery. For Wiman, love arrived with an inexplicable force, cracking open his existence and reacquainting him with the mystical spirit at the center of life. And it was then, in that "wonderful, terrible time when reason, if only for a moment, lost its claim," Wiman felt the pull of Christ. In an essay on his faith, Wiman quotes Elizabeth Bowen, the Irish novelist: "To turn from everything to one face is to find oneself face to face with everything."[75]

Everything includes death, which was now coming at Wiman from inside his own body, from inside his blood. Faith helped him cope, a "beacon and bulwark" against the pain.[76] It's not that Wiman was reassured by some particular vision of heaven. He admits that he has no idea what comes after, whether it's a soundless dark or a glittering light. And Wiman—whose cancer is currently in remission—acknowledges that the timing of his return to the fold is suspicious: "That conversions often happen after or during intense life experiences, especially traumatic experiences, is sometimes used as evidence against them. The sufferer isn't in his right mind. The mind, tottering at the abyss of despair or death, shudders back toward any simplicity, any coherency it can grasp, and the man calls out to God."[77]

But Wiman doesn't worry about the skeptics. He believes that faith, like love, is ultimately a private experience, knowable only from the inside. And his experience has been a blessing. "I was brought up with the poisonous notion that you had to renounce love of the earth in order to receive the love of God," Wiman writes. "My experience has been just the opposite." Religion has expanded Wiman's circle of sympathy; it has made him more hopeful; it has allowed him to get closer to those he is closest to.

What interests me about Wiman's religious journey—his arc away from belief and back toward it—is the way it illustrates the knotted nature of attachment and faith. It returns the need for love to the center of religion, reminding us that John 4:16 had a point: "And so we know and rely on the love God has for us. God is love. Whoever lives in love lives in God, and God in them."

Those lines are a mystery. They always will be. But I think they evince the roots of religious experience, how a faith in the ineffable emerges from the same instincts that bind us to family and friends. Even if we never understand why this happens, we can still marvel at its consequences, how a sense of connection to God can transform a life.

This doesn't mean God is the only means of opening the heart. It doesn't mean God is more effective than cognitive behavioral therapy or Transcendental Meditation or any of the secular strategies that people use to deal with their sorrow and despair and addictions. As William James observed long ago, the reason some believe and others doubt depends on their personal experience of a loving God; you either know Him or you don't, but you can't reason your way across the chasm of faith. "There are moments of sentimental and mystical experience . . . that carry an enormous sense of inner authority and illumination with them," James wrote in his 1901 lecture "Religion and Neurology." "But they come seldom, and they do not come to everyone; and the rest of life makes either no connection with them, or tends to contradict them more than it confirms them. Some persons follow more the voice of the moment in these cases, some prefer to be guided by average results. Hence the sad discordancy of so many of the spiritual judgments of human beings."

In his writing, Wiman seems a little surprised that he is one of those who follow "the voice of the moment." Shortly after his diagnosis, he started writing poems again. One of the first poems went like this:

Once more I come to the edge of all I know
And believing nothing believe in this:[78]

And there, Wiman says, the poem ends. On the cliff of a colon. Because what does he actually believe? What does he know for certain? His is a strange religion, a faith inspired by a conversation in a Chicago coffee shop and a walk after church. It began as a feeling of love, an urgent desire to be with his wife. And then, because our nerves are tangled in strange ways, that feeling inspired a belief in something else. All of a sudden, Wiman heard the tapping. Now he's just trying to get as close to the wall as he can.

INTERLUDE:

Love Lost

Consume my heart away; sick with desire
And fastened to a dying animal.

—W.B. YEATS, "Sailing to Byzantium"

L OVE does not last forever. This is a terrible truth, dictated by the briefness of life. "Love dies or else lovers die," writes Harold Bloom. "Those are the pragmatic possibilities."[1] Although love is the cause of our purest joys, its inevitable loss is also responsible for our most intense suffering. The worst wounds are those we cannot see, caused by someone who is no longer here.

This is the pain of a broken heart. It's a violent metaphor: here is the muscle at the center of us, the box that beats out our life, and it's been busted. Wrecked by a feeling. (Nearly every language uses a broken heart as the representation of a failed love affair.)* The metaphor has a physical explanation. One theory is that the anguish of a broken heart causes a simultaneous activation of the sympathetic nervous system, responsible for the fight-or-flight response, and the parasympathetic nervous system, which calms us down and regulates rest-and-digest behaviors.[2] In short, our world is so disrupted by the loss of love that the brain turns on everything at the same time, like taking one's Ambien with a double espresso. Heartbreak is the feeling of being caught in between.

The feeling of lost love is so awful that it seems to send many of us, at least temporarily, into a fugue of mental illness. In a study of 114 people who had recently been rejected by a lover, more than 40 percent met the criteria for clinical depression.[3] What's worse, in approximately 1 to 2 percent of people, severe emotional trauma causes the disease Takotsubo cardiomyopathy, in which the cardiac muscles weaken and degenerate.[4] For such people, the metaphor is not a metaphor at all. Their hearts are literally breaking.

In the midst of the loss, when the wound is raw, we usually assume that we will be miserable forever, that the absence will always be present. We take drugs, but the drugs wear off. We see a shrink, but the words don't work. Nothing works. The pain feels permanent. This loss is never going away.

But then something strange happens: the heart heals. The break is unbroken. We turn out to be far more resilient than we think. In recent years, scientists have begun to document this surprising recovery, as they study what happens to people in the aftermath of a terrible emotional event. (Researchers esti-

---

* One of the few exceptions is Indonesian, which refers to a broken liver (*patah hati*) instead.

mate that around 20 percent of people are likely to experience a potentially traumatic event every year.[5] The most common category of trauma, by far, is the loss of a loved one.) While researchers used to assume that such losses were disabling— we either moved on or suffered from post-traumatic stress disorder—study after study has found that grief and hurt can also leave us with surprising benefits. Nietzsche might have been exaggerating for rhetorical effect—what doesn't kill us doesn't *always* make us stronger—but he was conceptually accurate.

The technical term for this is post-traumatic growth. The phenomenon was discovered largely by accident, as researchers studied the aftereffects of a shipwreck. Stephen Joseph's *What Doesn't Kill Us* describes what happened in detail: On the evening of March 6, 1987, a ferry called the *Herald of Free Enterprise* set sail from Belgium. She was headed to Dover, just across the English Channel, carrying nearly five hundred passengers and eighty crew. Alas, one of those crew members was asleep in his cabin when he should have been securing the bow doors. The doors remained open as the ferry left the harbor, allowing water to gush in. The sinking happened fast. Within ninety seconds, the ship was listing thirty degrees. Joseph, a professor of social science at the University of Nottingham who closely followed the survivors for years, writes, "There was no time to sound alarms of any kind. Furniture, cars, trucks, and passengers alike were indiscriminately catapulted to port side. People collided with one another, crashed into walls, and slipped under the icy cold water as portholes imploded and water flooded the passenger areas. Electricity went out. The darkness reverberated with screams and shouts of pain and terror. As dead bodies floated in the icy water, many expected death, many lost loved ones, many witnessed unimaginable horrors."[6] The sinking of the *Herald* became one of the deadliest maritime disasters of the twentieth century, with 193 passengers and crew dying in the shallow waters of Zeebrugge harbor.

Shortly after the accident, Joseph and colleagues begun studying the survivors, looking for ways to help them cope with the tragedy and the loss of their loved ones. While Joseph set out to understand the factors that made post-traumatic stress disorder (PTSD) more likely—around 25 percent of survivors showed some signs of the disorder—he unexpectedly began to notice that many people mentioned, almost as an afterthought, that the accident had made them better people. This led Joseph to add new questions to his interview, asking subjects if their view of life had changed since the disaster and whether the changes were positive or negative.

The results, Joseph writes, were a shock: 43 percent of the *Herald* survivors said that they found potential benefits to being a trauma survivor. The tragedy was horrific, but it had made them kinder, tougher, less stressed about the little things. The suffering interrupted the busyness of their lives, forcing them to grapple with the big questions: What kind of life were they living? Whom did they want to be?

And it's not just shipwrecks. Since Joseph and colleagues first documented the positive outcomes triggered by adversity, other scientists have extended their findings. Richard Tedeschi and Lawrence Calhoun, clinical psychologists at the University of North Carolina in Charlotte, have repeatedly shown that a large proportion of people come to believe that these "highly stressful" life events have made them more resilient. (Although PTSD dominates the conversation around psychology and adversity—one literature review found twenty-five times more papers on PTSD than post-traumatic growth[7]—growth is a more common aftereffect.)[8] "Post-traumatic growth is not simply a return to baseline," write Tedeschi and Calhoun. "It is an experience of improvement that for some persons is deeply profound."[9] The details of the incident don't seem to matter that much: psychologists have observed post-traumatic growth in divorcées, prisoners of war in Vietnam, college students dealing with academic problems, HIV patients, grieving parents, cancer survivors, widows and widowers.[10] A common metaphor for post-traumatic growth is the rebuilding that occurs after a severe earthquake. While the seismic shock might challenge our fundamental assumptions about the world—the ground is not always still—it often leads to a more durable urban core. We see which structures survive and which ones crumble; what lasts and what falls apart. The city comes back stronger, just like the mind after a trauma.[11]

This newfound strength is not caused by the sorrow, which is useless and mute; misery should not be romanticized. Rather, the science shows that hardship leads to something better when it is used as an opportunity for self-assessment, a rare chance to reevaluate the basic premises of our life. (It's also essential that people have strong support networks to help them cope.) The pain becomes an engine of meaning, as people often discover in the aftermath of a great difficulty that life is brief, and that those we love matter more than anything else. It's not the most original wisdom, but it's what we learn from the darkness. "[Trauma survivors] take a new approach to their closest relationships," Joseph writes. "Now that they are newly aware that life is fragile, and that human connection is one of the most important aspects of life, they begin to value their family and friends more than they did before the traumatic event." The rupture of attachment makes us more determined than ever to attach ourselves to others.

This makes no sense. When confronted with the specter of loss and heartbreak, any reasonable person would learn to live alone. It's just so much safer that way.

But we don't want to be safe. When it comes to love, we are reckless creatures. The tragedy is plain as day—everyone we love will die, unless we die first—but we live in denial of this truth, for that is the only way to feel alive.

Thank God we never learn.

5

ON MEMORY

Perhaps I did not always love him so well as I do now. But in such cases as these, a good memory is unpardonable.

—Jane Austen, *Pride and Prejudice*

Love is so short, forgetting is so long.

—Pablo Neruda

T HE MEN FELL in love at the village feast. One was a few years older, already married, an accomplished poet and adviser to the Bordeaux court; the other was a recent law graduate, blessed with a vast family fortune. The older man was ugly; the younger man was handsome. Nobody knows what they talked about at their first meeting, but the conversation soon became quite intimate. The younger man remembered it this way: "We found ourselves so taken with each other, so well acquainted, so bound together, that from that time on nothing was so close to us as each other."[1]

It was the late 1550s. Southwest France. The king had just been killed in a jousting tournament; the country was heading toward a long religious war. Yet, these two men could think of little else but their friendship. They didn't worry about what others would think or try to hide the intensity of their feelings. It was an audacious love, but they didn't care. "Our friendship has no other model than itself, and can be compared only with itself," wrote the younger man.[2] "If you ask me why I loved him, I feel that it can only be explained by saying, because it was him, because it was me."[3]

They took long walks across the countryside. They rode horses through the Aquitaine forest. They talked about everything: politics, wine, the lure of the New World, Socrates, whether a man in a coma still felt pain. (The younger man said yes, the older man said no.) They wrote each other poems—most of them not very good—and long, florid letters in praise of their relationship. "Our souls mingle and blend with each other so completely that they efface the seam that joined them, and cannot find it again," wrote the younger.[4] The older man agreed, noting that they had attained "the highest point of love. . . . There is no reason to fear that our descendants, if only the fates permit, will begrudge placing our names among those of famous friends."[5]

And then, just like that, it was over. The bad news arrived on a Monday. The younger man invited his friend over for dinner. The older man responded that he wasn't feeling well. He had stomach pain and diarrhea. The next morning, he wrote that he felt even worse. He couldn't keep anything down, not even water. The younger man rushed over. The older man, worried that he had the plague, told him to go home. The younger man refused to leave.

The nightmares started a few days later. They were ter-rible hallucinations, "no better than death," said the older man. He had a shivering fever and was drenched in a "mortal sweat."[6] After nearly ten days of puke and torment, the older man heaved a great sigh and "gave up the ghost." It was three o'clock on a Wednesday morning. The older man—Étienne de La Boétie—had lived for thirty-two years, nine months, and seventeen days.* The younger man would live for another three decades. But he would never get over this loss.

The survivor was Michel Eyquem de Montaigne. We only know about this relationship because Montaigne couldn't stop writing about it. He wrote about it most famously in his *Essays*, but the loving friendship also echoes in the margins of his journals and letters. While Montaigne was visiting Italy, almost two decades after La Boétie's death, he was still think-ing constantly of his lost friend, confessing to his diary that he was "overcome by such painful thoughts about Monsieur de La Boétie, and I was in this mood so long, without recovering, that it did me much harm." He would later dedicate all of his work to his departed friend, writing that he "felt like no more than a half person" in the aftermath of La Boétie's death.[7]

Montaigne's genius was to turn this grief into a source of inspiration. The pain became a kind of art, as the memory of La Boétie helped Montaigne invent the personal essay form.**[8]

---

*La Boétie is best known for a manifesto entitled *The Anti-Dictator*, which is widely seen as the first anarchist tract. He believed that all leaders were corrupt, and that the only rational course of action was complete civil dis-obedience.

**If La Boétie had lived, Montaigne insisted that he would have focused on letter-writing instead; the *Essays* would not exist. Donald Murdoch Frame, *Montaigne: A Biography* (New York: Harcourt Brace, 1965), 83.

Because he could no longer talk to his beloved companion, Montaigne began talking to himself. His writing was born from these lonely soliloquies.[9] As the biographer Donald Frame notes, Montaigne's work is premised on a simple substitution, in which "the reader takes the place of the dead friend." When La Boétie passed away, Montaigne lost a loved one, but he gained a philosophical technique. "He [La Boétie] alone enjoyed my true image and carried it away," Montaigne wrote. "That is why I myself decipher myself so painstakingly."[10]

The *Essays* are a record of that deciphering. The past could not be changed; La Boétie was never coming back; death is a locked door. But by searching for himself so relentlessly, by mining the veins of his memory for the rest of his days, Montaigne kept his friend alive. "Here I am," Montaigne's words call out. "And as long as I am here, so are you."

Plastic Memories

That a man would spend most of his life in mourning, lamenting the loss of the "fullest soul" he would ever meet, is undeniably sad. Yet despite the persistence of his grief, Montaigne's writing never lapses into self-pity. He never seems bitter about life or angry at God. Instead, Montaigne comes across as a man impressed by the strange tenacity of his attachment, curious as to how his best friend was "still lodged in me so entire and so alive" years after his death. Montaigne had nothing to go on but recollection, but that turned out to be enough. His love survived, even if his lover did not.

Such devotion might seem extreme, but it's also proof of an ordinary truth: *memory sustains love.* Although we think of love in the present tense, the endurance of the feeling depends on the past, on all those scenes and stories we do not forget. We form attachments slowly, over time; we maintain those attachments by reflecting on what we've done together, recalling all those moments that made us close. Intimacy is made possible by history, for the feeling of love is as much a memory as it is an experience.

Why are memory and love so intertwined? The answer involves a deeply unsettling aspect of human recollection, which is that the act of remembering changes the memory itself.[11] This is known as memory reconsolidation, and it represents a dramatic break from the old metaphors of recall. Ever since Plato, we've imagined our memories as literal recordings of the past; the brain is a vast hard drive, faithfully storing all the data.* Once a memory is formed, it's supposed to stay the same, an immutable file locked away inside the head.

But this model is false. If you can remember it, then what you remember is changing. Our recollections might feel accurate and stable, but they are always being revised, rewritten, remade. That two-letter prefix changes everything.

Here's an example of reconsolidation at work. I can remember the first time I kissed my wife. It feels like a cheesy movie scene. We were lying on the carpet of my dorm room; *Astral Weeks* was playing in the background. I leaned forward over a bowl of half-eaten spaghetti and, in a moment of unusual boldness, pressed my lips against hers. My left hand went to the back of her neck. I can still smell the soap on her skin.

This memory is embedded deep in my cortex, in a circuit

---

*The details of the metaphor depend on the technology of the time. Plato compared memory to impressions in a wax tablet, while current analogies almost always involve the digital world, as if our memories were made of zeros and ones.

of connected cells that I will contain forever. Yet the science of reconsolidation suggests that this memory—which feels so fixed—is altered every time I think of it. Whenever I remember the kiss, I re-create the scene and modify its map of neural connections. Some details get reinforced—I'm reminded that we started kissing during "Cyprus Avenue"—while others get erased or added. This means that every memory is less like a movie, a permanent emulsion of chemicals on celluloid, and more like a play, subtly different each time it's performed.

One of the first scientists to propose this unsettling theory of memory was Frederic Bartlett, a psychologist at Cambridge University. His discovery was made possible by a subtle twist in experimental procedure. While previous memory research had focused on rote memorization, often involving a long list of random numbers, Bartlett gave his subjects *stories*. In one clever study, first conducted in 1917, he asked his students to read a short folk tale about a river battle involving Indians from a place called Egulac. Fifteen minutes later, he asked the students to repeat the narrative. To Bartlett's surprise, the tale had been utterly transformed in the telling. Although the subjects routinely omitted irrelevant details, they almost always heightened the drama and inserted a didactic moral.[12] Based on his research, Bartlett concluded that the standard view of human memory was wrong. "Remembering is not the re-excitation of innumerable fixed, lifeless and fragmentary traces," he wrote. "It is an imaginative reconstruction."[13]

What does this have to do with loving relationships? If our memories never changed, then we might adapt to their pleasures. We would probably lose interest in revisiting our favorite moments, or in reliving our favorite scenes with other people. I'd get bored thinking of that first kiss, or my son's first smile. (He was two weeks old and passing gas.) But memories are not faithful or immaculate. Rather, they are always getting reinterpreted in light of what we know now, altered by casual conversations and random thoughts and recent experiences.

These changes are usually seen as a bad thing since it means that our version of history is fickle and untrustworthy, that remembering is inseparable from *mis*remembering. Yet, even as Montaigne complained about his "marvelously treacherous" memory, he came to appreciate the upside of its lapses. They allowed him to reflect on his past and still have these memories "smile upon me with a fresh novelty."[14] This lack of habituation proved particularly important when it came to his best friend. Montaigne could no longer share long walks with La Boétie, but he found a way to keep the conversation going by himself, in his own head. As long as Montaigne could remember, he would not be alone.

But the mutability of memory is not just about sustaining our nostalgia, those pleasures we want to remember forever. When done right, our plastic recollections also offer us a chance at recovery and forgiveness, a means of telling a story that lets us cope with the most difficult parts of life. Because our memories are always changing, we can change them for the better, finding ways to make sense of what we cannot forget.

The Importance of Coherence

The past is never past. In *Civilization and Its Discontents*, Freud compared the adult mind to the city of Rome, arguing that the self was best understood as a series of archaeological layers. Although most of these layers are no longer visible—Roman apartments have been built over ancient ruins; new highways hide old aqueducts; Catholic churches are layered on top of pagan temples—the ancient designs still shape the modern metropolis, determining the grid of its streets and the layout of its parks. "Nothing that has once come into existence will have passed away," Freud wrote. "All the earlier phases of development continue to exist alongside the latest one."[15]

The importance of the past helps explain Freud's faith in talk therapy. For the psychiatrist, the talking cure was just an archaeology of the mind, a means of excavation that used words instead of shovels. Most of what is found will be pointless, boring, the meaningless litter of yesterday. But sometimes all the digging leads to discoveries. What we thought we'd forgotten has not been forgotten at all. The hope of therapy, then, is not for closure, for the past is not a door that can be shut. Rather, Freud imagined the therapist as an enabler of change, helping us build something out of the ruins.

Why is remembering at the root of healing? Freud's logic was straightforward. The patient must confront what happened because it cannot be willfully forgotten; repression never works.* Freud would later insist that the impossibility of repression was the "corner-stone on which the whole structure of psychoanalysis rests."[16] Because people could not choose what to forget, they had to find ways to live with what they remembered, which was what the talking cure was all about. As Freud came to refine his psychiatric techniques, he concluded that making sense of our personal history was one of the basic challenges of being human, and that a person unaware of his or her past

---

*As Montaigne remarked, "Nothing fixes a thing so intensely in the memory as the wish to forget it."

would not be able to handle the challenges of intimacy. Before we can learn how to love, we need to learn how to remember.

Freud was wrong about many things, but he was right about the impact of memory. Consider the lives described by the Minnesota Longitudinal Study of Risk and Adaptation, which has followed 267 children born to single mothers in the mid-1970s. (We encountered some of the major findings of this study in chapter 1.) In one, Alan Sroufe, Glenn Roisman, Elena Padron, and Byron Egeland described what happened when they gave their subjects an assessment known as the Adult Attachment Interview, or AAI.[17] The interview is little more than a structured conversation about our childhood memories, with a focus on our closest relationships. (That it resembles a Freudian therapy session is not an accident.) Here are a few of the suggested questions:

"I'd like to ask you to choose five adjectives or words that reflect your relationship with your mother starting from as far back as you can remember in early childhood."

"What is the first time you remember being separated from your parents?"

"Did you experience the loss of a parent or other close loved one while you were a young child?"

The interviews were recorded and then transcribed. The dialogue was often quite intense, as subjects opened up about their childhood traumas and familial wounds. Based on these conversations, Sroufe and colleagues slotted the adults into the same basic categories first described by Ainsworth: secure, avoidant, and anxious-resistant. Not surprisingly, secure adults describe secure childhoods. They dwell on happy scenes—birthday parties, Christmas dinner, weddings—and typically describe the positive influence of family members. Life isn't perfect, but it has been made better by love.

Now come the problematic attachment styles. Avoidant subjects are defined by the negative space of their descriptions. They have few childhood memories and give short, banal accounts of what they can recall. Anxious adults, meanwhile, suffer from the opposite problem. Their accounts of childhood overflow with detail and description. They slide from one charged scene into the next, often with little thought as to how the scenes connect. In many instances, they remain emotionally invested in the past event.

So far, so obvious: our early attachments shadow our lives. The Minnesota scientists, however, were most interested in those kids who changed over time. In particular, they wanted to focus on subjects whose lives began badly but who still managed to become emotionally healthy adults, able to form secure attachments. These people, the "earned-secures" as they are known in the scientific literature, have found a way to rise above the sadness and insecurity of their childhoods. As the Minnesota researchers note, such progress is the stated goal of psychotherapy, which attempts to help patients get over what has gone wrong.

How did these children earn their security? One key variable was the "coherence" of their memories, at least as reflected in the AAI. "It is not the *content* of early memories but rather *the coherence with which they are described* that provides an accurate depiction of states of mind," write the scientists. Furthermore, by looking at how these adults discussed their past traumas, and whether their wounds had been "successfully integrated" into a larger life story, one could make sense of their eventual attachment outcomes. We carry our origins to our graves, but the *meaning* of our origins—the lessons of our childhood—can always be revised.

But this raises the obvious question: where does the coher-

ence come from? How did these people find the strength to revise their life narratives? The Minnesota scientists conclude that
their security is typically rooted in the support of other people,
who helped them cope with their difficult childhoods. "Some of
them had early, security promoting experiences prior to the period of difficulty," Alan Sroufe wrote in an email. "For others the
supports emerged later." However, he notes that there is little
evidence that many people are able to earn their security on their
own. In the end, the experience of love is what gave their stories
coherence, the through line that held everything else together.

In a separate study by the psychiatrist Daniel Siegel, a patient describes her tumultuous relationship with her father:
"My father was very troubled by his being unemployed. For
several years, I think that he was depressed. He wasn't very fun
to be around. He'd go out looking for work, and when he didn't
find any, he would yell at us. When I was young, I think that it
was very upsetting to me. I didn't feel close to him."[18]

However, as the interview continues, the patient places her
"less-than-ideal parenting experience" in a broader context.
She doesn't deny the hurt, but she does explain how it eventually made her stronger: "I had to deal with my anger with him
before we could have the relationship we developed after my
teen years. I think that my drive today is in part due to how
difficult that period was for all of us."

In parsing her AAI transcript, Siegel focuses on the structure and tone of her recollections. Nobody is blamed and nothing is idealized. Instead, the patient unfurls a narrative that
integrates the distinct aspects of her experience, revealing all
the lessons she's learned from her attachment relationships.
The resilience of her life—she's also an earned-secure—is
rooted in her *story* of resilience.

The implication of this research is that the true impact of childhood events is not determined by the events themselves. Rather, what matters most is how those events are remembered, the way they've been written into memory. Although many earned-secures suffered from the same tragedies as their troubled peers—abuse, neglect, parents in prison—they found a way to tell a meaningful tale about their early life, making sense of the turbulence and pain. As the years passed, the nature of this narrative was what proved most predictive of their adult attachments. "We tell ourselves stories in order to live," wrote Joan Didion. Or, put another way, we tell ourselves stories because life is rife with pain, but we've got to go on living anyway.

The Minnesota subjects are an extreme example. Their lives have been marked by difficulty from the start. But the same logic applies to everyone, for how we describe the past of a relationship shapes its future. Our memories are so important that one of the most predictive tests of divorce is incredibly simple: researchers bring a newlywed couple into a room and ask them to tell the story of their marriage from their first encounter to the last bad fight. Then, their dialogue is scored on seven different dimensions, from levels of affection to a sense of "life chaos," which describes whether people feel in control of their lives. The following transcript is from a couple who scored high on the chaos metric:

Interviewer: How did the two of you meet? And what were your first impressions of one another?

Lenny: We met at a party. She was nice.

Wendy: Yeah, we didn't talk much then.

Interviewer: And then?

Lenny: She moved in with me the next week because there was a fire in her apartment.

Interviewer: Wow, that was fast. How was that decision made?

Wendy: I just had to move somewhere, and he said, "Well, okay, you can stay here for a while."

Interviewer: And your impressions of him?

Wendy: He was okay. Nice, I guess.

Interviewer: Then what happened?

Lenny: Her mom got cancer and we decided to move up there to Wisconsin to take care of her.

Interviewer: That's amazing that you both did that. How long had you been together at that point?

Wendy: About a year.

Interviewer: How did you decide to do that together?

Lenny: I don't remember.

Wendy: It just kind of happened. Like the fire.[19]

Notice the sense of chaos, which manifests itself as a lack of control. When Wendy and Lenny describe their relationship, it is merely something that happened to them. They didn't decide to live together, or to move to Wisconsin. Unfortunate life events made these choices for them. Fire. Cancer. *It just kind of happened.*

In contrast, here is a transcript of a couple who scored low in "chaos" and high on a metric called Glorifying the Struggle, which refers to a shared sense of pride in overcoming adversity.

Randy: Jonine was four months pregnant when we got married.

Interviewer: So did you think you "had to" get married?

Jonine: No, not at all.

Randy: I think it was more of me respecting Jonine. I don't think it was a "Well, you guys have to get married now." [He emphasizes his respect for his wife at the time.]

Jonine: And I think it was kind of protective, right?[20]

It later becomes clear that their shotgun wedding was fraught, as both of their families disapproved and skipped the event. Nevertheless, Randy's and Jonine's memories reflect a sense of control over their lives, an ability to cope with the unexpected turns of life. The unplanned pregnancy was a crisis, but they found a way to make it work. "Couples who Glorify the Struggle . . . may be in the same turmoil as the couples who score high in chaos," write the scientists, "but the difference is their perception of the hardships." These differences are obvious in the interviews. When Randy and Jonine are asked about their wedding day, they focus on the pleasures, not the turmoil. "It was an awesome wedding," Randy remembers. "There was a boat, all decorated."[21]

After assessing fifty-two couples based on their oral history interviews, the psychologists Kim Buehlman, John Gottman, and Lynn Katz at the University of Washington found that the way spouses described their history predicted whether they would get divorced within the next three years with *94 percent* accuracy.[22] It's an astonishing statistic: by simply looking at how couples speak about their past, the scientists could foresee their future.

What were the crucial tells? One important variable was whether a couple could fit the stories of their life—both the ups and downs—into a larger tale of love and redemption. The happiest couples didn't talk only about happy times, but they did find a positive frame for their struggles. (As the scientists write, "Glorifiers" such as Randy and Jonine "go on to tell in detail how certain traumas and intense experiences made them feel closer to one another. Hence marriages with this outlook on hardships grow stronger and get better as time goes on.") Another key variable was "we-ness." When the most satisfied spouses discussed their history, the narratives were filled with the first-person plural; they focused on how events affected them as a couple, and not as individuals. *We learned to make do. That was a hard time for us. We got through it.*

The moral of these studies is that the past requires constant upkeep. Life is messy. It is full of contingency and randomness and accidents. And that's why the coherence of our past is something we must create for ourselves, a meaning chiseled out of experience, carved out of the confusion of our relationships. Sometimes, this means resolving a fight before falling asleep, or weaving a "glorifying" tale about a difficult time. It's insisting that there must be a lesson to learn and thinking about life as a shared journey. It's not about forced forgetting, although much is bound to be forgotten. It's about finding a way to weave together what we remember.

Montaigne's writing is a model here. His prose is famously discursive, winding its way among an esoteric collection of subjects, including cannibals, thumbs, Seneca, farts, and repentance. In an essay on solitude, for instance, Montaigne begins by pondering the nature of evil, then transitions to Socrates, before speculating on the best way to secure a ship's cargo.

It's the usual digressiveness until, about halfway through the piece, Montaigne unfurls one of his most famous lines: "The greatest thing in the world is to know how to belong to oneself."[23] It's as if, while writing that aphorism, Montaigne cut through the clutter of his mind: this is what he'd been trying to say all along.

How did Montaigne find that line? By writing and then rewriting. Montaigne never stopped altering his work. ("I cannot keep my subject still," he confessed. "It goes along befuddled and staggering, with a natural drunkenness.")[24] The hard copies of his *Essays* document their endless revisions, as he added new quotes in the margins, crossed out sentences, and pasted in additional paragraphs. Many of the pages in the printed final folio are covered with handwritten edits. If Montaigne had had more time, one imagines him ending up like the mad artist in Balzac's short story, who keeps on reworking his painting until it's a meaningless mess of color.[25]

But this was not Montaigne's fate. There are certainly moments when all the additions stretch the limits of our comprehension, but mostly his changes make the *Essays* even wiser. "It is life that emerges more and more clearly as these essays reach not their end, but their suspension in full career," wrote Virginia Woolf, in an appreciation of Montaigne.[26] She was right to emphasize his fidelity to life. While Montaigne's critics attacked his illogic and imprecisions, such criticism missed the point, for Montaigne wasn't trying to construct a flawless argument. He was attempting to write his mind onto the page, using free association as a philosophical technique.[27]

The narratives of memory require a similar approach. Before we can make sense of the past, we need to revisit it, following the mind into all sorts of sentimental corners and nostalgic culs-de-sac. Most of these memories will mean little; almost all of them could easily be forgotten. This is why talk therapy is often so tedious. Yet if we spend enough time remembering, if we keep reworking the rough drafts of the past, then we might eventually stumble upon a little wisdom, just like Montaigne. Revision is a kind of revealing. "If others examined themselves attentively, as I do, they would find themselves, as I do, full of inanity and nonsense," Montaigne wrote. "Get rid of it I cannot without getting rid of myself. We are all steeped in it, one as much as another, but those who are aware of it are a little better off—though I don't know."[28]

Besides, what's the alternative? The past can't be undone or repressed, which means we have to find a way to deal with it. James Pennebaker, a social psychologist at the University of Texas at Austin, has spent decades studying the tangible benefits of confronting our memories, especially when we'd rather forget them. One of the inspirations for his research was an undergraduate student named Warren.[29] Although Warren had received excellent grades during his freshman year, he developed severe test anxiety as a sophomore. Before long, he had to withdraw from school. Pennebaker began studying Warren in the lab, hooking him up to a heart-rate monitor and asking him assorted questions about his emotional life. Most of the questions triggered little response. When asked about problems with his girlfriend, for instance, Warren replied that they had "some disagreements about sexuality," but nothing too serious. (His pulse barely budged, ticking upward to seventy-seven.) The same pattern continued as Pennebaker asked Warren about college, the future, and even his testing failures—Warren's answers were calm and collected; his heart rate stayed mostly steady. However, one question triggered a dramatic spike in Warren's heart rate: whenever Pennebaker asked him about his parents' divorce, Warren's pulse spiked nearly thirty points, fluttering at more than one hundred beats per minute. This massive physiological response came despite Warren's insistence that the divorce was not traumatic at all. "It was no big deal," he said. Not even worth discussing. When Pennebaker confronted Warren with the heart-rate data, the student was astonished. He had no idea he was so upset. These results convinced Warren to reflect on his negative emotions, to try to figure out where they were coming from. While the introspection didn't make his feelings disappear, his test anxiety soon vanished. "Confronting a trauma helps people to understand and ultimately assimilate the event," Pennebaker writes. "By talking or writing about previous inhibited experiences, individuals translate the event into language. Once it is language-based, people can better understand the experience and ultimately put it behind them."[30] It's a literary model of healing, in which the mere attempt at description—trying to put the feeling into words—comes with significant benefits.

In one of his most influential studies, Pennebaker and Sandra Beall asked a random sample of undergraduates to undergo writing therapy. Those assigned to the control group were told to write about a superficial subject, such as how they use their time. Those assigned to the experimental group were given a version of the following instructions: "I want you to write continuously about the most upsetting or traumatic experience of your entire life," Pennebaker told them. "You can write about anything you want. But whatever you choose, it should be something that has affected you very deeply. Ideally, it should be about something you have not talked about with others in detail. It is critical, however, that you let yourself go and touch those deepest emotions and thoughts that you have."[31]

These writing sessions took place for four consecutive days. The participants shared dark secrets. One woman told the story of how, when she was ten years old, her mother asked her to clean up her toys before her grandmother arrived for a visit. She didn't listen. Her grandmother then tripped on a toy, fractured her hip, and died during surgery. The woman wrote about how she still blamed herself every single day. Other subjects described sexual molestation or the toll of alcoholism. The researchers were "stunned and depressed" by the outpouring: "That our college students had experienced so many horrors and, at the same time, had so readily revealed them to us was remarkable. The grim irony is that, by and large, these were 18-year-old kids attending an upper-middle-class college with above-average high school grade-point averages and college-board scores. These are the people who are portrayed as growing up in the bubble of financial security and suburban tranquility."[32] Yet despair seemed to find everyone. They all had something to confess.

Pennebaker then followed up with the students. The initial results were not promising: the subjects said they felt much worse after opening up. Catharsis was a curse. However, as the months passed, the benefits of writing therapy started to accumulate. After four months, those students who had written about their traumas were significantly less likely to get sick, at least when compared to those asked to write about superficial things. This correlation held for serious conditions such as depression, but also for the common cold. (Subsequent studies helped to explain these correlations, with writing therapy leading to higher levels of immune function, at least as measured by the amount of antibodies in the blood following vaccination.)[33] Additionally, students in writing therapy got better grades and drank less alcohol.*

Why does confessing to a journal make people feel better? The main benefit of catharsis is that it gives people the opportunity to shape a new narrative. "The people who benefited from writing were constructing stories," Pennebaker writes in his book *Opening Up*.[34] "On the first day of writing, they would often tell about a traumatic episode that simply described an experience. . . . But day by day, as they continued to write, the episode would take on shape as a coherent story with a clear beginning, middle, and end."[35] What started as a secret list of past traumas—a source of chronic stress that wrecked their health—morphed into a life-affirming lesson, which made these people better at handling future struggles. (As John Updike once wrote, "Composition, in crystallizing memory, displaces it.")[36] If nothing else, Pennebaker notes, the misfortune led his writing subjects to notice what lasted, what mattered the most.

Such is the wisdom that emerges from a coherent past. Erik Erikson, one of the most influential psychoanalysts of the twentieth century, believed that being able to make sense of our memories was the essential task of maturity, which he called integrity. As Erikson saw it, the goal of talk therapy was to help people tell a story about themselves that they could live

---

*These results have led Pennebaker to recommend that people find time to write in the aftermath of a difficult event. Even if we only have fifteen minutes, we should attempt to describe what happened, and how we feel about it, and why we feel that way. The crucial caveat, Pennebaker told me, is that the writing doesn't need to be done right after the trauma occurred: "If you feel as if you are overwhelmed immediately afterwards and think writing is a bad idea, don't write. It's sometimes good to get a little distance before putting feelings into words." Regardless of when the writing takes place, the benefits will likely last long after we put the pen down.

with, even if it was still stained with regrets. (The alternative to integrity, Erikson said, was bitterness and despair.) "It [integrity] is the acceptance of one's own and only life cycle and of the people who have become significant to it as something that had to be and that, by necessity, permitted of no substitutions," he wrote. "It thus means a new and different love of one's parents, free of the wish that they should have been different, and an acceptance of the fact that one's life is one's own responsibility."[37] Although we think of memory as immutable, Erikson realized that our recollections could always be rewritten. The ink never dries. And so we must keep telling our story until we find a version that gives us peace and solace and meaning.

Dinner

The importance of remembering raises a practical question: How do we learn how to do it? Storytelling is a skill. It requires role models and practice.

The answer is not surprising: we learn how to remember from our families. That is the conclusion of the psychologists Marshall Duke, Jennifer Bohanek, and Robyn Fivush, who have been working at the Family Narratives Project at Emory University. One of the scientists' most striking findings features a survey called the Do You Know? scale.[38] The quiz consists of twenty yes-or-no questions that measure a child's knowledge of his or her family history. Here's a sample:

"Do you know where some of your grandparents grew up?"

"Do you know some of the lessons that your parents learned from good or bad experiences?"

"Do you know the names of the schools that your mom went to?"

"Do you know where some of your grandparents met?"

Despite the simplicity of the survey, the scientists documented an impressive statistical link between the scores of children on the Do You Know? scale and various measures of mental health and well-being. According to the data, children with higher scores showed higher levels of self-esteem and felt more in control of their lives. They were less anxious, had fewer behavioral problems, and were more resilient.

But it's important not to confuse correlation and causation. As the researchers note, we can't teach to the test; telling your children about their genealogy won't magically help them get better grades. Rather, a knowledge of family history is a side effect of the real cause: *conversation*. "It is not the *content* of what is known that is the critical factor, but the *process* by which these things came to be known," writes Marshall Duke. "This process is, in our opinion, the causational factor. In order to hear family stories, people need to sit down with one another and not be distracted. Some people have to talk and some have to listen. The stories need to be told over and over and the times of sitting together need to be multiple and occur over many years."[39]

For many families, this reminiscing process is most likely to take place during dinner. The rest of the day is simply too busy and frantic. This led the Emory researchers to study the conversations that took place during "family mealtimes" in forty middle-class households across Atlanta. By studying the transcripts of these conversations, the researchers found a link between the quality of discussion and the emotional life of the children. According to the data, one of the most useful forms of dinner talk was the construction of a "coherent family story," in which the past is told and retold until it makes sense. "In order for a family to construct a coherent narrative together, each part of the story must be explained, and the members of the family may challenge what was told, may add in different pieces, or may critique and rework the current theory of what happened," write Bohanek and coauthors, in their paper "Narrative Interaction in Family Dinnertime Conversations."[40] It doesn't matter what's remembered. The families in the study talked about everything from trips to Disney World to the events of the last weekend. What matters is that they remember *together*, and that they do this every day.

Put this way, it can all seem daunting, as if nostalgia time needs to be scheduled in alongside homework and piano lessons. But the transcripts of dinner conversations reveal that this remembering usually works best when it unfolds naturally, as a by-product of the most routine talks. The scientists noticed that many meaningful dialogues began with a version of the same basic question: How was your day? In this exchange, for instance, the father begins by asking Becca, his thirteen-year-old daughter, about her band competition:

Becca: Well, we didn't get to hear any other bands. We would have liked to, but, you know, we had to leave.

Father: Hmm. I remember when I was in choir, when I was in high school.

Becca: Uh-huh.

Father: We didn't do so good. [He and Becca laugh] I think we got threes and fours.

Becca: Yeah, yeah, see, the thing I don't like about our choir is, uh, they sound really nice, but they're all whispering, you know [in a whispering voice].[41]

Notice how Becca's short initial answer could easily have ended the conversation. But her father doesn't let that happen. Instead, he segues into a dialogue about the past, as he recounts his own school memories. What's more, his candid sharing of failure ("We didn't do so good") encourages Becca to voice her misgivings about the day. ("The thing I don't like about our choir is . . .") This mundane scene, say the scientists, is an example of how our personal memories are always being integrated into family conversation, which helps children make sense of their own life experiences.

The benefits of all this memory-sharing are impressive.[42] Children raised in households that engage in the most recollection report higher levels of emotional well-being and a stronger sense of personal identity. The family unit also becomes stronger, as those children and parents who know more about the past also scored higher on a widely used measure of "reported family functioning."[43] This research is buttressed by related surveys showing the widespread benefits of family dinner. According to data compiled by Sandra Hofferth and John Sandberg, the single best predictor of a young child's academic achievement is the amount of mealtime they experience with their family at home.[44] Shared dinners were a better predictor of classroom performance than time spent in school, doing homework, playing organized sports, or going to church. (This correlation holds steady after controlling for race, gender, income, parental education, and family size.) Other researchers find that the trend persists into adolescence, as teenagers who have five or more dinners per week with a parent get better grades and are far less likely to experiment with alcohol and cigarettes.[45]

Alas, shared family meals are becoming increasingly rare. Hofferth, for instance, has found a 33 percent drop between

1981 and 1997 in the amount of time parents and children spent talking during meals.[*46] Another study, led by the Sloan Center on Everyday Lives of Families at UCLA, found that only 17 percent of middle-class families ate dinner together regularly, even when all the family members were at home. (The single most common meal setup was for family members to eat the same meal at different times or in different rooms of the house.)[47] Although almost all the parents said they wanted to talk more with their kids, they struggled to spend more than ten minutes a day in conversation without distractions. Technology kept making the problem worse. There were too many goddamn gadgets.

Virginia Woolf once wrote, "On or about December 1910 human character changed." It's one of her most famous lines, occurring in the midst of a defense of modernist literature. It's also a reminder that every age is convinced it's on the verge of becoming a New Age, a technology or two away from total transformation. The twenty-first century is no exception. Our lives have been upended by the digital screen, these panes of glowing pixels we can't stop staring at. If Woolf were alive today, she might note that human character changed on or about June 2007, when the first iPhone was released.

Yet amid all these gizmos and machines, it's more important than ever to remember which parts of human character have *not* changed. Because technology does not alter everything. We still live in desperate need of attachments. Our lives are still shaped by the stories we tell. And we still tend

---

*What were we doing instead? Children reported spending more time on computers, participating in "structured activities," such as Little League and doing homework.

to tell these stories while eating together. It's such a primal act, breaking bread, but it seems to connect us in all sorts of mysterious ways. When we share a meal, we end up sharing our past, too. So our separate narratives get woven together, each story becoming a thread of a larger one, which we tell again and again until we know it all by heart.

I've got a selfish interest in all this memory research. I think a lot about how, one day, I'm going to have to tell my children the story of my mistakes. I'm going to have to tell them what I lost and how I lost it, how I hurt their mother and so many people I love. I will tell them about my regrets, which remain raw and potent, years later.

But I also hope that it might also be a story of what I gained. A story about how I learned to be a decent dad and husband, which is so much harder than I thought it would be. A story about all the time I got to spend telling *My Little Pony* stories and building with LEGOs and going for afternoon hikes. (And carrying my kids on my shoulders when they were tired of hiking.) A story about the consolations of being here, being home, becoming a little more aware of what matters.

That's the story I want to tell. I could tell another story, but I'm choosing this one. Because there is a choice. We are the stars of the tales we tell, but we are also the authors, searching for a way through. We write the words that define our lives.

Montaigne is testament to this possibility. He lost his great love as a young man. He could have given up. He could have let the melancholy take over. Instead, he sublimated all that sadness into his writing, composing sprawling essays that echoed their conversations. He was consoled by his worn memories of

La Boétie, but what he learned is that memory is how we come to understand ourselves.

Toward the end of his life, as he was wracked with pain from kidney stones, Montaigne began to reflect on ultimate questions. There he was, hunched over the piss bowl, cursing the "sharp rough stone that cruelly pricks and flays the neck of my penis," thinking all sorts of deep thoughts. Montaigne knew that he was dying, but he wasn't scared. The death of La Boétie, he said, had taught him the essential truth of life, which is that nothing lasts forever. One day, his castle would crumble, the grapevines would wither, even the wine in his cellar would rot. Time is the sharpest scythe. It cuts down everything. And the sooner we learn to accept its brutal edge, the sooner we can get on living. As Montaigne once wrote in an echo of Cicero, "To philosophize is to learn how to die."

At first glance, this line makes no sense. We don't need philosophy to become a corpse; death requires no education. Yet Montaigne was besotted with the aphorism, even using it as the title of a chapter in the *Essays*. I'm guessing he liked its stoic tone, how it summarized philosophy as a means of reconciling ourselves to loss, coping with the brevity of everything. For Montaigne, this was what wisdom was all about—the acceptance of brute facts. If life were easy, if the heart were never broken, our stories wouldn't matter; we could survive on our own without them. But life is not easy, and the heart is constantly broken, which is why our stories matter so much.

Dan McAdams, a psychologist at Northwestern University, has spent years studying the uncanny power of these stories. For the last few decades, he has focused on people who score particularly high in "generativity," a character trait associated with generosity and selflessness. "Generative adults seek to give something back to society," McAdams writes in his book *The Redemptive Self*.[48] "They work to make their world a better place, not just for themselves but for future generations." Such selflessness comes with real benefits, as McAdams has found a strong link between generativity in middle age and mental health. In particular, those people who devote themselves to others are far less likely to be depressed.[49]

McAdams argues that generativity is often rooted in a specific type of life story, which he refers to as a "redemption narrative." While these narratives begin with tales of hardship and sin—popular examples include addiction, divorce, and illness—they end with absolution and grace, or what McAdams describes as the "deliverance from suffering to an enhanced status or state." (Interestingly, stories of redemption are a much better predictor of well-being than straightforward stories of happiness.)[50] As with post-traumatic growth, this enhanced state is not rooted in the suffering itself. Rather, it emerges over time, as people learn from their most trying experiences. McAdams quotes one highly generative adult on the lessons he gleaned from his hard times: "When I die, I guess the chemicals in my body, well, they'll go to fertilize some plants, you know, some ears of corn, and the good deeds I do will live through my children and through the people I love."[51]

Stories of redemption can feel self-serving. They can seem like excuses for past misdeeds, a flattering way to excuse our sins. Yet such stories about the past—even when they are subjective, biased, and filled with inevitable inaccuracies—shape who we are and the people we become. It says in Romans 5:3–4, "We also glory in our sufferings, because we know that suffering produces perseverance, and perseverance, character, and character, hope." Is that biblical equation always true? Does suffering always lead to something better? Of course not. But sometimes we need to believe it does.

I'm reminded here of another study of life narrative, this one from the Family Narratives Project at Emory University. After tape-recording dinnertime conversations, and listening to the children tell stories about their parents' childhoods, the researchers sorted families into three basic categories.[52] Some parents told stories of ascent, how a relative began with nothing and worked hard for what he or she got. Other families focused on the downfall: here's what we had and this is how we lost it. The most useful family stories, however, involved a complex mixture of success and failure. Known as oscillating narratives, these family histories had sweep: they told of rises and falls, triumphs and disappointments, failures and forgiveness. "There are heroes in these stories, there are people who faced the worst and made it through," said Marshall Duke in a recent interview with Elizabeth Kurylo. "And this sense of continuity and relatedness to heroes seems to serve the purpose in kids of making them more resilient."[53]

Why are oscillating narratives so useful? In part, it's because of their honesty. If we want our children to learn about life and love, we need to teach them that life is not easy and that love is hard work. There will be sweat and acrimony and moments of near defeat. People are flawed and fucked-up. This is what you need to deal with if you want to make it through.

But sharing memories with highs and lows, happiness and heartbreak, has another virtue. When we remember the flux of life, we also shift attention to what's most important: those feelings that persist. Amid the tales of incessant change, we come to see what counts, which is all that stays the same. We end up talking about the attachments that last, the desires that survive, the relationships that endure. Every story becomes a love story.

INTERLUDE:

The Opposite of Love

WHAT is the opposite of love? The answer seems obvious: hate. If love is the desire for closeness— we want to kiss, hold, touch—then hate is the desire for distance, or at least a fist to the face.

But the obvious answer is wrong. Love and hate are bound together in the brain, potent feelings sourced from the same knot of nerves. The first evidence for this unsettling fact emerged from the frustration-aggression hypothesis, outlined in a series of papers by John Dollard, Neal Miller, and colleagues in the late 1930s. The scientists used an electrode to stimulate the reward circuits in the brain of a rodent; the animal soon went quiet with bliss. That's not surprising. However, when they turned off the electricity, the animal would often become violent, lashing out at the same wires that had just delivered so much joy.

This is the lab rat version of the enraged lover. The anthropologist Helen Fisher calls it "love hatred" and argues that it's a common symptom of a broken heart, or just a difficult relationship. Maybe an attachment has been ended. Or perhaps we're just pissed at a spouse. Either way, it's shocking how easily the affection slips into righteous anger. This flip can be switched, Fisher writes, because the "primary rage network is closely linked to centers in the prefrontal cortex that anticipate rewards," including the reward of being in love.[1]

Leo and Sonya Tolstoy remain one of the great literary examples of a love-hate relationship. The couple met in the summer of 1862, when Sonya was eighteen. (Her birth name was Sofia Behrs, but most people knew her as Sonya.) After a brief courtship, Leo wrote her a formal letter of proposal. He began with a confession, lamenting how the sexual attraction was more than he could bear. After stalling for another few paragraphs—he describes his insomnia, complains about her family, celebrates his work—Tolstoy gets to the point, pleading, "Tell me, your hand on your heart—without hurrying, for the love of God, without hurrying—tell me what I must do. . . . Tell me as an honest woman, do you wish to be my wife?" Sonya's reply was an ecstatic yes.[2]

Before long, however, scenes of fury and despair interrupted the happy romance. Because Leo and Sonya were compulsive diarists, it's possible to trace, in excruciating detail, the ebb and flow of their feelings. Some entries drip with affection. Sonya describes the thrill of seeing Leo after a long day of writing—"I always feel sick with happiness when he returns home"[3]—and the pleasure of staying up late, copying out his cursive sentences by candlelight.* Leo was just as ef-

---

*As William Shirer observes in his moving biography of their marriage, Sonya was an invaluable assistant and editor. By her own estimates, she

fusive. In a passage from early 1863, he sounds like a blissed-out newlywed: "I love her when I wake up at night or in the morning and see her. . . . I love it when she is a girl in a yellow dress and sticks out her lower jaw and tongue. . . . I love it when . . ." The entry ends with an ellipsis, as if Leo was too in love to explain.[4]

But the diaries also describe a montage of battles, how the walls of the house would shake with screams.[5] The two squabbled over sex—Leo wanted it, Sonya didn't—with resentments over her chronic pregnancies. (She had thirteen children in twenty-five years, which perhaps explains her lack of desire.) Leo came to see Sonya as a spoiled countess, more interested in comfort and luxury than in helping others. They fought over the kids and money and his vegetarian diet. Sonya thought he was a slob and should bathe more often; Leo didn't care. For the most part, these are survivable problems, which is why the couple were constantly reconciling, telling themselves that their relationship was back on track. Love became hate, which became love again.

It stayed this way until the bitter end. When Leo was dying, he decided to run away from home. He took the train south but got stranded at a stationmaster's house in the middle of nowhere. Sonya begged to see him, but Leo refused, saying that a "meeting would be fatal." (They'd been married for forty-eight years, but Leo was still playing games.) In a desperately sad photograph, Sonya is outside the train station, on her tiptoes, trying to peer inside. Her arms rest on a windowsill

---

copied drafts of *War and Peace* at least seven times, which amounts to approximately twenty-one thousand pages in her notebook. William Shirer, *Love and Hatred: The Stormy Marriage of Leo and Sonya Tolstoy* (New York: Simon & Schuster, 1994), 69.

coated with snow; her head is covered with a white scarf; next to her is a basket of dirty laundry. All she wants is to see him, one last time.[6]

The Tolstoys are an extreme example of a universal phenomenon: every attachment is mixed up with darker stuff. (As Fyodor Dostoyevsky, another Russian realist, once wrote, "Love in action is a harsh and dreadful thing compared with love in dreams.")[7] To be close is to see the flaws, to get furious at all those imperfections we only notice because we're living together, sharing a bed and a bathroom. What's more surprising, perhaps, is that this anger can endure for a long time, just like those feelings of love. While every other emotion is subject to habituation, love and hate linger in the head: those people we feel passionate about (even when the passion is rage) keep demanding more and more of our attention. The nerves keep firing.

This returns us to the original question: What is the opposite of love? Here's one speculative answer, first put forth by Elie Wiesel: indifference.[8] Apathy. Ennui. Heidegger once said that boredom is the awareness of time passing. The charm of love is that it leaves us unaware. The feeling doesn't stop time—nothing stops time—but it does have the uncanny power to distort it. This happens first when we fall in love, during those ecstatic early days when the days are never long enough. And then it happens again when love persists, when it outlives every other urge, itch, and pleasure. The clock is still ticking, but true love doesn't notice. It goes on until time runs out.

And even when the love doesn't last, it still leaves a lasting mark. To be in love is to forever lose the capacity not to care. You might be furious at him, or jealous of her, but he or she will never become boring. Years pass; you change; this doesn't. For reasons you can't explain, your ex-lover will remain strangely interesting, a figure you can't quite forget. You will stalk him on Facebook; follow her on Instagram; he will continue to appear in your dreams. And if you ever see him on the street, or spy her at a class reunion, or on the arm of someone else, you will not be able to look away or feign indifference. Your beating heart will give you away.

6

GOING ON

What is to give light must endure burning.

—Viktor Frankl

Strongly spent is synonymous with kept.

—Robert Frost[1]

V iktor Frankl trained as a psychiatrist in Vienna in the early 1930s, during the peak of Freud's influence. He internalized the great man's theories, writing at one point that "all spiritual creations turn out to be mere sublimations of the libido." The human mind, powered by its id engine, was a simple machine. Mostly, it just wanted sex and sugar and shiny things.

Unfortunately, Frankl didn't find this therapeutic framework useful. While working as a doctor in the "suicide pavilion" at the Steinhof hospital—he treated thousands of at-risk Viennese women over four years—Frankl began to question his training.[2] Despite his interventions, his patients weren't getting better; the women were still suicidal. So Frankl concluded that the pleasure principle must not be the main motive of existence. The despair of these women was about more than a thwarted id.

So what were these women missing? Frankl answered that their depression was caused by a lack of *meaning*. His diagnosis was deliberately vague, for he knew there was no universal fix; every person's source of meaning was different. For some people, it was another person to care for, or a lasting relationship. For others, it was an artistic skill or a religious belief or an unwritten novel. But the point was that meaning was at the center, for "life can be pulled by goals as surely as it can be pushed by drives." What we craved wasn't happiness for its own sake, Frankl said, but something to be happy about.

Inspired by this insight, Frankl began developing his own school of psychotherapy, which he called logotherapy. (*Logos* is Greek for "meaning"; *therapeia* means "to heal or make whole." *Logotherapy* literally translates as "healing through meaning.") As a clinician, Frankl's goal was not the elimination of pain or worry. Rather, it was showing patients how to locate a sense of purpose in their lives. As Nietzsche put it, "He who has a why to live can bear with almost any how."[3] Frankl wanted to help people find their why.

His timing couldn't have been worse. Shortly after Frankl opened his first logotherapy clinic, in early 1938, the Nazis "annexed" Austria, marching into Vienna to the sound of applause. Like all Jewish men, Frankl was assigned an additional middle name (Israel) and forced to wear a yellow Star of David. He was fired from the prestigious Steinhof hospital and told to open a new office in his tiny apartment, where he was listed as a "Jew-Caretaker."

Yet even in these darkening times, life went on. Frankl continued to see patients—he could only treat Jews—and began writing a book about the clinical applications of his theories. The following year, Frankl fell in love with a nurse named Tilly. They married in December 1941, the last Viennese Jews to marry under the Nazis.[4]

A few months later, Frankl and his family were deported to the Theresienstadt concentration camp. In this hellish place, nearly fifty-three thousand "residents" were crammed into a town built for four thousand.[5] To keep busy, Frankl worked in a psychiatric clinic to treat new arrivals and delivered free lectures on everything from the psychology of mountain climbing to the problem of suicide in the Jewish ghetto. Frankl even continued working on his book. In an early draft, Frankl described what he'd learned so far from his time at Theresienstadt: "There is nothing in the world that can so much enable a person to overcome outer difficulties and inner troubles as the awareness of having a mission in life."[6] Because the Nazis couldn't steal his meaning—he was still working, still writing, still in love with his wife—they couldn't take away what mattered most.

But they kept taking. In October 1944, Viktor and Tilly were sent to Auschwitz. They stepped off the cattle trains and were separated immediately by the Nazi guards. There wasn't even time for a kiss good-bye. Frankl was ordered to strip naked and surrender all of his clothing. He was used to such indignities, but he didn't want to give up the coat, as it contained the only copy of his book. Frankl pleaded and begged. At first, a guard seemed sympathetic. But then a cruel smile spread across his face. "First [it was] piteous, then more amused, mocking, insulting," Frankl remembered. "He bellowed one word at me in answer to my question, a word that was ever present in the vocabulary of the camp inmates: 'Shit!' "[7] Frankl watched as his book was thrown onto the pile of rags. In exchange, he was given the filthy uniform of an inmate who had just been sent to the gas chambers.

After three days at Auschwitz, Frankl was ordered onto another train, bound for the work camps of Kaufering III, part of the Dachau concentration camp. Because Frankl remained reasonably healthy compared to many of his fellow prisoners, he was sentenced to the hardest labor, digging underground tunnels. One night, the SS guards were in a particularly cruel mood, shouting at the prisoners and beating them with the butts of their rifles. Frankl was contemplating suicide—if he stepped out of line, he would be shot—when a simple thought transfixed him:

> For the first time in my life I saw the truth as it is set into song by so many poets, proclaimed as the final wisdom by so many thinkers. The truth—that love is the ultimate and the highest goal to which man can aspire. Then I grasped the meaning of the greatest secret that human poetry and human thought and belief have to impart: *The salvation of man is through love and in love*. I understood how a man who has nothing left in this world still may know bliss, be it only for a brief moment, in the contemplation of his beloved.[8]

The power of the idea is not the idea itself, which is sappy and sentimental. Rather, it's that such a cliché kept a man alive in the worst possible circumstances. Because Frankl did not step out of line. He did not die. We are reading his memoir.

The rest of Frankl's life was devoted to the implications of his survival. He wanted to understand the mystery of endurance, why those recurring thoughts of his wife and parents kept him alive in hell. So the psychiatrist began studying himself, trying to decipher how love allowed him to go on.

Frankl wasn't searching for final answers. He knew his questions might never get answered. Yet he also knew that the questions must still be asked. Because we do get glimmers. Not solutions, just glimmers. Glances of self-understanding.

Here is one glimmer.

The Beast

The story begins on the steps of Eisenhower Hall, a colossal brick theater on the bank of the Hudson River at West Point. Here new army cadets arrive on their first day, showing up at six thirty in the morning. After a short briefing, they are told to say good-bye to their families: they have ninety seconds. Then the cadets are bused across campus to Thayer Hall, where they are "processed" for the military. They are given short haircuts and a slew of vaccinations and are told to change into Gym Alpha, a uniform consisting of a white T-shirt, black shorts, shined formal shoes, and knee-high black socks. A booklet is attached with a safety pin to their clothes; as they progress through the stations, tabs are torn off one by one until, by the end of the afternoon, only stubs remain. That evening, the cadets march onto the Plain—a sprawling grass field that was the site of the original army garrison in 1778—and take the Oath of Allegiance.

The following day, and every day for the next six weeks, the young soldiers are woken at 5:30 a.m. They are sent on twelve-mile marches in the summer heat and offered constant corrections by their superiors. They learn how to quickly assemble their M4 rifles and fire at moving targets; how to march in formation and sleep in the wilderness in a wet uniform. They are isolated from the outside world, unable to use e-mail and cell phones or to receive packages from their parents. At West Point, this difficult period is known as Beast Barracks, or the Beast.

"We want them to feel overwhelmed during basic training," Mike Matthews, a professor of engineering psychology at West Point, told me. "That's why we wake them up early and keep them busy until late at night. Maybe we'll give them ten assignments when there's only time for seven. How do they prioritize? Can they deal with the stress?"[9]

Not every soldier can. Historically, some 5 percent of cadets drop out during the Beast, with more than 20 percent leaving over the next four years. Because West Point is highly selective during the admissions process, and because it spends hundreds of thousands of dollars educating each cadet, the institution has sought ways to reduce its level of attrition. For decades, West Point relied on a system known as the Whole Candidate Score to predict which students were most likely to succeed at the academy. The score involved a complex statistical weighting of every measurable attribute of a cadet—physical aptitude, performance in one-on-one interviews, and academic variables such as SAT scores and high school rank.[10]

By 2003, however, Matthews had concluded that the score and other traditional selection models were rather limited and that a new approach was needed if the army was going to more accurately predict which soldiers would make it through their training. "I'd come to believe that persistence was a black box," Matthews says. "We'd never know why some cadets couldn't make it."

The problem reached a crisis point as the Iraq War dragged on, with the army experiencing a serious recruiting shortfall, especially at the officer level. The Pentagon projected that, within five years, nearly 20 percent of positions at the rank of major would be vacant or staffed by junior officers.[11] This projected shortage gave Matthews's interest in persistence at West Point a new urgency; he began asking many of the psychologists who worked with the army about his dilemma. Was there a test for persistence? Why did some people quit, while others refused to give up? How could he get his cadets to survive the Beast?

That's when Matthews heard about a graduate student at the University of Pennsylvania, Angela Duckworth.

Angela Duckworth grew up in suburban Cherry Hill, New Jersey, just across the river from Philadelphia. The child of Chinese immigrants—her father was a color chemist at DuPont, specializing in automotive refinishing—she was raised in a family with high academic expectations. The expectations paid off; Duckworth excelled in the classroom. She was accepted at Harvard, graduated magna cum laude with a degree in neurobiology, and received a Marshall Scholarship to study at Oxford. After two years of graduate school, however, she grew tired of research and accepted a position as a management consultant at McKinsey & Company.[12]

The work proved unsatisfying. Duckworth did not want to spend her life this way. She decided to make a drastic change and fastened on the idea of teaching in the inner city. She joined the Learning Project One, a struggling middle school on the Lower East Side of New York City. Duckworth taught math to seventh graders, giving lessons on fractions, decimals and solving for x. Her students showed a significant bump in test scores, but Duckworth left the school when she moved across the country.

After another few career experiments—Duckworth taught at a high school in San Francisco and then joined an educational start-up—she decided to try something completely different. In 2002, at the age of thirty-two, Duckworth applied to graduate school in psychology at the University of Pennsylvania.

Just as Duckworth began yet another new career, she started to contemplate the successes and failures of her classmates from Harvard and Oxford. Looking at the life stories of her peers, Duckworth was struck by a startling disconnect between talent and achievement. Some of her brightest, most impressive contemporaries seemed to have floundered in adult life, flitting in and out of jobs, graduate programs, even relationships. Others, who had seemed unexceptional at school, seemed to have fared far better. They had patiently worked their way up in their chosen careers and now, in their early thirties, had lives that seemed stable and even eminent. Duckworth had always thought of herself as a high achiever, but looking around, she reluctantly realized that she now belonged in the other group—the smart people who hadn't found their way.

At Penn, Duckworth started working with Martin Seligman, a psychology professor known for his work in the field of positive psychology, which seeks to apply scientific principles to the pursuit of happiness. But Duckworth wasn't interested in fleeting pleasure. She was interested in persistence, how we summon the strength to keep working when the work isn't fun at all.

Duckworth had a tough time measuring persistence in the lab. In her first experiments she asked middle-school students to solve tedious puzzles that took several minutes to complete. The data, however, had little variation. Most of the kids simply refused to quit. They could fake persistence for an afternoon.

Duckworth was discouraged, but she'd found a pursuit worth the struggle. After reflecting on the experimental mishap, Duckworth realized that her failure was actually an insight, and that the kind of persistence she was interested in was defined by its *time scale*. If self-control was about not eating a marshmallow for fifteen minutes, and conscientiousness was about following the rules during a short test, Duckworth was determined to study whatever allowed us to pursue those "higher-order" goals that take years to achieve. Life is a marathon, not a sprint, and Duckworth wanted to understand how people run the full race. What keeps us from quitting?

Experimental psychology tends to focus on measurements that can be made fast, studying differences that can be quantified before subjects get bored by the task, or before they get claustrophobic in a brain scanner. Alas, these differences are often not the differences that count most in life. It's like clocking someone in the 100-yard dash and then expecting those results to predict his or her endurance over twenty-six miles.

Here's an example of this research bias, and the blind spots it creates. In the early 1980s, Paul Sackett, a psychologist at the University of Minnesota, was asked by a group of supermarket chains to develop a method for measuring the speed of their cashiers.[13] Sackett soon came up with a clever strategy. He would use the newly installed electronic scanners to automatically record the number of items checked out by each employee during an average workday. Sackett used the scanner data to rank hundreds of cashiers according to their *typical* productivity, or how they performed day in, day out, when they didn't even know they were being monitored.

But not every supermarket had installed the new checkout machines, so Sackett had to come up with a second form of measurement. His solution was straightforward: instead of relying on the scanners, he filled several shopping carts with twenty-five items each and then asked the cashiers to check out the carts as quickly as possible. (The manager was standing nearby with a stopwatch.) This sort of measurement is known as a *maximum* test. The name is literal, as the quick test seeks to record peak performance. Because employees are being closely watched by their boss, they are highly motivated, trying to check out items as fast as possible.

Sackett began to wonder about the potential differences between the maximum and typical measures. They were supposed to be tracking the same thing—employee productivity—but Sackett worried that they were spitting out contradictory results. So he decided to give twelve hundred cashiers both measurements and compare the results. He soon discovered that the maximum and typical tests generated different rankings; the correlation between the two was shockingly small. "I'd stumbled into a big practical problem," Sackett told me. "Let's say you're a supermarket chain and you need to let go of the bottom twenty-five percent of cashiers. Depending on which test you use, you're going to come up with a very different list of employees."[14]

Sackett refers to this as the typical-maximum distinction. In recent years, it has become a major issue in the assessment of human nature. We assume that all of our maximum data will give us insight into behavior, but that assumption is often incorrect. A troubling mismatch occurs between what we attempt to quantify—those sudden peaks in performance—and what we want to know, which is how we will perform in everyday life. "These high-stakes tests can do a good job of assessing talent," Sackett says. "But typical performance isn't just about talent. It's about *talent plus effort*." It's about putting in the work over the long term, and not just during quick tests, or at the start. Emerson was right: "The years teach much which the days never know."

To understand the importance of Sackett's finding, it helps to think about close relationships. Although we attempt to make sense of the short bursts of love—it's the ecstatic high, the initial passion, the early ardor—the true import of the feeling can only be revealed over time. (Intimacy is an exercise in typical performance.) Because here is the disappointing truth: every love has its own Beast, a period of struggle that will test our commitment. What happens then is most telling, since it reveals our willingness to put in the effort, to fix what is broken, to keep going on. The surest measure of our love is not what we say. It is what we are willing to endure.

Duckworth's adviser, Martin Seligman, was intrigued by her line of speculation, but cautious about the proposal to study a trait over such an extended time, in an environment unbounded by the exacting controls of the lab. He refused to even talk with her about the subject until she found a compelling name for the attribute she wanted to study. Duckworth started proposing various words—*pluck? perseverance? courage?*—before settling on one that felt right. She was going to study *grit*.

The Search for Meaning

Frankl's death camp was liberated by American troops on April 27, 1945. He slowly made his way back to Vienna, hitchhiking on the back of an open troop transport truck. The city was in ruins—nearly a third of its residential buildings had been damaged by bombs—but Frankl returned to find news of his wife and family. The news was tragic: nearly everyone he loved was dead. His mother, his father, his brother, even Tilly.

Frankl was heartbroken. Visions of his wife had kept him alive during the war, and now she was gone. "In the camp, we believed that we had reached the lowest point—and then, when we returned, we saw that nothing has survived, that that which had kept us standing has been destroyed, that at the same time as we were becoming human again it was possible to fall deeper, into an even more boundless suffering," Frankl wrote in a letter dated September 1945. "There remains perhaps nothing more to do than cry a little and browse a little through the Psalms."[15]

Once again, Frankl considered suicide. He decided, however, that before he killed himself, he needed to finish the book that was lost in Auschwitz. "This was the only thing I wanted to do before dying," he remembered decades later. "Beyond that I didn't want to exist."[16]

So his work kept him going, if only for a little while. While most of the book was a technical introduction to logotherapy— it would eventually be called *The Doctor and the Soul*—a few pages

confronted the horrors of the war, as Frankl attempted to describe the "psychology of the concentration camp." In unsparing prose written in the present tense, Frankl investigated the
dream life of prisoners—"Usually they dream of bread, cake,
cigarettes, and a good warm bath in a tub"[17]—and the way their
waking thoughts "fasten again and again upon the same details
of past experiences," obsessing over "the most commonplace
trivialities of the past."[18] He concluded that the ultimate cru-
elty of the camps was not the misery, for man can habituate
to pain. Rather, it was a creeping nihilism among prisoners, a
conviction that all their suffering was in vain. "The character
changes in the concentration-camp inmate are both the consequences of physiological changes of state (hunger, lack of sleep,
etc.) and expression of psychological data," Frankl wrote. "But
ultimately and essentially they are a spiritual attitude."[19] The
tragedy of that sentence is that Frankl wrote it as a man whose
own spirit had been broken. This book was his last reason for
living. He would finish it and then die.

But that's not what happened. Meaning kept leaking back
into his life. After *The Doctor and the Soul* was published, Frankl's
friends insisted that he write more about his wartime experience. They said the world needed to know about the Holocaust.
So, over nine frantic days, Frankl poured out his memories to
a crew of secretaries taking dictation in his tiny apartment.[20]
Frankl talked for hours at a time, writing and rewriting out
loud; the only breaks came when he would start to weep.[21]

These spoken words would later become *Man's Search for
Meaning*, Frankl's Holocaust memoir. In the text, Frankl focused on the existential questions, how the prisoners survived
in such a hopeless place. Not surprisingly, he concluded that a
sense of meaning was the key to endurance. Frankl describes

two men on the verge of suicide. Both of the prisoners used the same argument: "They had nothing more to expect from life," so they might as well stop living in pain. Frankl, however, used his therapeutic training to convince his fellow prisoners that "life was still expecting something from them."[22] For one man, that meant thinking about his beloved child, who was waiting for him abroad. For the other man, it was his scientific research, which he wanted to finish after the war. Because these prisoners remembered that their life still had meaning, they were able to resist the temptation of suicide.

Meaning didn't save everyone. In his writings, Frankl made it clear that a sense of purpose was necessary but not sufficient, and that his survival in the Holocaust was also due to chance and guile. There was the kind capo and the stolen potatoes, which kept him from starving at Dachau. There were the little tricks to avoid the gas chambers—Frankl shaved regularly, even if it meant shaving with broken glass, because a bare face made him look healthier—and the dumb luck of not dying from dysentery. Yet Frankl continued to believe that his ability to "squeeze out some meaning," even in Auschwitz, helped keep him alive in a camp devoted to his death.[23]

After the war, Frankl's experiences in the Holocaust led him to pioneer a therapeutic technique he called dereflection. Many of his Viennese patients, he said, were stuck in self-absorption, obsessed with their own unhappiness. Frankl's solution to such crises was to "dereflect" attention from the self. While conventional psychiatric treatments focused on fixing the internal problems of the mind, Frankl insisted that the solutions to our misery were *out in the world*, and not just inside our head. The good life was not about avoiding the struggle—it was about finding something we were willing to struggle for.[24]

Dereflection represented a sharp break from conventional talk therapy. According to Freudian theory, mental health was the absence of internal conflict. But Frankl pointed out that conflict was part of the good life, and that what man needed most was a difficult goal for which to strive. "If architects want to strengthen a decrepit arch, they *increase* the load which is laid upon it, for thereby the parts are joined more firmly together," Frankl wrote. "So if therapists wish to foster their patients' mental health, they should not be afraid to create a sound amount of tension."[25]

One of Frankl's main intellectual influences was Hans Selye, an Austrian-Canadian endocrinologist who pioneered the study of animal stress. While Selye confirmed the devastating effects of chronic anxiety—it wrecked the flesh—he also realized that a certain amount of stress was necessary. (Selye dedicated his book "to those who are not afraid to enjoy the stress of a full life.")[26] In his writing, Selye distinguished between *distress* (negative) and *eustress* (positive). The difference was not in the chemistry, for most stressors led to a similar mixture of hormones in the blood. Rather, it was whether the difficult experience served a larger goal. A rat shocked at random would soon be crippled by its fear. But a rat given the same dose of stress while protecting its pups would show few side effects. Having a *reason* to suffer kept it safe.

Frankl extended this logic to human beings. He argued that modern man had misunderstood his nature. We'd come to imagine ourselves as merely a collection of primal drives, wired to seek out the simplest pleasures. But this was a tragic mistake. "Ever more people today have the means to live, but no meaning to live for," he wrote in one of his many critiques of society. Frankl believed that man craved more than food and sex and clothes, for we are material machines driven by immaterial desires. What we want most of all is not some superficial happiness, but a feeling that lasts. Someone to be happy *about*. We want this because we need it.

The Work of Love

Grit is a new name for an old idea. Duckworth knows this, which is why she's constantly citing nineteenth-century thinkers such as William James and Francis Galton. These men, she says, understood the necessity of persistence. (Galton, for instance, was convinced that "zeal" and the "capacity for hard labour" were the foundation of every success.)[27] However, Duckworth argues that we've come to neglect this virtue because persistence is hard to measure and we're obsessed with maximum tests.

Consider a largely forgotten study funded by the Educational Testing Service, which administers the SAT, GRE, and a long list of other tests designed to predict success at school and the workplace. In the early 1980s, a team of psychologists led by Warren Willingham began tracking nearly five thousand undergraduates from a variety of institutions, including Bucknell, Williams, and Kenyon.[28] They measured the college performance of the students in dozens of different ways, from grades to intramural athletics to writing samples. They generated ratings on more than one hundred different personal characteristics. The goal of the study was to identify those variables that were most predictive of undergraduate success. As expected, SAT scores were reasonably effective at predicting college grades. But they were not the best metric at predicting other forms of achievement, such as leadership positions and extracurricular accomplishments. When it came to these pursuits, one character trait proved to be far more important in shaping student outcomes. The psychologists called the trait follow-through, and they defined it as the ability to exert a "pattern of persistent effort."[29] (Interestingly, it didn't seem to matter what the students had shown persistence for, whether it was student government or cheerleading. It simply mattered that they had persisted.) Given the power of follow-through, the final report recommended that colleges and the College Board find ways to reliably measure it.[30] That never happened.

Duckworth set out to correct this oversight. She wanted to study persistence in the real world, with real people and real stakes. In 2004, she began working with Matthews on a survey to assess grit at West Point. The resulting questionnaire took only a few minutes to complete and required cadets to consider twelve straightforward statements, such as "New ideas and new projects sometimes distract me from previous ones" and "My interests change from year to year." Each statement had five possible answers, in a rising scale from "not like me at all" to "very much like me."[31] The goal of the survey was to measure two distinct aspects of personality: (1) Is a person passionate about his goals? and (2) Is he willing to sacrifice for the sake of these goals? Those high in grit are more likely to answer yes to both questions. They feel strongly about what they want—it's a persistent source of meaning—and are willing to suffer to get it.

West Point administered the grit survey on the second and third days of Beast Barracks in July 2004, sliding the test in between more than 113 other cognitive and personality measurements. After collecting the results from some twelve hundred new cadets, Duckworth and Matthews compared their grit scores to performance at the military academy. The results were convincing: those cadets who scored highest in grit (one standard deviation higher) were 60 percent more likely to survive Beast Barracks than those with average grit levels, while those low in grit were far more likely to drop out. The Grit Scale was more effective at predicting the retention of cadets than any of the Whole Candidate Score indicators, such as SAT scores or high school academic rankings.[32] "These results were a little bit humbling for the army," says Matthews. "We've spent decades fine-tuning our tests. But then this short, three-minute survey turns out to be the best predictor of summer retention."

Since pioneering the study of the character trait at West Point, Duckworth and her graduate students have shown that, in field after field, grit matters. A lot. They've demonstrated that levels of grit predict success among real estate agents, with grittier agents making more sales and sticking with the profession through the downturns. The character trait predicts completion of the army's Special Forces course[33] and advancement to the final rounds of the Scripps National Spelling Bee. It predicts graduation from the Chicago public schools[34] and retention among new teachers at Teach For America.*[35] In an early paper on grit, Duckworth and coauthors summarized the necessity of the character trait: "We suggest that one personal quality is shared by the most prominent leaders in every field. The gritty individual approaches achievement as a marathon; his or her advantage is stamina. Whereas disappointment or

---

*As Mike Matthews points out in his book *Head Strong*, grit scores increased in a "near linear fashion" with education levels, so that the group with the highest average grit scores are those who completed a postgraduate degree. The only exception to this rule, Matthews writes, are adults who reported that they had completed an associate degree from a community college— their average grit scores were roughly equal to those of adults with an advanced degree. "While this finding may seem odd," Matthews writes, "keep in mind that community college students often work full-time and have families. Anyone who can balance work, family, and school must be highly motivated to succeed." Michael D. Matthews, *Head Strong: How Psychology Is Revolutionizing War* (New York: Oxford University Press, 2013), 21.

boredom signals to others that it is time to change trajectory and cut losses, the gritty individual stays the course."[36]

There is something inherently appealing about the idea of grit. It describes a world in which talent is earned, a natural meritocracy in which those who are successful achieve their success through diligence and discipline. The science of grit affirms all of our maxims about achievement. It contradicts no clichés.

Except one. We tend to assume that career success requires dedication and perseverance—that's why those with grit do better—but that success at love is easy, effortless, a piece of cake. Once we fall in love, the love is supposed to take care of itself. If the love feels too hard—if the relationship demands grit—then it surely wasn't meant to be. We give up on people who make us work.

This is wrong on every level. One of the most surprising aspects of grit is the way it seems to shape our closest relationships. Succeeding at love is just as difficult as preparing for the Scripps National Spelling Bee or practicing jump shots or marching in the summer heat at West Point. The reality of romance is that it's not just about romantic things: every relationship is also a test of stubbornness and endurance, a measure of our willingness to stay committed even when we'd rather run away.

Duckworth and colleagues demonstrated the importance of grit in loving relationships by collecting grit scores from 6,362 middle-aged adults. After analyzing the data, and controlling for the influence of other personality traits and demographic factors, the scientists found that gritty men were 17 percent more likely to stay married.[37] If you're not gritty, then you might be passionate about your wife, but the passion will never become sustainable. When the relationship requires exertion, you will be more likely to disappear, succumbing to the temptation of disengagement and extramarital affairs. Love is the ultimate source of lasting pleasure, but let's be honest: it's also the hardest work. That's why it takes grit.

And sometimes gritted teeth. When it comes to human relationships, invocations of "hard work" are usually a euphemism for conflict and arguments. In one study, the psychologists John Gottman and Lowell Krokoff looked at the correlation between the amount of "verbal conflict" experienced by couples and the duration and happiness of their marriage. At first, the statistics seemed straightforward: spouses who fought more often were less satisfied with their relationship. However, when the scientists repeated the survey with the same couples three years later, the effect had *reversed*, as the spouses who argued the least were now more likely to have got divorced.[38] The psychologist John Gottman summarizes the results: "For a marriage to have real staying power, couples need to air their differences. In other words, what may lead to temporary misery in a marriage—disagreement and anger—may be healthy for it in the long run. Rather than being destructive, occasional anger can be a resource that helps the marriage improve over time."[39] The moral is that relationships only survive when spouses confront their failings, when they have the grit to talk about their mistakes and regrets. Such confrontation is stressful, but it's also essential, at least if we want the attachment to last.

True love, in this model, is best understood as a test of stamina. *Literally*. In the Grant Study, that epic longitudinal project run by George Vaillant, the Harvard men were subjected to an arduous treadmill task while still in college. (They had to run up a 6 percent incline at seven miles per hour for five minutes, or until they gave up.) While the men were running, the scientists measured their pulse and blood lactate levels. To the surprise of the scientists, fitness levels didn't predict physical health. However, the passage of time revealed a much stranger correlation: those men who lasted longer on the treadmill were far more likely to have successful attachments.[40] And this wasn't just about running—Vaillant notes that, in general, measures of "endurance and stoicism" among the Grant subjects were closely linked to measures of love.[41] "These [running] tests were telling us something about toughness," Vaillant says. "They show us that toughness is not just about running fast, but that it also helps us in the realm of relationships." In one of his most recent write-ups of the Grant Study, Vaillant concludes that there are only "two pillars of happiness." "One is love," he says. "The other is finding a way of coping with life that does not push love away."[42]

Vaillant's point is that making love endure, especially when life is difficult, requires an inner strength. It takes sinewy muscles and a sturdy spine, just like running a marathon or finishing basic training. The question is, where does this strength come from? How do we develop the toughness that relationships require? What allows us to stay committed?

The answer is a paradox, a line of circular logic: *we learn how to love by being loved*. While John Watson and his cohort believed that love made us soft and weak and spoiled, it actually does the opposite. Unless we experience the tenderness of another person, then we won't have the fortitude to love someone else or have the audacity to stay devoted. We won't understand what it takes. Attachment is a great rewiring, altering all the parts of us that it touches. It is the why that lets us bear with almost any how.

This theme repeats throughout life, like a tonic chord in

a symphony. Again and again, the science reveals a correlation between the presence of loving relationships and the ability to handle stressful events, from missile attacks to money problems, chronic pain to diabetes, combat training to college exams.[43] (As the psychiatrist Eric Berne once said, "Love is nature's psychotherapy."[44]) It's what allows those securely attached children to become more independent in their kindergarten classroom; it's why the sensitivity of parents is one of the best predictors of a child's graduation from high school; it's why people confident in the affection of their spouse also exhibit more confidence at work, less burdened by the fear of failure.[45]

The power of attachment holds even in the most extreme conditions. Mike Matthews, the West Point psychologist, interviewed 116 army captains and majors who had recently returned from combat operations in Iraq or Afghanistan. He asked the officers to write an essay about their most difficult wartime experience. Then he asked them which of twenty-four different character strengths had been most useful in dealing with the challenges of combat. Teamwork was number one, followed by bravery. But the third most important character strength was much more surprising, at least to me. According to the officers, the "capacity to love" was a critical skill on the battlefield. Because these men loved their fellow soldiers, they were able to handle the trauma and turmoil of war.[*46]

---

[*]Matthews also asked the army officers what they'd learned from war, how combat had improved their character. (He was interested in the mechanisms of post-traumatic growth.) The most popular answer was that battle had made them better at teamwork. The second most popular answer, however, involved the "capacity to love." It might seem like a contradiction, but the rigors of wartime had taught these men that there is no substitute for close relationships. You can't make it on your own.

Another study, by a team of scientists led by Zahava Solomon at Tel Aviv University, studied the resiliency of 164 Israeli prisoners of war from the 1973 Yom Kippur War.[47] Their goal was to understand the variation, to figure out why some soldiers suffered from the crippling symptoms of PTSD while others were able to lead healthy and productive lives after being released. They discovered that the "hardiest" soldiers—those who seemed best able to deal with their searing experiences—were more likely to have secure attachment styles. When the prisoners were later asked how they dealt with captivity, those who were securely attached were much more likely to say that they drew strength from memories of their loved ones.[48] These "imagined encounters" helped them cope, which is why a secure attachment style was associated with less severe PTSD symptoms.

Love, however, is not an anesthetic. Those securely attached POWs didn't suffer less because they loved someone on the outside. If anything, they probably suffered more, because they knew what they were missing. But they had a *reason* to suffer, and that made all the difference.

This doesn't mean we should never give up on anything, or that every relationship can be saved, or that attachment is always worth it. Rather, it suggests that we should take a constant inventory of whom and what we love, reflecting on that short list of people we can't live without. Grit is a scarce mental resource; we shouldn't squander it on bad pursuits or second-rate attachments, for even the best ones are hard enough.* Besides, unless

---

*Grit is not always a good thing. One study, led by Gale Lucas at USC, found that the grittiest people are sometimes too stubborn: because they hate quitting, they end up getting stuck with bad prospects. Gale M. Lucas et al., "When the going gets tough: Grit predicts costly perseverance," *Journal of Research in Personality* 59 (2015): 15–22.

we're truly in love—unless the feeling survives over time—then our endurance will eventually exhaust itself. Staying power can't be faked. It is just about the only thing that can't be faked.

The vision of love that emerges from these studies is a long way from Romeo and Juliet. Those teenagers pretended that love is a pleasure so intense it eclipses every pain. They assumed that relationships provide their own forward momentum, and that finding an enduring love was simply a matter of falling for the right person. But that is a fantasy, a most dangerous myth. Love is not something we solve at first sight—it is what solves us over time, revealing whom we can become, and what we cannot live without.

The Choice

There is a recurring thesis here, a shared concern that connects Frankl's search for meaning to the gritty loyalty described by Duckworth.[*49] The concern is the hardship of love, how what matters most in life also requires the most effort. (As Rilke wrote, "Trust in what is difficult.")[50] For Frankl, this meant that a good therapist should never undersell the struggle of meaning, for "what is to give light must endure burning."

---

[*]Duckworth has based her entire science on the challenge of achieving long-term goals, whether it's graduating from West Point or staying married. In one of her most recent studies, Duckworth found that levels of grit were unrelated to a pleasure-seeking lifestyle; the grittiest souls were the least likely to be hedonists, seeking out temporary fixes of dopamine in the kitchen and shopping mall. Instead, she found that grit was associated with a tendency to search for meaning and engagement, even when it made people a little miserable in the short term. Katherine R. Von Culin, Eli Tsukayama, and Angela L. Duckworth, "Unpacking grit: Motivational correlates of perseverance and passion for long-term goals," *Journal of Positive Psychology*, ahead-of-print (2014): 1–7.

To make his point, Frankl liked to tell a story about the time an American doctor showed up at his Viennese office. The doctor asked Frankl to explain, in a single sentence, the difference between Freudian psychoanalysis and logotherapy. Frankl's response was to first ask the American to describe, in one sentence, the essence of psychoanalysis. "This was his answer," Frankl writes. " 'During psychoanalysis, the patient must lie down on a couch and tell you things which sometimes are very disagreeable to tell.' "[51] The patients have to confess their secret desires and darkest wishes. Frankl wasted no time offering his reply: "In logotherapy, the patient may remain sitting erect but he must hear things which sometimes are very disagreeable to hear."

What are these "disagreeable" things? Although Frankl believed that human love gave us meaning in its most basic form—it is what kept him alive in the camps—he also knew that it tested us like nothing else. We will yell at our spouse and be disappointed by our kids. Our friends will let us down; our parents will fuck us up. Sometimes, loving will feel like too much, like more than we can bear. Some days all we feel is the burn.[52]

But at such low moments we must look for the light, even when it's faint and hard to see. If the meaning persists, if we are still in love, then we can't give up. Not yet. Instead, we have to trust in what lasts. We have to work to *make* it last. In the midst of the marital fight, we have to think about forgiveness, and maybe the makeup sex that comes after. In the middle of the night, when the toddler has puked in our bed, we have to remind ourselves that, one day, even this scene will make us laugh. When a friend doesn't call us back, and God feels far away, and we are wondering why the hell we bother, we have to remember what we once felt and what we will feel again. Love has no destination—it is a journey into itself, and on the most difficult days the best we can do is marvel at our slow progress, at all the ways we've been changed by a feeling.

I realize these words aren't very useful. I have so little practical advice. There is no five-step plan for increasing grit levels, nor is there a pill that can give us purpose. The science can offer us little more than perspective, reminding us of what matters amid so much that does not. Marriage is hard, kids are hard, faith is hard. *Life is hard*, at least if you're doing it right. But there is no other way. Frankl was once asked by students to summarize the lesson of his life and work. He wrote his answer down on a piece of paper and then asked the crowd to guess what he'd written. One student got his words exactly right: "The meaning of your life is to help others find the meaning of theirs."[53]

Frankl knew this was an unlikely sell. He knew how vague it sounded, that he was peddling romantic advice in a cynical age. But he also believed it. A man who survived the railway platform at Auschwitz, Frankl said, could not "avoid asking himself, day by day, whether he has been worthy of that [God's] grace."[54] The only way to be worthy is to search relentlessly for a purpose. To seek out attachments. To sacrifice for those we care most about.

None of us are here for long. Even when we are here, most of what we do will vanish, neglected by nerves always looking for the next new thing. It's possible to live a life in pursuit of these temporary pleasures, chasing after objects that will become as noticeable as our underwear. It's entirely possible to run away from every attachment, to lock down the heart so it will never get broken.

So we must choose. We can curse the pain. We can look at the light and think of the burning. Or we can marvel at our ability to make something of it all, to find a feeling that endures amid so much that does not.

From dust to dust, with just love in between.

There is no avoiding it: the story I've told is sentimental.

Love heals all. Love makes us strong. Love lets us go on.

These are clichés. They are also true.

For Frankl, these truths were not abstract. They defined his life. In 1946, the same year he wrote *Man's Search for Meaning*, Frankl met an operating-room assistant named Elly Schwindt. He courted her with a passion he didn't know he still had, dressing up for their dates in a ragged coat and a pair of women's shoes that fit his small feet. (He couldn't afford a better outfit.) The following year Viktor and Elly married. They didn't have enough money for a wedding, so they invited a few friends over to their studio apartment for "ice cream" made from water and sugar and food coloring. "We were so happy," Elly would later remember. "We had almost nothing, but you have no idea how happy we were."[55]

Viktor and Elly went on to have a remarkable fifty-two-year marriage and partnership. As Viktor was the first to admit, Elly pieced him back together; she became that source of meaning he couldn't exist without. Frankl's writing reflects this transformation. In his later essays, he spends less time on the horrors of Auschwitz and more on the ordinary pleasures of attachment; the Holocaust survivor had become a family man. He would eventually conclude that humans were built to crave "self-transcendence," which he defined as being in a relationship with "someone other than oneself."[56] This is what Elly had taught him.

In his early nineties, Viktor Frankl's heart began to give out. Before his last surgery—an operation from which he would never awake—he called Elly to his side. In *When Life Calls Out to Us*, Haddon Klingberg Jr.'s biography of the couple, Elly recounts their last conversation. "I have inscribed one of my books to you and I have hidden it in our apartment," Viktor whispered. "There you will find it."[57] It took a few months of searching, but Elly finally found the book. Viktor had chosen one of his more obscure titles, a collection of lectures published in 1950 on the treatment of *Homo patiens*, or suffering man. His scrawl was barely legible—Viktor had lost his eyesight years before—but Elly could make out the slanted markings on the last blank page:

For Elly,
Who succeeded in changing a suffering man into a loving man.[58]

It's the last line of a good life, a testament to the power of love. This is what the best relationships do: they save us. They give us a reason to go on.

I wish I'd learned this truth in a different way. But at least I learned it before it was too late. At least I know it now. That is my consolation. And so, late at night, I found myself drawn to this flickering screen. I sat down in the dark. I thought about all that I'd learned and everyone that I love. And I began typing these words.

CODA

Scarcity

1

I wrote this book during a difficult time. It reflects the preoccupations of a man in the middle of things:[1] chasing after his young kids, working on his marriage, trying to do decent work. The book was born from a few simple questions: How does love go on? What makes it last? Why can't we live without it?

I don't have many answers, but I have learned to find meaning in the questions. I have tried my best to live them out.* Most days, I don't have much of a choice. The glory of

---

*Here's Rilke, from his *Letters to a Young Poet*: "Try to love the questions themselves, like locked rooms, or books written in a foreign language. Do not now look for the answers. They cannot now be given to you, because you would not be able to live them. And the point is, to live everything. Live the questions now. Perhaps then, someday far in the future, you will gradually, without even noticing it, live your way into the answer."

the middle—being somewhere between the thrilling start of love and its tragic end—is that I'm fully absorbed in the labor of attachment. My days are defined by its demands and delights, swallowed whole by the rituals of diapers and naps and the drive to school. This time of life might not seem romantic, but I've found it to be inlaid with all sorts of tender pleasures.

I did not expect these pleasures. And they often catch me by surprise. But such is family life: sometimes, you can't believe whom you've become or what you're laughing at or where you most want to be. Our attachments bend us in funny ways.

People change. That simple fact is one of the great themes of the longitudinal studies in this book. When you study souls over time, you soon discover that time cannot be ignored, for nobody stays the same. People adapt to life, and life adapts to them. As George Vaillant writes, "Our journeys through this world are filled with discontinuities."[2]

This is affirming news: we never stop growing. The self is a verb. And yet, amid all the flux, it's only human to wish for a constant, some shard of truth that won't get worn down. So here is mine. This is what I've learned in the middle of things. This is what I hope I don't forget, no matter what happens next.

2

The world is defined by scarcity: there's never enough of anything. Living beings only evolve when demand exceeds supply; we exist in the shadow of want. The same principle exists at every layer and level. Economics is preoccupied with shortfall, but so is modern psychology, which treats the brain as a bounded machine. If we stare at this, we can't see that; if we're thinking of that, we can't think of this. There are trade-offs all the way down.

It's only natural to assume that love obeys the same dismal logic, that the human heart is a muscle of limited strength and even less capacity. This means that every new love must require the sacrifice of an old one; attachment is a zero-sum game.

But my experience suggests that love escapes the curse of scarcity. To fall in love with someone doesn't make it harder to love someone else. It makes it *easier*. We know what it takes; the sinew is there; the illusions are not. The feeling expands to fit the need.

The boundlessness of love is the mystery I think about now. If this book began with the paradox of love's endurance, it ends with the wonder of its abundance. It's the first truth you learn as a parent, and then—because it makes no sense—you have to learn it again. Before my son was born, I was convinced I could never love him the way I loved my daughter. My heart didn't have the space. My life didn't have the time. I was too attached to get attached all over again. But then he was here, a crying lump of need, and I felt all the same feelings, welling up from my most primal parts.

Isn't that the way of the world? We fall for another person. Maybe the person falls for us. Then, if we're lucky, the eros of those early days gives way to something stranger, stronger, more sustainable. The heart is full, but the heart is greedy. The heart has appetites. So we start a family. We love these little people we made; they are so delightful. Time passes. Everyone changes. The attachments remain.

One day, when I reread these words, I hope my heart and home are even more crowded. I hope I'm even more aware that love resists all the obvious constraints, that it does not get old and is not scarce.

The world has rules. This feeling breaks them all.

3

When I began this book, I wanted to understand the mysteries of love. I wanted to grasp its sly mechanics. But now I see there is no solution. The magic trick is actually magic. We can glimpse the power of love, the way it shapes our lives, but the feeling arises and endures for reasons we can't begin to explain.

The mystery of love is the mystery of our lives: we are bound by a force we cannot fathom, driven by desires we cannot deny. Because there is no resisting the feeling: our existence depends on it. So we keep falling in love and falling again. That, at least, is what it feels like to me. The best days are the ones when I look around at all these people in my life, these people in my heart, and I think, *This is it.*

NOTES

Introduction: *Habituation*

1   Arthur Rimbaud, *A Season in Hell*, "Hallucinations 1," as translated in Alan Badiou, *In Praise of Love* (New York: New Press, 2012).
2   Richard F. Thompson and William A. Spencer, "Habituation: A model phenomenon for the study of neuronal substrates of behavior," *Psychological Review* 73.1 (1966): 16.
3   Philip Brickman, Dan Coates, and Ronnie Janoff-Bulman, "Lottery winners and accident victims: Is happiness relative?," *Journal of Personality and Social Psychology* 36.8 (1978): 917.
4   Richard Thompson, "Habituation: A history," *Neurobiology of Learning and Memory*, 2008; and Mitch Griffin, Barry J. Babin, and Doan Modianos, "Shopping values of Russian consumers: The impact of habituation in a developing economy," *Journal of Retailing* 76.1 (2000): 33–52.
5   Lorne Campbell and Bruce J. Ellis, "Commitment, Love, and Mate Retention," in *The Handbook of Evolutionary Psychology*, ed. David Buss (New York: John Wiley & Sons, 2005).
6   Helen Fisher, *Why We Love: The Nature and Chemistry of Romantic Love* (New York: Macmillan, 2004); and Arthur Aron et al., "Reward, motivation, and emotion systems associated with early-stage intense romantic love," *Journal of Neurophysiology* 94.1 (2005): 327–37.
7   Andreas Bartels and Semir Zeki, "The neural correlates of maternal and romantic love," *NeuroImage*, November 2004; Andreas Bartels and Semir Zeki, "The neural basis of romantic love," *NeuroReport*, November 2000; and Helen Fisher, Arthur Aron, and Lucy L. Brown, "Romantic love: An fMRI study of a neural mechanism for mate choice," *Journal of Comparative Neurology* 493.1 (2005): 58–62.
8   E. E. Cummings, *No Thanks* (New York: Liveright, 1998), 61.

1: Attachment

1   Emily Dickinson, *The Complete Poems* (Boston: Back Bay Books, 1976), 433.

2   Steven J. Haggbloom et al., "The 100 most eminent psychologists of the 20th century," *Review of General Psychology* 6.2 (2002): 139.

3   Kerry W. Buckley, *Mechanical Man: John Broadus Watson and the Beginnings of Behaviorism* (New York: Guilford Press, 1989), 1–3.

4   Ibid., 5.

5   Ibid., 7.

6   Ibid., 10–12.

7   Ibid., 15.

8   Ibid., 39.

9   Ibid., 40.

10 Ibid., 81.

11 John B. Watson, "Psychology as the behaviorist views it," *Psychological Review* 20 (1913): 158–77.

12 Ibid., 158.

13 Buckley, *Mechanical Man*, 75.

14 Ibid., 86.

15 John B. Watson and Rosalie Rayner, "Conditioned emotional reactions," *Journal of Experimental Psychology* 3.1 (1920): 1.

16 Ben Harris, "Whatever happened to Little Albert?," *American Psychologist* 34.2 (1979): 151.

17 Ibid.

18 Buckley, *Mechanical Man*, 124, 128.

19 Ann Hulbert, *Raising America* (New York: Knopf, 2003), 125.

20 John Watson and Rosalie Watson, *Psychological Care of Infant and Child* (New York: W. W. Norton, 1928), 82.

21 Ibid., 43.

22 http://www.jhu.edu/jhumag/0400web/35.html.

23 Mark Rilling, "John Watson's paradoxical struggle to explain Freud," *American Psychologist* 55.3 (2000): 301, http://www.ncbi.nlm.nih.gov/pubmed/10743249.

24 Suzan Van Dijken, *John Bowlby: His Early Life* (London: Free Association Books, 1998), 20.

25 Ibid., 21.

26 Ibid., 27.

27 John Bowlby, *Can I Leave My Baby?* (London: National Association for Mental Health, 1958), 7; and Frank C. P. van der Horst, *John Bowlby—from Psychoanalysis to Ethology: Unraveling the Roots of Attachment Theory* (New York: Wiley, 2011), 6.

28 Robert Karen, *Becoming Attached* (Oxford: Oxford University Press, 1994), 31.
29 Ibid.
30 Van Dijken, *John Bowlby*, 85.
31 Ibid., 90.
32 Ibid., 87.
33 Ibid., 51.
34 John Bowlby, "Forty-four juvenile thieves: Their characters and home life," *International Journal of Psychoanalysis* 25.19–52 (1944): 107–27.
35 Karen, *Becoming Attached*, 52.
36 Bowlby, "Forty-four juvenile thieves," 107–27.
37 http://www.bbc.co.uk/history/british/britain_wwtwo/evacuees_01 .shtml.
38 John Bowlby, Emanuel Miller, and Donald W. Winnicott, "Evacuation of small children," *British Medical Journal* 2.4119 (1939): 1202, http:// www.ncbi.nlm.nih.gov/pmc/articles/PMC2178618/?page=2.
39 Geoffrey G. Field, *Blood, Sweat, and Toil: Remaking the British Working Class, 1939-1945* (Oxford: Oxford University Press, 2011), 35.
40 John Bowlby, *The Making and Breaking of Affectional Bonds* (New York: Routledge Classics, 2005), 109.
41 Frank van der Horst and Rene van der Veer, "Changing attitudes towards the care of children in hospital: a new assessment of the influence of the work of Bowlby and Robertson in the UK, 1940–1970," *Attachment & Human Development* 11.2 (2009): 128.
42 Jeremy Holmes, *John Bowlby and Attachment Theory* (New York: Routledge, 1993), 37; and John Bowlby, *Maternal Care and Mental Health* (Geneva, Switzerland: World Health Organization, 1951), 59, http:// whqlibdoc.who.int/monograph/WHO_MONO_2_(part1).pdf.
43 Bowlby, *Maternal Care and Mental Health*, 27.
44 John Sudbery, *Human Growth and Development: An Introduction for Social Workers* (New York: Routledge, 2010), 57.
45 John Bowlby, *The Making and Breaking of Affectional Bonds* (New York: Routledge, 2012), 61.
46 Bowlby, *Maternal Care and Mental Health*, 11.
47 Deborah Blum, *Love at Goon Park* (New York: Perseus, 2002), 231.
48 Ibid., 146.
49 Harry F. Harlow, "The nature of love," *American Psychologist* 13.12 (1958).
50 Ibid.
51 Ibid.
52 Blum, *Love at Goon Park*, 231.

53   A. N. O'Connell and N. F. Russo, eds., *Models of Achievement: Reflections of Eminent Women in Psychology* (New York: Columbia University Press, 1983), 200–19, http://www.psychology.sunysb.edu/attachment/pdf/mda_autobio.pdf.

54   Gregory A. Kimble and Michael Wertheimer, eds., *Portraits of Pioneers in Psychology,* vol. 5 (Mahwah, NJ: Erlbaum, 2003), http://www.psychology.sunysb.edu/attachment/pdf/mda_inge.pdf.

55   Inge Bretherton, "The origins of attachment theory: John Bowlby and Mary Ainsworth," *Developmental Psychology* 28.5 (1992): 759.

56   O'Connell and Russo, eds., *Models of Achievement,* 200–19.

57   Mary Ainsworth, "The development of infant-mother interaction among the Ganda," in *Determinants of Infant Behavior,* ed. B. M. Foss (New York: John Wiley & Sons), 67–104.

58   Karen, *Becoming Attached,* 134.

59   Mary D. Salter Ainsworth, *Infancy in Uganda: Infant Care and the Growth of Love* (Baltimore: Johns Hopkins Press, 1967).

60   Main, "Mary D. Salter Ainsworth: Tribute and portrait," 682–736.

61   Mary Ainsworth and B. A. Wittig, "Attachment and exploratory behavior of one-year-olds in a strange situation," in *Determinants of Infant Behavior, IV,* ed. B. M. Foss (London: Methuen, 1969), 111–36.

62   Bretherton, "Origins of attachment theory," 759.

63   Mary Ainsworth, Mary C. Blehar, Everett Waters, and Sally Wall, *Patterns of Attachment: A Psychological Study of the Strange Situation* (New York: Psychology Press, 2014).

64   Gottfried Spangler and Klaus E. Grossmann, "Biobehavioral organization in securely and insecurely attached infants," *Child Development* 64.5 (1993): 1439–50; and Ashley L. Hill-Soderlund et al., "Parasympathetic and sympathetic responses to the Strange Situation in infants and mothers from avoidant and securely attached dyads," *Developmental Psychobiology* 50.4 (2008): 361–76.

65   Inge Bretherton, "Mary Ainsworth: Insightful Observer and Courageous Theoretician," in *Portraits of Pioneers in Psychology,* vol. 5, ed. Gregory A. Kimble and Michael Wertheimer (Mahwah, NJ: Erlbaum, 2003), http://www.psychology.sunysb.edu/attachment/pdf/mda_inge.pdf.

66   Ainsworth et al., *Patterns of Attachment.*

67   O'Connell and Russo, eds., *Models of Achievement,* 200–19.

68   Ibid.

69   Ainsworth et al., *Patterns of Attachment.*

70   M. D. S. Ainsworth, "Maternal sensitivity scales," 1969, http://www.psychology.sunysb.edu/attachment/measures/content/maternal%20sensitivity%20scales.pdf.

71   Ibid.

72 John Bowlby, *A Secure Base: Parent-Child Attachment and Healthy Human Development* (New York: Basic Books, 1988), 11.

73 Ibid.

74 Brooke C. Feeney, "The dependency paradox in close relationships: Accepting dependence promotes independence," *Journal of Personality and Social Psychology* 92.2 (2007): 268.

75 Bretherton, "Mary Ainsworth."

76 L. Alan Sroufe et al., *The Development of the Person: The Minnesota Study of Risk and Adaptation from Birth to Adulthood* (New York: Guilford Press, 2005), 52.

77 Ibid., 8.

78 Ibid.

79 Telephone interview, August 14, 2013.

80 Karen, *Becoming Attached*, 184.

81 Marinus Itzendoorn et al., "The relationship between quality of attachment in infancy and IQ in kindergarten," *Journal of Genetic Psychology* 1 (1988).

82 Richard Arend, Frederick Gove, and Alan Sroufe, "Continuity of individual adaptation from infancy to kindergarten: A predictive study of ego-resiliency and curiosity in preschoolers," *Child Development* 4 (1979); and Karen, *Becoming Attached*, 185.

83 Sroufe et al., *Development of the Person*, 126.

84 Ibid., 156.

85 Shane Jimerson et al., "A prospective longitudinal study of high school dropouts examining multiple predictors across development," *Journal of School Psychology* 38 (December 2000); and Sroufe et al., *Development of the Person*, 187.

86 Telephone interview, August 14, 2013.

87 K. Lee Raby et al., "The enduring predictive significance of early maternal sensitivity: Social and academic competence through age 32 years," *Child Development* 86.3 (2014).

88 http://www.cehd.umn.edu/icd/research/parent-child/docs/SRA%20 2010/Puig_SRA_2010.pdf.

89 K. Lee Raby et al., "Greater maternal insensitivity in childhood predicts greater electrodermal reactivity during conflict discussions with romantic partners in adulthood," *Psychological Science* 26.3 (2015).

90 Raby et al., "Enduring Predictive Significance."

91 Jeffry Simpson et al., "The impact of early interpersonal experience on adult romantic relationship functioning: Recent findings from the Minnesota Longitudinal Study of Risk and Adaptation," *Current Directions in Psychological Science* 20.6 (2011), http://www.psych.uncc .edu/acann/Simpson2011.pdf.

92 L. A. Sroufe et al., "Placing early attachment experiences in developmental context," in *Attachment from Infancy to Adulthood: The Major Longitudinal Studies*, ed. K. E. Grossmann, K. Grossman, and E. Waters (New York: Guilford Press, 2005), 63–64.

93 Ibid.

94 Sroufe et al., *Development of the Person*, 11.

95 Dong Liu et al., "Maternal care, hippocampal glucocorticoid receptors, and hypothalamic-pituitary-adrenal responses to stress," *Science* 277.5332 (1997): 1659–62.

96 Christian Caldji et al., "Maternal care during infancy regulates the development of neural systems mediating the expression of fearfulness in the rat," *Proceedings of the National Academy of Sciences* 95.9 (1998): 5335–40.

97 Carine I. Parent and Michael J. Meaney, "The influence of natural variations in maternal care on play fighting in the rat," *Developmental Psychobiology* 50.8 (2008): 767–76.

98 Liu et al., "Maternal care, hippocampal glucocorticoid receptors," 1659–62.

99 Marilee D. Zaharia et al., "The effects of early postnatal stimulation on Morris water-maze acquisition in adult mice: Genetic and maternal factors," *Psychopharmacology* 128.3 (1996): 227–39.

100 Charlotte M. Lindeyer, Michael J. Meaney, and Simon M. Reader, "Early maternal care predicts reliance on social learning about food in adult rats," *Developmental Psychobiology* 55.2 (2013): 168–75.

101 Dong Liu et al., "Maternal care, hippocampal synaptogenesis and cognitive development in rats," *Nature Neuroscience* 3.8 (2000): 799–806.

102 http://www.nature.com/neuro/journal/v7/n8/abs/nn1276.html; and Tamara B. Franklin et al., "Epigenetic transmission of the impact of early stress across generations," *Biological Psychiatry* 68.5 (2010): 408–15.

103 Anu-Katriina Pesonen et al., "Depressive symptoms in adults separated from their parents as children: A natural experiment during World War II," *American Journal of Epidemiology* 166.10 (2007): 1126–33.

104 Hanna Alastalo et al., "Cardiovascular health of Finnish war evacuees 60 years later," *Annals of Medicine* 41.1 (2009): 66–72.

105 Anu-Katriina Pesonen et al., "Childhood separation experience predicts HPA axis hormonal responses in late adulthood: A natural experiment of World War II," *Psychoneuroendocrinology* 35.5 (2010): 758–67.

106 Pesonen et al., "Depressive symptoms in adults," 1126–33.

107 Clancy Blair and C. Cybele Raver, "Child development in the context of adversity: Experiential canalization of brain and behavior," *American Psychologist* 67.4 (2012): 309.

108 George Vaillant, *Aging Well* (New York: Little, Brown, 2002), Appendix A.

109 George Vaillant, *Triumphs of Experience* (Cambridge, MA: Belknap Press, 2012), 67.

110 The precise criteria used to select Harvard students for the Grant Study have never been fully explained.

111 Vaillant, *Triumphs of Experience*, 65.

112 Ibid., 71–73.

113 Ibid., chap. 3, 78.

114 Ibid., 86.

115 Joshua Wolf Shenk, "What makes us happy?," *Atlantic*, June 2009, 36–53.

116 Ibid.

117 Vaillant, *Aging Well*, 97.

118 George Vaillant, *Adaptation to Life* (New York: Little, Brown, 1974), 38.

119 Vaillant, *Triumphs of Experience*, 86.

120 Interview at George Vaillant's home, July 8, 2013.

121 Vaillant, *Adaptation to Life*, 3.

122 Vaillant, *Triumphs of Experience*, 267–69.

123 Ibid., 52.

124 Ibid., 123.

125 Ibid., 134.

126 Ibid., 113.

127 Ibid., 41.

128 Vaillant, *Adaptation to Life*, 306.

129 Ibid., 301.

130 Interview at George Vaillaint's home, July 8, 2013.

131 Vaillant, *Adaptation to Life*, 302.

132 Vaillant, *Aging Well*, 133.

133 Ibid., 133–39.

134 Vaillant, *Triumphs of Experience*, 27.

135 Shenk, "What makes us happy?," 36–53.

136 Vaillant, *Triumphs of Experience*, 179.

137 Mufid James Hannush, "John B. Watson remembered: An interview with James B. Watson," *Journal of the History of Behavioral Science* 23 (1987).

138 Buckley, *Mechanical Man*, 180–83.

139 Ibid.

140 Ibid.

141 Ibid.

Interlude: *Limerence*

1 Dorothy Tennov, *Love and Limerence* (Lanham, MD: Scarborough House, 1998), 82.
2 Ibid., 23–24.
3 Ibid., 19–20.
4 Ibid.
5 Ibid., 59.
6 Dorothy Tennov, *A Scientist Looks at Love and Calls It "Limerence": The Collected Works of Dorothy Tennov* (Greenwich, CT: Great American Publishing Society, 2005).
7 Tennov, *Love and Limerence*, 104.

2: The Abraham Principle

1 Dale Peterson, *Jane Goodall: The Woman Who Redefined Man* (Boston: Houghton Mifflin Harcourt, 2006), 619–20.
2 Jane Goodall, interviewed by Andrea Miller, *Shambala Sun*, July 2013.
3 Jane Goodall, *Through a Window: My Thirty Years with the Chimpanzees of Gombe* (Boston: Houghton Mifflin Harcourt, 2010), 245.
4 Konrad Z. Lorenz, "The companion in the bird's world," *Auk* 54.3 (1937): 245–73.
5 Deborah Blum, *Love at Goon Park* (New York: Perseus, 2002), 168.
6 John Bowlby, *Can I Leave My Baby?* (London: National Association for Mental Health, 1958).
7 Suzan Van Dijken, *John Bowlby, His Early Life: A Biographical Journey into the Roots of Attachment Theory* (London: Free Association Books, 1998), 5.
8 Goodall, *Through a Window*, 245.
9 Anna Blackburn Wittman and L. Lewis Wall, "The evolutionary origins of obstructed labor: Bipedalism, encephalization, and the human obstetric dilemma," *Obstetrical & Gynecological Survey* 62.11 (2007): 739–48.
10 David F. Bjorklund, *Why Youth Is Not Wasted on the Young: Immaturity in Human Development* (New York: John Wiley & Sons, 2009), 51.
11 Hillard Kaplan, "Evolutionary and wealth flows theories of fertility: Empirical tests and new models," *Population and Development Review* 20.4 (1994): 753–91.
12 Jennifer Senior, *All Joy and No Fun* (New York: Ecco, 2014), 61.
13 Brian D. Doss et al., "The effect of the transition to parenthood on relationship quality: An 8-year prospective study," *Journal of Personality and Social Psychology* 96.3 (2009): 601.

14   Daniel Kahneman et al., "A survey method for characterizing daily
     life experience: The Day Reconstruction Method," *Science* 306.5702
     (2004).
15   http://news.harvard.edu/gazette/story/2013/02/money-marriage-kids/.
16   Personal communication, November 2012.
17   Jeffrey S. Cramer, ed., *Walden: A Fully Annotated Edition* (New Haven,
     CT: Yale University Press, 2008); and http://thoreau.eserver.org/
     walden07.html.
18   http://www.bradleypdean.com/research_writings/Bean_Field_Article
     .pdf.
19   Cramer, *Walden*, 150.
20   John Bowlby, *A Secure Base* (New York: Basic Books, 1988), 2.
21   Kerstin Erlandsson et al., "Skin-to-skin care with the father after
     cesarean birth and its effect on newborn crying and prefeeding behav-
     ior," *Birth* 34.2 (2007): 105–14.
22   Catherine Tamis LeMonda et al., "Fathers and mothers at play
     with their 2 and 3 year olds: contributions to language and cogni-
     tive development," *Child development* 75.6 (2004): 1806–20; Jacinta
     Bronte-Tinkew et al., "Involvement among resident fathers and links
     to infant cognitive outcomes," *Journal of Family Issues* (2008); and
     Michael Yogman, Daniel Kindlon, and Felton Earls, "Father involve-
     ment and cognitive/behavioral outcomes of preterm infants," *Journal
     of the American Academy of Child & Adolescent Psychiatry* 34.1 (1995):
     58–66.
23   Jeffrey Rosenberg and W. Bradford Wilcox, *The Importance of Fathers in
     the Healthy Development of Children* (Washington, DC: US Department
     of Health and Human Services, 2006), 11.
24   Edward Tronick et al., "The infant's response to entrapment between
     contradictory messages in face-to-face interaction," *Journal of the Amer-
     ican Academy of Child Psychiatry* 17.1 (1979): 1–13.
25   E. Tronick et al., "Infant emotions in normal and perturbated inter-
     actions" (paper presented at the biennial meeting of the Society for
     Research in Child Development, Denver, CO, April 1975).
26   Tronick et al., "Infant's response to entrapment," 1–13; and Daniel
     Stern, *The Interpersonal World of the Infant* (New York: Basic Books,
     1985), 150.
27   Stern, *Interpersonal World*, 150.
28   Thomas Lewis, Fari Amini, and Richard Lannon, *A General Theory of
     Love* (New York: Random House, 2007), 61.
29   Donald Winnicott, "The capacity to be alone," *International Journal of
     Psycho-Analysis* 39 (1958): 416–20, http://icpla.edu/wp-content/uploads
     /2012/10/Winnicott-D.-The-Capacity-to-be-Alone.pdf.

30 Jonas Chatel-Goldman et al., "Touch increases autonomic coupling between romantic partners," *Frontiers in Behavioral Neuroscience* 8 (2014).

31 Stern, *Interpersonal World*, 152.

32 Margaret O'Brien Caughy, Keng-Yen Huang, and Julie Lima, "Patterns of conflict interaction in mother-toddler dyads: Differences between depressed and non-depressed mothers," *Journal of Child and Family Studies* 18.1 (2009): 10–20.

33 Roshi P. Kapleau, *The Three Pillars of Zen* (New York: Anchor, 2013), 11.

34 Carroll Lachnit, "The Sunday Profile: Adopting a New Outlook: Sharon Kaplan Roszia Has Made a Career of Building Families, but Her Own Experiences Have Changed Her Approach," *Los Angeles Times*, May 14, 1995, http://articles.latimes.com/print/1995-05-14/news/ls-705_1_adoptive-parent.

35 Personal interviews, November 10, 2013, and March 5, 2014.

36 Sigmund Freud, *Reflections on War and Death* (New York: Moffat, Yard, 1918).

37 Rozsika Parker, *Mother Love, Mother Hate: The Power of Maternal Ambivalence* (New York: Basic Books, 1996), 133; and John Bowlby, *The Making and Breaking of Affectional Bonds* (New York: Routledge Classics, 2005), 10–15.

38 Parker, *Mother Love, Mother Hate*, 7.

39 Maurice Sendak, *Where the Wild Things Are* (New York: HarperCollins, 1984).

40 http://adoptionvoicesmagazine.com/adoptive-parents/adoption-makes-strange-relationships/#.UqjqKqSYZ74.

41 Jerome Kagan, *The Nature of the Child* (New York: Basic Books, 1994), 60–61.

42 Robert Karen, *Becoming Attached* (Oxford: Oxford University Press, 1994), 260.

43 Kagan, *Nature of the Child*, 62.

44 Karen, *Becoming Attached*, 261.

45 Klaus Grossmann, Karin Grossmann, and Everett Waters, eds., *Attachment from Infancy to Adulthood: The Major Longitudinal Studies* (New York: Guilford Press, 2005), 125.

46 Ibid., 130.

47 Karin Grossmann and Klaus E. Grossmann, "The impact of attachment to mother and father at an early age on children's psychosocial development through young adulthood," *Encyclopedia on Early Childhood Development*, 2005, 1–6, http://www.child-encyclopedia.com/Pages/PDF/GrossmannANGxp_rev.pdf.

48 K. Grossmann et al., "Maternal sensitivity and newborns' orientation responses as related to quality of attachment in northern Germany," *Monographs of the Society for Research in Child Development* 50.1–2 (1985): 233–56.

49 Karen, *Becoming Attached*, 264.

50 Suzanne M. Bianchi, "Family change and time allocation in American families," *The Annals of the American Academy of Political and Social Science* 638.1 (2011): 21–44.

51 Dong Liu et al., "Maternal care, hippocampal synaptogenesis and cognitive development in rats," *Nature Neuroscience* 3.8 (2000): 799–806.

52 James R. Flynn, *What Is Intelligence?: Beyond the Flynn Effect* (Cambridge: Cambridge University Press, 2007), 43, 104–5.

53 Richard Lynn, "What has caused the Flynn effect? Secular increases in the Development Quotients of infants," *Intelligence* 37.1 (2009): 16–24.

54 Senior, *All Joy and No Fun*, 128.

55 Dymphna C. van den Boom, "Neonatal irritability and the development of attachment," in *Temperament in Childhood*, ed. G. A. Kohnstamm et al. (New York: John Wiley & Sons, 1989), 299–318.

56 Karen, *Becoming Attached*, 304.

57 Dymphna C. van den Boom, "The influence of temperament and mothering on attachment and exploration: An experimental manipulation of sensitive responsiveness among lower-class mothers with irritable infants," *Child Development* 65.5 (1994): 1457–77.

58 Ibid., 1472.

59 Dante Cicchetti, Fred A. Rogosch, and Sheree L. Toth, "Fostering secure attachment in infants in maltreating families through preventive interventions," *Development and Psychopathology* 18.03 (2006): 623–49.

60 Ibid., 636.

61 Ibid., 637.

62 Richard Reeves and Kimberly Howard, "The parenting gap," Center on Children and Families at the Brookings Institution, 11, http://www.brookings.edu/research/papers/2013/09/09-parenting-gap-social-mobility-wellbeing-reeves.

63 Shanta R. Dube et al., "Adverse childhood experiences and personal alcohol abuse as an adult," *Addictive Behaviors* 27.5 (2002): 713–25.

64 Shanta R. Dube et al., "Childhood abuse, neglect, and household dysfunction and the risk of illicit drug use: The adverse childhood experiences study," *Pediatrics* 111.3 (2003): 564–72.

65 Ralph Waldo Emerson, *The Spiritual Emerson: Essential Writings by Ralph Waldo Emerson* (Boston: Beacon Press, 2003), 215.

66   Randall Jarrell, *No Other Book: Selected Essays* (New York: HarperCollins, 2000), 185.

3: The Marriage Plot

1   http://www.darwinproject.ac.uk/darwins-notes-on-marriage.
2   Ibid.
3   http://sites.duke.edu/theatrst130s02s2011mg3/files/2011/05/McPherson-et-al-Soc-Isolation-2006.pdf.
4   Robert D. Putnam, *Bowling Alone: The Collapse and Revival of American Community* (Simon & Schuster, 2001), 98–100.
5   Claire Cain Miller, "The Divorce Surge Is Over, but the Myth Lives On," *New York Times*, December 2, 2014, http://nyti.ms/1rSon3Y.
6   Michel Montaigne, *The Complete Essays of Montaigne* (Palo Alto, CA: Stanford University Press, 1958), 647.
7   Ibid.
8   K. Daniel O'Leary et al., "Is long-term love more than a rare phenomenon? If so, what are its correlates?," *Social Psychological and Personality Science* 3.2 (2012): 241–49.
9   Christine M. Proulx, Heather M. Helms, and Cheryl Buehler, "Marital quality and personal well-being: A meta-analysis." *Journal of Marriage and Family* 69.3 (2007): 585.
10   http://faculty.wcas.northwestern.edu/eli-finkel/FinkelAIF_AllOrNothingMarriage.mp4, at 15:45.
11   Cindy Hazan and Phillip Shaver, "Romantic love conceptualized as an attachment process," *Journal of Personality and Social Psychology* 52.3 (1987): 511.
12   Marco Del Giudice, "Sex differences in romantic attachment: A meta-analysis," *Personality and Social Psychology Bulletin* 37.2 (2011): 193–214.
13   Phillip Shaver and Mario Mikulincer, *Attachment in Adulthood: Structure, Dynamics and Change* (New York: Guilford Press, 2007), 308.
14   Ibid., 314.
15   Ibid., 301–23, 350–53.
16   Jeffry A. Simpson, William S. Rholes, and Julia S. Nelligan, "Support seeking and support giving within couples in an anxiety-provoking situation: The role of attachment styles," *Journal of Personality and Social Psychology* 62.3 (1992): 434.
17   http://psycnet.apa.org/journals/psp/62/3/434/.
18   John Bowlby, *A Secure Base* (New York: Basic Books, 1988), 61.
19   Cindy Hazan and Phillip R. Shaver, "Attachment as an organizational framework for research on close relationships," *Psychological Inquiry* 5.1 (1994): 1–22.

20 Ibid., 14.

21 Ellen Berscheid and Elaine (Walster) Hatfield, "A little bit about love," *Foundations of Interpersonal Attraction* 379 (1974).

22 Elaine Hatfield and G. William Walster, *A New Look at Love* (Lanham, MD: University Press of America, 1985), 9.

23 Bianca P. Acevedo et al., "Neural correlates of long-term intense romantic love," *Social Cognitive and Affective Neuroscience* (2011).

24 Edward Carr et al., "The cellular composition of the human immune system is shaped by age and cohabitation," *Nature Immunology* (2016).

25 Joseph Alpert, "Philematology: the science of kissing," *American Journal of Medicine* 126.6 (2013): 466.

26 Erich Fromm, *Art of loving* (New York: Continuum, 2000), vii.

27 Ibid., 97.

28 Tara Parker-Pope, *For Better* (New York: Plume, 2011), 275.

29 Scott Coltrane, "Research on household labor," *Journal of Marriage and the Family* 62.4 (2000).

30 John Gottman and Nan Silver, *What Makes Love Last?* (New York: Simon & Schuster, 2012), 101.

31 Duane W. Crawford et al., "Compatibility, leisure, and satisfaction in marital relationships," *Journal of Marriage and Family* 64.2 (2002): 433–49.

32 Daniel Wile, *After the Honeymoon: How Conflict Can Improve Your Relationship* (Daniel Wile Publisher, 2008).

33 John Gottman, *The Marriage Clinic* (New York: W. W. Norton, 1999), 56.

34 R. Chris Fraley and Phillip R. Shaver, "Adult romantic attachment: Theoretical developments, emerging controversies, and unanswered questions," *Review of General Psychology* 4.2 (2000): 132, 148.

35 Christina Stefanou and Marita McCabe, "Adult attachment and sexual functioning: A review of past research," *Journal of Sexual Medicine* 9 (2012).

36 Shaver and Mikulincer, *Attachment in Adulthood*, 356.

37 Ibid., 350.

38 George Loewenstein et al., "Does increased sexual frequency enhance happiness?," *Journal of Economic Behavior & Organization* 116 (2015): 206–18.

39 David G. Blanchflower and Andrew J. Oswald, "Money, sex and happiness: An empirical study," *Scandinavian Journal of Economics* 106.3 (2004): 393–415; and http://nyti.ms/1LlWuuw.

40 Amy Muise et al., "Keeping the spark alive: Being motivated to meet a partner's sexual needs sustains sexual desire in long-term romantic relationships," *Social Psychological and Personality Science*, August 2012.

41 Sue Johnson, *Hold Me Tight: Seven Conversations for a Lifetime of Love* (New York: Little, Brown, 2008), 185–86.
42 Ibid., 186–87.
43 Ibid., 7.
44 Amy Sohn, "First Comes Sex Talk with These Renegades of Couples Therapy," *New York Times*, July 1, 2015.
45 Telephone interview with Farahad and Sameera Zama, September 7, 2013.
46 Stephanie Coontz, *Marriage, a History: How Love Conquered Marriage* (New York: Penguin, 2006), 6.
47 Ibid., 147.
48 Tulika Jaiswal, *Indian Arranged Marriages: A Social Psychological Perspective* (New York: Routledge, 2014), 1.
49 Ibid., 12.
50 Paul Yelsma and Kuriakose Athappilly, "Marital satisfaction and communication practices: Comparisons among Indian and American couples," *Journal of Comparative Family Studies* 19.1 (1988): 37–54; and Usha Gupta and Pushpa Singh, "An exploratory study of love and liking and type of marriages," *Indian Journal of Applied Psychology* 2 (1982); and http://www.scientificamerican.com/podcast/episode.cfm?id=arranged-marriages-can-be-real-love-10-03-11.
51 Robert Epstein, "How science can help you fall in love," *Scientific American Mind* 20.7 (2010): 26–33.
52 Pamela Regan et al., "Relationship outcomes in Indian-American love-based and arranged marriages," *Psychological Reports* 110 (2012).
53 Robert Epstein, Mayuri Pandit, and Mansi Thakar, "How love emerges in arranged marriages: Two cross-cultural studies," *Journal of Comparative Family Studies* 44.3 (2013).
54 http://www.nytimes.com/2009/06/07/fashion/07love.html?page wanted=all.
55 http://www.jstor.org/discover/10.2307/3773618?uid=2&uid=4&sid=21102635755277.
56 *Plato's* Symposium: *A Translation by Seth Benardete with Commentaries by Allan Bloom and Seth Benardete* (University of Chicago Press, 2001), 21.
57 http://www2.warwick.ac.uk/fac/soc/economics/staff/phd_students/backus/girlfriend/why_i_dont_have_a_girlfriend.pdf.
58 C. Raymond Knee, "Implicit theories of relationships: Assessment and prediction of romantic relationship initiation, coping, and longevity," *Journal of Personality and Social Psychology* 74.2 (1998): 360.
59 Rebecca Fishbein. "Man behind 'Why I Don't Have a Girlfriend' theory to marry," Today.com, May 24, 2013.

60   Harville Hendrix, *Getting the Love You Want* (New York: Macmillan, 2009), 50.

61   Eli Finkel et al., "Online dating: A critical analysis from the perspective of psychological science," *Psychology Science in the Public Interest* 13 (2012); and Paul Eastwick and Eli Finkel, "When and why do ideal partner preferences affect the process of initiating and maintaining romantic relationships?," *Journal of Personality and Social Psychology* 101 (2011).

62   http://nyti.ms/19twg80.

63   Portia Dyrenforth et al., "Predicting relationship and life satisfaction from personality in nationally representative samples from three countries," *Journal of Personality and Social Psychology* 99.4 (2010).

64   http://www.pewinternet.org/2013/10/21/online-dating-relationships/.

65   Eli Finkel et al., "Online dating: A critical analysis from the perspective of psychological science," *Psychology Science in the Public Interest* 13 (2012).

66   http://www.scientificamerican.com/article.cfm?id=scientific-flaws-online-dating-sites&page=2.

67   Jordi Quoidbach, Daniel T. Gilbert, and Timothy D. Wilson, "The end of history illusion," *Science* 339.6115 (2013): 96–98.

68   Richard Jenkyns, *A Fine Brush on Ivory: An Appreciation of Jane Austen* (Oxford: Oxford University Press, 2007), ix.

69   Jane Austen, *Emma* (New York: W. W. Norton, 2000), 56.

70   Ibid., 77.

71   Ibid., 295–96.

72   Ibid., 15.

73   Ibid., 1.

74   Jane Austen, *Sense and Sensibility: An Annotated Edition*, ed. Patricia Meyers Sparks (Cambridge, MA: Belknap Press, 2013), 103.

75   Austen, *Emma*, 234.

76   Ibid.

77   William Deresiewicz, *A Jane Austen Education: How Six Novels Taught Me about Love, Friendship, and the Things That Really Matter* (New York: Penguin, 2011), 225.

78   Ibid., 223.

79   Claire Tomalin, *Jane Austen: A Life* (New York: Knopf, 1997), 183.

80   John Mordechai Gottman, Lynn Fainsilber Katz, and Carole Hooven, *Meta-emotion: How Families Communicate Emotionally* (New York: Psychology Press, 1997), 45–85.

81   Telephone interview, September 3, 2013.

82   Gottman, Katz, and Hooven, *Meta-emotion*, 45–85.

83   Gottman, *Marriage Clinic*, 320.

84   Ibid., 307; and John Gottman et al., *What Predicts Divorce?* (Hillsdale, NJ: Lawrence Erlbaum Associates, 1996).

85   Gottman, Katz, and Hooven, *Meta-emotion*, 210.

86   Jane Austen, *Pride and Prejudice: An Annotated Edition* (Cambridge, MA: Belknap Press, 2010), 22.

87   Hannah Fry, *The Mathematics of Love* (Simon & Schuster/TED Books, 2015), 102–6.

88   http://greatergood.berkeley.edu/article/item/john_gottman_on_trust _and_betrayal.

89   http://www.nytimes.com/2015/02/08/opinion/sunday/in-defense-of-tinder.html?hp&action=click&pgtype=Homepage&module=c-col umn-top-span-region&region=c-column-top-span-region&WT.nav= c-column-top-span-region.

90   Jeffrey Eugenides, *The Marriage Plot* (New York: Farrar, Straus and Giroux, 2011), 22.

91   http://www.pemberley.com/janeinfo/brablt15.html.

92   William Farr, *Vital Statistics: A Memorial Volume of Selections from the Reports and Writings of William Farr* (London: Sanitary Institute, 1885), 396.

93   As cited in Wolfgang Stroebe and Margaret S. Stroebe, *Bereavement and Health: The Psychological and Physical Consequences of Partner Loss* (Cambridge: Cambridge University Press, 1987), 3.

94   http://www.nytimes.com/2010/04/18/magazine/18marriage-t.html; Norman J. Johnson et al., "Marital status and mortality: The national longitudinal mortality study," *Annals of Epidemiology* 10.4 (2000): 224–38; and Robert M. Kaplan and Richard G. Kronick, "Marital status and longevity in the United States population," *Journal of Epidemiology and Community Health* 60.9 (2006): 760–65.

95   James Coyne, et al., "Prognostic importance of marital quality for survival of congestive heart failure," *The American Journal of Cardiology* 88 (2001): 526–29.

96   Walter Grove, Michael Hughes, and Carolyn Briggs Style, "Does marriage have positive effects on the psychological well-being of the individual?," *Journal of Health and Social Behavior* 24 (1983); http://wrap .warwick.ac.uk/315/1/WRAP_Oswald_finaljpubecwellbeingjune2002 .pdf; and Christopher Peterson et al., "Orientations to happiness and life satisfaction: The full life versus the empty life," *Journal of Happiness Studies* 6 (2005).

97   Martin Seligman, *Authentic Happiness* (New York: Atria Books, 2003), 187; and Eli J. Finkel et al., "A brief intervention to promote conflict reappraisal preserves marital quality over time," *Psychological Science* 24.8 (2013): 1595–1601.

98   Shawn Grover and John F. Helliwell, *How's Life at Home? New Evidence*

on Marriage and the Set Point for Happiness, no. 20794 (Cambridge, MA: National Bureau of Economic Research, 2014).

99 Meena Kumari et al., "Association of diurnal patterns in salivary cortisol with all-cause and cardiovascular mortality: Findings from the Whitehall II study," *Journal of Clinical Endocrinology & Metabolism* 96.5 (2011): 1478–85; and Michael R. Jarcho et al., "Dysregulated diurnal cortisol pattern is associated with glucocorticoid resistance in women with major depressive disorder," *Biological Psychology* 93.1 (2013): 150–58; and Ruth A. Hackett, Andrew Steptoe, and Meena Kumari, "Association of diurnal patterns in salivary cortisol with type 2 diabetes in the Whitehall II study," *Journal of Clinical Endocrinology & Metabolism* 99.12 (2014): 4625–31.

100 Richard B. Slatcher, Emre Selcuk, and Anthony D. Ong, "Perceived partner responsiveness predicts diurnal cortisol profiles 10 years later," *Psychological Science* (2015), doi:10.1177/0956797615575022.

101 Nicholas Christakis and Paul Allison, "Mortality after the hospitalization of a spouse," *New England Journal of Medicine*, February 16, 2006; and Felix Elwert and Nicholas Christakis, "The effect of widowhood on mortality by the causes of death of both spouses," *American Journal of Public Health* 98 (2008).

102 Charles Darwin, Frederick Burkhardt, and Sydney Smith, *The Correspondence of Charles Darwin*, vol. 5 (Cambridge: Cambridge University Press, 1990), 24.

103 Francis Darwin, "Reminiscences of the everyday life of my father," in *The Autobiography of Charles Darwin* (Cambridge: Icon, 2003), 97–98.

104 Deborah Heiligman, *Charles and Emma: The Darwins' Leap of Faith* (London: Macmillan, 2009), 200.

105 Adrian Desmond and James Moore, *Darwin* (London: Penguin, 1991), 662.

106 Ibid., 661.

Interlude: *Divorce*

1 John Updike, *The Early Stories* (New York: Knopf, 2003), 441.

2 Ibid., 372.

3 Adam Begley, *Updike* (New York: HarperCollins, 2014), 236–38.

4 John Updike, "Why Write?," in *Picked-Up Pieces* (New York: Knopf, 1975), 31.

5 John Updike, *Endpoint* (New York: Knopf, 2009), p. 10.

6 Begley, *Updike*, 351.

7 Updike, *Early Stories*, 792.

8 Ibid., 797.

9   Ibid., 798.
10 Begley, *Updike*, 356.
11 John Updike, *Couples* (New York: Random House, 1996), 111.
12 http://www.census.gov/prod/2011pubs/11statab/vitstat.pdf.
13 E. Mavis Hetherington and John Kelly, *For Better or for Worse: Divorce Reconsidered* (New York: W. W. Norton, 2003), 40.
14 Ibid., 7.
15 Ibid., 3.
16 I. L. Wooten, "Hetherington's groundbreaking work shows how families cope with divorce," retrieved from http://www.virginia.edu/insideuva/2000/09/hetherington.html.
17 Ibid.
18 Hetherington and Kelly, *For Better or for Worse*, 5.
19 Howard Friedman and Leslie Martin, *The Longevity Project* (New York: Hudson Street Press, 2011), 83.
20 Ibid., 80.
21 Judith S. Wallerstein and Sandra Blakeslee, *Second Chances: Men, Women, and Children a Decade after Divorce* (Boston: Ticknor & Fields, 1989), xvii.
22 Ibid.
23 Stephanie Coontz, *Marriage, a History: How Love Conquered Marriage* (New York: Penguin, 2006), 121.
24 George Vaillant, *Triumphs of Experience* (Cambridge, MA: Belknap Press, 2012), 196.
25 Ibid., 197.
26 Ibid., 198.
27 Ibid., 220.
28 Updike, *Early Stories*, 441.

4: Moments of Grace

1   J. David Hacker, "A census-based count of the Civil War dead," *Civil War History* 57.4 (2011): 307–48.
2   Drew Gilpin Faust, *This Republic of Suffering: Death and the American Civil War* (New York: Knopf, 2008).
3   Ibid., 171.
4   Ibid., 186.
5   Elizabeth Stuart Phelps, *The Gates Ajar* (Boston: Fields, Osgood, 1870), 49.
6   Faust, *This Republic of Suffering*, 185.
7   Randall M. Miller, Harry S. Trout, and Charles Reagan Wilson, eds., *Religion and the American Civil War* (Oxford: Oxford University Press, 1998), 31.

8   Phelps, *Gates Ajar*, 51.
9   William James, *The Varieties of Religious Experience*, vol. 13 (Cambridge, MA: Harvard University Press, 1985), chap. 20.
10 Ibid., chap. 14.
11 Ibid.
12 Ibid., chap. 18.
13 Lee A. Kirkpatrick, *Attachment, Evolution, and the Psychology of Religion* (New York: Guilford Press, 2005).
14 Ibid., 67.
15 G. D. Kaufman, *The Theological Imagination: Constructing the Concept of God* (Philadelphia: Westminster, 1981), 67.
16 Ibid.
17 Andreas Birgegard and Pehr Granqvist, "The correspondence between attachment to parents and God: Three experiments using subliminal separation cues," *Personality and Social Psychology Bulletin* 30.9 (2004): 1122–35.
18 Pehr Granqvist, Cecilia Ljungdahl, and Jane R. Dickie, "God is nowhere, God is now here: Attachment activation, security of attachment, and God's perceived closeness among 5–7-year-old children from religious and non-religious homes," *Attachment & Human Development* 9.1 (2007): 55–71.
19 Pehr Granqvist et al., "Experimental findings on God as an attachment figure: Normative processes and moderating effects of internal working models," *Journal of Personality and Social Psychology* 103.5 (2012): 804.
20 Nicholas Epley et al., "Creating social connection through inferential reproduction loneliness and perceived agency in gadgets, gods, and greyhounds," *Psychological Science* 19.2 (2008): 114–20.
21 David Hacker, "A census-based count of the civil war dead," *Civil War History* 57.4 (2011): 307–48.
22 Thomas McDermott, *Filled With All the Fullness of God: An Introduction to Catholic Spirituality*. (New York: Bloomsbury, 2013), 15.
23 George E. Vaillant, *Adaptation to Life* (Boston: Little, Brown, 1977), 253.
24 George E. Vaillant, *Triumphs of Experience: The Men of the Harvard Grant Study* (Cambridge, MA: Harvard University Press, 2012).
25 Vaillant, *Adaptation to life*, 251–55.
26 George Vaillant, *Spiritual Evolution: A Scientific Defense of Faith* (New York: Random House Digital, 2008), 83.
27 George E. Vaillant, *Aging Well: Surprising Guideposts to a Happier Life from the Landmark Study of Adult Development* (New York: Hachette Digital, 2008), 271.
28 Vaillant, *Adaptation to Life*, 257.
29 Vaillant, *Triumphs of Experience*, 48.

30   Ibid.
31   Ibid., 49.
32   Ibid., 48.
33   Daniel N. McIntosh, Roxane Cohen Silver, and Camille B. Wortman, "Religion's role in adjustment to a negative life event: Coping with the loss of a child," *Journal of Personality and Social Psychology* 65.4 (1993): 812.
34   Pehr Granqvist and Lee A. Kirkpatrick, "Religious conversion and perceived childhood attachment: A meta-analysis," *International Journal for the Psychology of Religion* 14.4 (2004): 235.
35   Ibid., 226.
36   T. M. Luhrmann, *When God Talks Back: Understanding the American Evangelical Relationship with God* (New York: Random House Digital, 2012), 41.
37   Ibid., 60.
38   T. M. Luhrmann, Howard Nusbaum, and Ronald Thisted. ""Lord, teach us to pray": Prayer practice affects cognitive processing." *Journal of Cognition and Culture* 13.1–2 (2013): 159–77.
39   Lynn Underwood, *Spiritual Connection in Daily Life* (West Conshohocken, PA: Templeton Press, 2013), 107–9.
40   Lee A. Kirkpatrick and Phillip R. Shaver, "An attachment-theoretical approach to romantic love and religious belief," *Personality and Social Psychology Bulletin* 18.3 (1992): 266–75.
41   Kirkpatrick, *Attachment, Evolution*, 69.
42   http://www.nytimes.com/2010/04/20/health/20drunk.html.
43   Robert Thomsen, *Bill W.: The Absorbing and Deeply Moving Life Story of Bill Wilson, Co-founder of Alcoholics Anonymous* (Center City, MN: Hazelden Publishing, 2010), 222–24.
44   *The Big Book*, fourth ed. (Alcoholics Anonymous World Services, 2002), 10.
45   Ernest Kurtz, *Not God: A History of Alcoholics Anonymous* (Center City, MN: Hazelden Publishing, 2013), 311.
46   Ibid., 20.
47   Ibid., 20.
48   Ibid., 21.
49   Ibid., 23.
50   Ibid., 29.
51   Rudolf H. Moos and Bernice S. Moos, "Long-term influence of duration and frequency of participation in Alcoholics Anonymous on individuals with alcohol use disorders," *Journal of Consulting and Clinical Psychology* 72.1 (2004): 81.
52   Paul E. Bebbington, "The efficacy of Alcoholics Anonymous: The elusiveness of hard data," *British Journal of Psychiatry* 128.6 (1976):

572–80; and Lee Ann Kaskutas, "Alcoholics Anonymous effectiveness: Faith meets science." *Journal of Addictive Diseases* 28.2 (2009): 145–57.

53   Charlotte Davis Kasl, *Many Roads, One Journey: Moving beyond the Twelve Steps* (New York: HarperPerennial, 1992), 10.

54   Rudolf H. Moos and Bernice S. Moos, "Participation in treatment and Alcoholics Anonymous: A 16-year follow-up of initially untreated individuals," *Journal of Clinical Psychology* 62.6 (2006): 735–50.

55   Scott Tonigan, Radka Toscova, and William R. Miller. "Meta-analysis of the literature on Alcoholics Anonymous: sample and study characteristics moderate findings." *Journal of Studies on Alcohol* 57.1 (1996): 65–72.

56   Vaillant, *Triumphs of Experience*, 315.

57   Ibid., 314.

58   Personal correspondence, "Positive Emotions and the Success of AA Full Draft."

59   George E. Vaillant, *The Natural History of Alcoholism Revisited* (Cambridge, MA: Harvard University Press, 2009), 243.

60   J. Scott Tonigan, Kristina N. Rynes, and Barbara S. McCrady, "Spirituality as a change mechanism in 12-step programs: A replication, extension, and refinement," *Substance Use & Misuse* 48.12 (2013): 1161–73.

61   Matthew J. Raphael, *Bill W. and Mr. Wilson: The Legend and Life of AA's Cofounder* (Amherst: University of Massachusetts Press, 2002), 92.

62   Ibid.

63   Vaillant, *Natural History of Alcoholism Revisited*, 244.

64   Maria E. Pagano et al., "Helping other alcoholics in Alcoholics Anonymous and drinking outcomes: Findings from Project MATCH," *Journal of Studies on Alcohol* 65.6 (2004): 766.

65   David Foster Wallace, *Infinite Jest* (Boston: Back Bay Books, 2006), 369.

66   Daniel T. Max, *Every Love Story Is a Ghost Story: A Life of David Foster Wallace* (New York: Penguin, 2012), 315.

67   Simone Weil, *Gravity and Grace* (Lincoln: University of Nebraska Press, 1997), 200.

68   Christian Wiman, "Gazing into the abyss: The sudden appearance of love and the galvanizing prospect of death lead a young poet back to poetry and a 'hope toward God,'" *American Scholar* (2007): 61–65.

69   Christian Wiman, *Ambition and Survival: Becoming a Poet* (Port Townsend, WA: Copper Canyon Press, 2007), 241.

70   Ibid., 241–42.

71   Christian Wiman, *My Bright Abyss: Meditation of a Modern Believer* (New York: Farrar, Straus and Giroux, 2013), 68.

72   Wiman, *Ambition and Survival*, 243.

73 Wiman, *My Bright Abyss*, 68.
74 http://www.onbeing.org/program/remembering-god/transcript /4537#main_content.
75 Wiman, *My Bright Abyss*, 67.
76 Ibid., 68.
77 Ibid., 146.
78 Ibid., 3.

Interlude: *Love Lost*

1 Harold Bloom, *The Invention of the Human* (New York: Riverhead Books, 1999), 88.
2 Megan Laslocky, *The Little Book of Heartbreak* (New York: Plume, 2012).
3 Jack Mearns, "Coping with a breakup: Negative mood regulation expectancies and depression following the end of a romantic relationship," *Journal of Personality and Social Psychology* 60.2 (1991): 327.
4 Abhiram Prasad, Amir Lerman, and Charanjit S. Rihal, "Apical ballooning syndrome (takotsubo or stress cardiomyopathy): A mimic of acute myocardial infarction," *American Heart Journal* 155.3 (2008): 408–17.
5 Stephen Joseph, *What Doesn't Kill Us: The New Psychology of Posttraumatic Growth* (New York: Basic Books), 19.
6 Ibid., 3.
7 Michael D. Matthews, *Head Strong: How Psychology Is Revolutionizing War* (New York: Oxford University Press, 2013), 74.
8 Ibid., 74–75.
9 Richard Tedeschi and Lawrence Calhoun, "Posttraumatic growth: Conceptual foundations and empirical evidence," *Psychological Inquiry* 15.1 (2004): 1–18.
10 Ibid.; Lawrence G. Calhoun and Richard G. Tedeschi, *Handbook of Posttraumatic Growth: Research and Practice* (New York: Routledge, 2014).
11 Jim Rendon, "Post-Traumatic Stress's Surprisingly Positive Flip Side," *New York Times Magazine*, March 22, 2012.

5: On Memory

1 Michel Montaigne, *The Complete Essays of Montaigne* (Palo Alto, CA: Stanford University Press, 1958), 139.
2 Donald Murdoch Frame, *Montaigne: A Biography* (New York: Harcourt Brace, 1965), 74.
3 Montaigne, *Complete Essays*, 139.
4 Ibid.

5   Frame, *Montaigne*, 74–75.
6   Ibid., 77–80.
7   Sarah Bakewell, *How to Live, or, A Life of Montaigne* (New York: Other Press, 2010), 107.
8   Frame, *Montaigne*, 83.
9   Bakewell, *How to Live*, 108.
10 Montaigne, *Complete Essays*, 752.
11 Karim Nader and Oliver Hardt, "A single standard for memory: The case for reconsolidation," *Nature Neuroscience Reviews*, March 2009.
12 Frederic C. Bartlett, "Some experiments on the reproduction of folk-stories," *Folklore* 31.1 (1920): 30–47.
13 Frederic C. Bartlett, *Remembering: A Study in Experimental and Social Psychology*, vol. 14 (Cambridge: Cambridge University Press, 1995), 213.
14 Michel de Montaigne, *Essays of Montaigne*, trans. Charles Cotton, http://archive.org/details/essaysofmontaign00mont, 34–37.
15 Sigmund Freud, *Civilization and Its Discontents* (New York: W. W. Norton, 2005), 34.
16 Sigmund Freud, *On the History of the Psycho-analytic Movement* (New York: W. W. Norton, 1989).
17 Glenn Roisman et al., "Earned-secure attachment status in retrospect and prospect," *Child Development*, July 2002.
18 Daniel J. Siegel, *The Developing Mind*, vol. 296 (New York: Guilford Press, 1999), 118–20.
19 John Mordechai Gottman, John Gottman, and Nan Silver, *What Makes Love Last?: How to Build Trust and Avoid Betrayal* (New York: Simon & Schuster, 2013), 215.
20 Ibid., 216.
21 Ibid., 217.
22 Kim T. Buehlman, John M. Gottman, and Lynn F. Katz, "How a couple views their past predicts their future: Predicting divorce from an oral history interview," *Journal of Family Psychology* 5.3–4 (1992): 295.
23 Montaigne, *Complete Essays*, 178.
24 Ullrich Langer, ed., *The Cambridge Companion to Montaigne* (Cambridge: Cambridge University Press, 2005), 173.
25 Thomas Newkirk, "Montaigne's revisions," *Rhetoric Review* 24.3 (2005): 298–315.
26 Virginia Woolf, *The Common Reader*, First Series (Boston: Mariner Books, 2002), 66.
27 Montaigne, *Complete Essays*, 611.
28 Bakewell, *How to Live*, 43.
29 James W. Pennebaker, *Opening Up: The Healing Power of Expressing Emotions* (New York: Guilford Publications, 1997), 8.

30   Ibid., 10.
31   Ibid., 32.
32   Ibid., 33.
33   James Pennebaker, "Writing about emotional experiences as a thera-
     peutic process," *Psychological Science* 3 (May 1997); and Keith J. Petrie et
     al., "Disclosure of trauma and immune response to a hepatitis B vaccina-
     tion program," *Journal of Consulting and Clinical Psychology* 63.5 (1995): 787.
34   Pennebaker, *Opening Up*, 103.
35   Ibid.
36   Adam Begley, *Updike* (New York: HarperCollins, 2014), 14.
37   Erik Homburger Erikson, *Identity and the Life Cycle*, vol. 1 (W. W. Nor-
     ton, 1980), 104.
38   Robyn Fivush, Jennifer G. Bohanek, and Marshall Duke, "The inter-
     generational self: Subjective perspective and family history," in *Self
     Continuity: Individual and Collective Perspectives*, ed. Fabio Sani (Mahwah,
     NJ: Erlbaum, 2008).
39   http://www.huffingtonpost.com/marshall-p-duke/the-stories-that-
     bind-us-_b_2918975.html.
40   Jennifer Bohanek, Robyn Fivush, Widaad Zaman, Caitlin E. Lepore,
     Shela Merchant, and Marshall P. Duke. "Narrative interaction in
     family dinnertime conversations." *Merrill-Palmer Quarterly* (Wayne
     State University Press) 55, no. 4 (2009): 488.
41   Fivush, Bohanek, and Duke, "Intergenerational self."
42   Robyn Fivush et al., "The power of family history in adolescent iden-
     tity and well-being," *Journal of Family Life*, February 2010.
43   Fivush, Bohanek, and Duke, "Intergenerational self."
44   Sandra L. Hofferth and John F. Sandberg, "How American children
     spend their time," *Journal of Marriage and Family* 63.2 (2001): 295–308;
     and John F. Sandberg and Sandra L. Hofferth, "Changes in chil-
     dren's time with parents: United States, 1981–1997," *Demography* 38.3
     (2001): 423–36.
45   "The importance of family dinners," National Center on Addiction
     and Substance Abuse at Columbia University, 2007, http://www.casa
     columbia.org/newsroom/press-releases/2007-family-dinners-4.
46   Marshall P. Duke et al., "Of ketchup and kin: Dinnertime conversa-
     tions as a major source of family knowledge, family adjustment, and
     family resilience," Emory Center for Myth and Ritual in American
     Life Working Paper no. 26 (May 2003); Sandra L. Hofferth and John
     F. Sandberg, "How American children spend their time," *Journal of
     Marriage and Family* 63.2 (2001): 295–308; and John F. Sandberg and
     Sandra L. Hofferth, "Changes in children's time with parents: United
     States, 1981–1997," *Demography* 38.3 (2001): 423–36.

47 Kathleen Christensen and Barbara L. Schneider, eds., *Workplace Flexibility: Realigning 20th-Century Jobs for a 21st-Century Workforce* (Ithaca, NY: ILR Press, 2010), 63–65.

48 Dan McAdams, *The Redemptive Self* (Oxford: Oxford University Press, 2007), 5.

49 Dan P. McAdams, "Narrating the generative life," *Psychological Science*, 2015; and Dan P. McAdams, "The positive psychology of adult generativity: Caring for the next generation and constructing a redemptive life," in *Positive Psychology*, ed. Jan D. Sinnott (New York: Springer, 2013), 191–205.

50 Dan P. McAdams, "The redemptive self: Generativity and the stories Americans live by," *Research in Human Development* 3.2–3 (2006): 81–100, https://www.sesp.northwestern.edu/docs/publications /954596231490a0bf9677c7.pdf, 90.

51 McAdams, *Redemptive Self*, 10.

52 Jennifer Bohanek et al., "Narrative interaction in family dinnertime conversations," *Merrill-Palmer Quarterly* 4 (2009); and R. Fivush, J. G. Bohanek, and W. Zaman, "Personal and intergenerational narratives in relation to adolescents' well-being," *New Directions for Child and Adolescent Development* 131 (2010): 45–57.

53 Elizabeth Kurylo, "Profile: Marshall Duke," Emory Center for Myth and Ritual in American Life, accessed December 2013, http://web .archive.org/web/20051121090343/http://www.marial.emory.edu/ faculty/profiles/duke.html.

Interlude: *The Opposite of Love*

1 Nan Bauer Maglin, ed., *Cut Loose:(Mostly) Older Women Talk about the End of (Mostly) Long-Term Relationships* (New Brunswick, NJ: Rutgers University Press, 2006), 188.

2 William Shirer, *Love and Hatred: The Stormy Marriage of Leo and Sonya Tolstoy* (New York: Simon & Schuster, 1994), 57.

3 Ibid., 33.

4 Ibid., 32.

5 Reginald Frank Christian, ed., *Tolstoy's Diaries* (New York: HarperCollins, 1994), entry: January 15, 1863.

6 Shirer, *Love and Hatred*, 361.

7 Fyodor Dostoyevsky, *The Brothers Karamazov* (Mineola, NY: Dover, 2005), 45.

8 Susan Ratcliffe, *Oxford Dictionary of Quotations by Subject* (Oxford: Oxford University Press, 2010), 249.

6: Going On

1   Robert Frost, *The Collected Prose of Robert Frost*, ed. Mark Richardson (Cambridge, MA: Belknap Press, 2008), 147.
2   http://www.viktorfrankl.org/e/chronology.html.
3   Viktor E. Frankl, *Man's Search for Meaning* (Boston: Beacon Press, 2006), 9.
4   Haddon Klingberg, *When Life Calls Out to Us: The Love and Lifework of Viktor and Elly Frankl* (New York: Doubleday Books, 2001), 104.
5   Ibid., 112.
6   Ibid., 117.
7   Frankl, *Man's Search for Meaning* (New York: Simon & Schuster, 1985), 14.
8   Ibid., 37.
9   Telephone interviews, April 2, 2012, and June 1, 2012.
10 Michael D. Matthews, *Head Strong: How Psychology Is Revolutionizing War* (New York: Oxford University Press, 2013), 17.
11 Charles Henning, "Army Officer Shortages: Background and Issues for Congress," CRS Report for Congress; http://www.fas.org/sgp/crs/natsec/RL33518.pdf.
12 Personal interviews, March 1–4, 2012, and December 5, 2012.
13 Paul R. Sackett, Sheldon Zedeck, and Larry Fogli, "Relations between measures of typical and maximum job performance," *Journal of Applied Psychology* 73.3 (1988): 482; and Paul R. Sackett, "Revisiting the origins of the typical-maximum performance distinction," *Human Performance* 20.3 (2007): 179–85.
14 Personal interview, March 29, 2012.
15 Viktor Frankl, *Man's Search for Meaning: Gift Edition* (Boston: Beacon Press, 2014), 159.
16 Klingberg, *When Life Calls Out to Us*, 151.
17 Viktor E. Frankl, *The Doctor and the Soul: From Psychotherapy to Logotherapy* (New York: Vintage, 1986), 95.
18 Ibid., 98.
19 Ibid., 98.
20 Klingberg, *When Life Calls Out to Us*, 2.
21 Ibid.
22 Frankl, *Man's Search for Meaning*, 79.
23 Klingberg, *When Life Calls Out to Us*, 238.
24 Roy F. Baumeister et al., "Some key differences between a happy life and a meaningful life," *Journal of Positive Psychology* 8.6 (2013): 505–16.
25 Frankl, *Man's Search for Meaning*, 105.

26 Hans Selye, *The Stress of Life*, rev. ed. (New York: McGraw-Hill, 1976).

27 Katherine R. Von Culin, Eli Tsukayama, and Angela L. Duckworth, "Unpacking grit: Motivational correlates of perseverance and passion for long-term goals," *Journal of Positive Psychology*, ahead-of-print (2014): 1–7.

28 Warren W. Willingham, *Success in College: The Role of Personal Qualities and Academic Ability* (New York: College Board Publications, 1985).

29 Ibid., 90.

30 Willingham recommended a five-point scale based on extracurricular achievement. Ibid., 213.

31 Angela L. Duckworth et al., "Grit: Perseverance and passion for long-term goals," *Journal of Personality and Social Psychology* 92.6 (2007): 1087.

32 Ibid.

33 Lauren Eskreis-Winkler et al., "The grit effect: Predicting retention in the military, the workplace, school and marriage," *Name: Frontiers in Psychology* 5 (2014): 36.

34 Ibid.

35 Here's a recent PowerPoint presentation of Duckworth's forthcoming data: http://www.corpu.com/documents/Angela_Duckworth_True _Grit.pdf.

36 Duckworth et al., "Grit," 1087.

37 Eskreis-Winkler et al., "Grit effect," 36.

38 John Gottman and Lowell J. Krokoff, "Marital interaction and satisfaction: a longitudinal view," *Journal of Consulting and Clinical Psychology* 57.1 (1989): 47.

39 John Gottman, *Why Marriages Succeed or Fail* (New York: Simon & Schuster, 1995), 66.

40 George E. Vaillant, *Triumphs of Experience: The Men of the Harvard Grant Study* (Cambridge, MA: Harvard University Press, 2012), 73.

41 Ibid.

42 Ibid., 50.

43 Mario Mikulincer and Phillip R. Shaver, *Attachment in Adulthood: Structure, Dynamics, and Change* (New York: Guilford Press, 2007), 201.

44 As cited in Neil Strauss, *The Truth: An Uncomfortable Book about Relationships* (New York: Dey Street Press, 2015), 405.

45 Cindy Hazan and Phillip Shaver, "Love and work: An attachment-theoretical perspective," *Journal of Personality and Social Psychology* 59.2 (1990).

46 I want to thank Professor Matthews for sharing his data. "Character Strengths and Post-Adversity Growth in Combat Leaders."

47 Giora Zakin, Zahava Solomon, and Yuval Neria, "Hardiness, attach-

ment style, and long term psychological distress among Israeli POWs and combat veterans," *Personality and Individual Differences* 34.5 (2003): 819–29; and Zahava Solomon et al., "Coping with war captivity: The role of attachment style," *European Journal of Personality* 12.4 (1998): 271–85.

48 Zahava Solomon et al., "Coping with war captivity: The role of attachment style," *European Journal of Personality* 12.4 (1998): 271–85.
49 Von Culin, Tsukayama, and Duckworth, "Unpacking grit," 1–7.
50 Rainer Maria Rilke, *Letters to a Young Poet*, trans. Stephen Mitchell (New York: Merchant Books, 2012), 41.
51 Viktor E. Frankl, "Logotherapy in a Nutshell," in *Man's Search for Meaning* (Simon & Schuster, 1985), 103.
52 Anna Redsand, *Viktor Frankl: A Life Worth Living* (Boston: Clarion Books, 2006), 114.
53 Frankl, *Man's Search for Meaning* (Boston: Beacon Press, 2006), 165.
54 Klingberg, *When Life Calls Out to Us*, 297.
55 Ibid., 214.
56 Ibid., 288.
57 Ibid., 330–31.
58 Ibid., 335.

Coda: *Scarcity*

1 I got the evocative phrase "middle of things" from Andrew Solomon's talk at the Whiting Writers' Awards on March 5, 2015.
2 George E. Vaillant, *Triumphs of Experience: The Men of the Harvard Grant Study* (Cambridge, MA: Harvard University Press, 2012), 52.